HOLLYWOOD

THRESHOLD EDITIONS

NEW YORK   LONDON   TORONTO   SYDNEY   NEW DELHI

THE DEVASTATING TRUTH
ABOUT OBAMA'S BIGGEST BACKERS

HYPOCRITES

jason
mattera

Threshold Editions
A Division of Simon & Schuster, Inc.
1230 Avenue of the Americas
New York, NY 10020

First Threshold Editions paperback edition February 2013

THRESHOLD EDITIONS and colophon are trademarks of Simon & Schuster, Inc.

For information about special discounts for bulk purchases,
please contact Simon & Schuster Special Sales at
1-866-506-1949 or business@simonandschuster.com.

The Simon & Schuster Speakers Bureau can bring authors to your live event. For more information or to book an event, contact the Simon & Schuster Speakers Bureau at 1-866-248-3049 or visit our website at www.simonspeakers.com.

Designed by Ruth Lee-Mui

Manufactured in the United States of America

10   9   8   7   6   5   4   3   2

Library of Congress Cataloging-in-Publication Data

Mattera, Jason.
   Hollywood hypocrites : the devastating truth about Obama's biggest backers / Jason Mattera.—1st Threshold Editions hardcover ed.
      p. cm.
   1. Motion picture industry—Political aspects—United States—History—21st century.   2. Motion picture actors and actresses—Political activity—United States.   3. Motion picture producers and directors—Political activity—United States.   4. Celebrities—Political activity—United States.   5. Right and left (Political science)—United States—History—21st century.   6. United States—Politics and government—2009–   7. Presidents—United States—Election—2008.   I. Title.
   PN1993.5.U6M28 2012
   384'.8097309005—dc23   2011043107
ISBN 978-1-4516-2561-5
ISBN 978-1-4516-2562-2 (pbk)
ISBN 978-1-4516-2563-9 (ebook)

To Joe and Joyce Mattera:
You raised me to fear no man.

Acknowledgments

Without the numerous and public O-basms of young people across the country, my first book, *Obama Zombies,* would've never come to fruition. So to the emasculated college dudes still waiting for President Obama to hand-deliver them strawberry-scented welfare checks in order that they can buy another pair of skinny jeans, I thank you. Similarly, without the mind-boggling duplicity and absolute absurdity of the Tinseltown crowd, there would be no *Hollywood Hypocrites.* So in a show of appreciation, I hope that all of you celebrities I unmask in the pages herewith score the mother of all coke highs. Now run along and get working on *Pirates of the Caribbean 6,* or whatever the number is at this point.

In all sincerity, I would've never thought I'd be writing books. Ever. And if you saw my high school grades, you'd be thinking the same thing! But here I am, on my second book, and there are plenty of people whom I need to acknowledge.

The entire team at Threshold—you guys totally rock. Anthony Ziccardi, the vice president, my deep gratitude for believing in me from the very beginning. I still remember our initial lunch like it was yesterday. Mitchell Ivers, my trusty editor. As was the case with *Obama Zombies,* this book is better with your input. You are a consummate professional. Thank you! Kristin Dwyer, my awesomely awesome publicist. You make promoting a book fun! And you also arrive at the television studios with me at 6:00 a.m. Seriously, who does that? You do! Also a big shout-out to Natasha Simons, editorial assistant; Tom Pitoniak, my copy editor; and Jonathan Nicholson, who helped with research. Of course, Louise Burke, the publisher, without your blessing, none of my projects would've ever gotten off the ground. Thank you!

Glen Hartley and Lynn Chu, two of the best agents around. Thanks for looking out for me.

I'm also blessed to work with a fantastic team at *Human Events.* To Jeff Carneal, president of Eagle Publishing, I know I give you heartburn at times, but thanks for being in this young buck's corner anyway. Joe Guerriero, the publisher: oh, man, what a wild ride it's been these past two years. Thanks for defending me! Then there's Allan Ryskind and Tom Winter. I've been fortunate to work with both of you. Your wisdom and passion are infectious. I hope to hate liberalism the way you two do when I'm your age.

No writer is on an island unto himself. We all build off the work of someone great who has gone before us. And let me tell you, I've had the privilege of working closely with some of the sharpest minds in politics today: Mark Levin, Michelle Malkin, Andrew Breitbart, and Ann Coulter. Thank you all for using your platform to help me build mine.

To Laurie Cantillo, the former program director at New York City's flagship radio station, 77 WABC: I can't begin to express how grateful I am to you for giving me a shot in radio. You were right. It is addicting! I'm sure we'll reunite in the future.

AJ Rice and Matt Fox, two of the most creative and talented people I know. One of these days you'll give Howard Stern a run for his money. To my college buddy Nick Yousif, thanks for your friendship and Biggie Smalls impersonations.

While humbled by the trajectory of my career, it's not the most important aspect of my life. That designation goes to family. To my siblings—Charissa, Rachel, Justin, Becky, and Kristian—I love you all dearly. To my parents, Joe and Joyce, you've spent a lifetime sacrificially giving of yourselves. Love you both!

Then there's my brother from another mother, who has guided me through two books now and lends his ear when I need to vent. Thx, bro!

To Daris and Cindy, your ongoing life advice has turned me into a better man and your willingness to cook me dinner ensures that I eat something other than Lucky Charms. Muchas gracias!

Last, but certainly not least: to God, the giver of life. I do not deserve your grace and mercy, but You bestow it on me still the same.

> Peace, love, and Obama granola goodness,
> Jason Mattera

Contents

Introduction

Two things keep me awake at night: 1) the gut-churning thought of Barack Obama being reelected in 2012 and 2) the fear that next season's *Dancing with the Stars* will feature Janet Napolitano.

I'll get over the latter.

The former, however, is serious. Dead serious.

In four years, Barack Hussein Obama has done more to destroy American freedom and flourishing than even his most committed Marxist zealots dreamed possible. He has increased the debt more than the first forty-one U.S. presidents—from George Washington to George H. W. Bush—combined.[1]

When Obama entered office, the national debt stood at $10.626 trillion. In his first two years in office, Barack sent that figure soaring to a jaw-dropping $14.071 trillion—a jump of $3.445 trillion in only 735 days. That works out to $5 billion a *day*.[2] And now the debt has exploded past $15 trillion.

Following his castration of American capitalism, Barack set his sights on socializing health care. And socialize he did. With the help of former Madame Speaker Nancy Pelosi—or, "Mommy" as Rahm Emanuel calls her (no, I'm not joking, and yes, I just threw up a little in my mouth)—Obama rammed through the Congress his unconstitutional Obamacare boondoggle, a legislative Leviathan that, according to the nonpartisan Congressional Budget Office (CBO), will slay some 800,000 American jobs.[3] Worse, Obamacare will destroy the finest health-care system in the world, wrest away patient choice, and burn through more money than Charlie Sheen at a strip club.

When he wasn't busy steamrolling free enterprise and the one sixth of our economy that is the U.S. health-care system, Dear Leader took it upon himself to make good on his 2008 campaign promise to heal the planet and oceans by . . . sitting idly by as the biggest natural disaster in American history took place on his watch. Barack's bumbling during the BP oil spill was so bad that even Chris "Tingle Up My Leg" Matthews blasted Oilbama. "The president scares me," Matthews said on *The Tonight Show*. "When is he actually going to do something? And I worry, I know he doesn't want to take ownership of it."[4]

And of course, who could forget Obama's stellar foreign policy leadership. When he's not out golfing eighty-seven times in his first three years, sending his wife on $350,000 trips to Spain (on your dime), or working up his NCAA brackets while Japan burns, Obama has managed to achieve incredible foreign policy feats.[5] Let's see, to date Barack Obama has: trashed our allies Israel and Britain; remained silent when freedom movements in Iran launched a democratic revolution because he didn't want to offend the biggest state sponsor of terrorism and that wonderful American ally, Mahmoud Ahmadinejad; deposed Muammar Gaddafi (a man who called Obama "our son") in Libya, where the United States had no national interest, but issued only a strongly worded letter to Bashar Assad in Syria (a close friend of Iran) for mowing down thousands of protesters with tanks; watched his director of "intelligence" James Clapper manage to out-clueless even himself by having to rely on one of the world's most knowledgeable terrorism experts, ABC News reporter Diane Sawyer, to learn about Britain detaining terrorists; and continued to promulgate the charade that radical Muslims hellbent on murder are not, in fact . . . radical Muslims hell-bent on murder.

And of course, who could forget Obama's orgy of buffoonery, ranging from him chastising the Cambridge, Massachusetts, police for acting "stupidly," mocking special needs children on *The Tonight Show*, telling us about his adventures visiting all "fifty-seven states," or talking about the valor of our Navy "Corpse-man," or, as the rest of planet earth calls them, Navy Corpsman. But none of that matters or registers on the media's "idiot-o-meter," of course, because Barack's last name isn't Bush.

But Jason, you say, *surely with a record as abysmal as his, there's no way this socialist Marxist will get reelected. Republicans will win in 2012. It's a slam dunk.*

To that I say, "Not so fast there, George Tenet."

First, as the last presidential cycle proved, if Republicans are good at anything it's choosing a bum of a candidate. John "Gramps" McCain was about as riveting to listen to on TV as actor-turned-Liberty Medical pitchman Wilford Brimley talking about his "diabeetus."

So, memo to RNC headquarters: "Choose a *real* conservative this time, would ya? If the GOP runs another squish, Republicans will get squished."

But let's assume for a moment that the GOP gets it this time and that they learned their lesson. Furthermore, let's assume that Republicans run a candidate with a pulse. What then? What could possibly revive the debacle that is the Obama presidency and breathe life back into his candidacy?

Answer: Obama's strongest weapon heading into the 2012 presidential election. The same weapon that helped him amass a $750 million campaign war chest unlike any ever achieved in American campaign history. The same media "Yes, We Can" marketing marvel that this time stands ready to help him rake in and run the first-ever billion-dollar presidential campaign.[6]

I'm speaking, of course, of the Hollywood Left. Never before have Hollywood progressives been as excited about a Democrat candidate as they were in 2008 for Barack Hussein Obama. As I recounted in my last book, *Obama Zombies: How the Liberal Machine Brainwashed My Generation*, 2008 brought the most expensive, high-tech, laser-focused marketing assault in presidential history. Twitter messages were machine-gunned to cell phones at Mach speed. Facebook groups spread across the Internet like digital fire. And of course, YouTube videos featuring the most reliable Obama Zombies of all, Hollywood celebrities, ricocheted across the globe and into college students' in-boxes with devastating regularity. But the inside Hollywood story goes deeper—much deeper—than even I initially understood. So I dove headlong into an ocean of investigative research to connect all the dots. The first of those dots begins with a critical moment that launched Obama's entire presidency and, ultimately, reshaped the contours of American history toward ignoble ends.

"WHEN HISTORIANS START looking for turning points in the trajectory of the Obama campaign for the presidency," writes *Los Angeles Times* reporter Patrick Goldstein, "they will inevitably turn to Feb. 21, 2007, the day that the *New York Times'* Maureen Dowd ran a column where [David] Geffen blasted then-Democratic presidential front-runner Hillary Clinton." [7]

Billionaire media mogul David Geffen and Bill and Hillary Clinton go way back. David Geffen, who is, among other things, joint owner of Dream Works along with Steven Spielberg and Jeffrey Katzenberg, spent much of the 1990s raising millions of dollars for Bill Clinton and myriad Democrat Party causes. Geffen and Bill Clinton were so close, in fact, that Clinton called Geffen incessantly, whether the latter was at his Beverly Hills mansion (previously owned by Jack Warner) or driving his car, or if it was late in the evening. When Clinton was in Hollywood he would crash at David Geffen's pad. When Geffen was in Washington, D.C., on more than one occasion he stayed at the White House in the Lincoln Bedroom. [8] Serious man-crush, these two.

But by the end of Bill Clinton's second term in office, the Geffen-Clinton lovefest began to wane. All of Clinton's triangulating irked the die-hard progressive Hollywood mogul. In 2001, Bill Clinton finally committed an unforgivable sin, one that would send the billionaire entertainment executive searching for a new progressive puppet to control. Clinton's sin? On the heels of pardoning fugitive financier Marc Rich, Clinton refused to extend a presidential pardon to one of progressivism's patron saints, radical Leonard Peltier, the member of the American Indian Movement who was convicted of aiding and abetting the execution-style murders of not one but two FBI agents.[9] (Few things excite the far Left quite as much as cop killers. Just ask that other progressive hero, convicted cop killer Mumia Abu-Jamal, who gunned down Philadelphia police officer Daniel Faulkner in 1981 in cold blood. Even though Abu-Jamal has been on death row for thirty years, liberals herald him as a downtrodden brother from the hood symbolizing the fight against white oppression. Or something like that.)

It was all downhill from there; Geffen knew that it was time to go searching for a true-blue, dyed-in-the-wool Leftist who would stay loyal to the progressive cause. When the Hollywood rumor mill began to buzz about Bill Clinton hitting the town womanizing with Geffen's party animal neighbor, Ron Burkle, people asked the Hollywood titan whether he thought the buzz about Clinton still cheating on Hillary was true. Geffen's answer: "Do you think the Pope's a Catholic?"[10]

Flash forward to 2004. When David Geffen laid eyes on Barack Obama delivering his much-ballyhooed speech at the Democrat National Convention, Geffen instantly fell in love. "I thought he was a remarkable guy," said Geffen. "After I heard him give that speech, I called him up and said, 'You're going to run for president and I'm going to support you.'"[11]

Within a year, Geffen arranged a private dinner meeting at his home with Barack, Jeffrey and Marilyn Katzenberg, and Warren Beatty. Geffen was "swept away" by Obama's chill, laid-back style and his "lack of entitlement or self-importance."[12] In other words, Geffen was clearly taking hallucinogenic drugs that night.

In early 2005, while speaking in New York at the 92nd Street Y, an audience member asked Geffen about Hillary Clinton's chances at winning the White House. "I said that Hillary was an incredibly polarizing figure and that if she ran, she'd never be elected president," Geffen recalls. "And when I said it, the audience broke into applause."[13] The reaction surprised the billionaire, because he had assumed that New York's Upper East Side was solidly in Clinton's corner.[14] But one member of that audience, Geffen's close friend, liberal *New York Times* columnist Maureen Dowd, saw Geffen's comments and the audience's reaction differently. "Afterwards she said to me, 'We oughta do a column about that.'" At the time Geffen declined. Dowd, however, persisted. "You have to say what you're thinking," Dowd urged. "It could have a real impact on the race."[15]

For two years, Maureen Dowd pestered David Geffen to let her interview him so she could include his support for Obama in her *New York Times* column. On February 19, 2007, Geffen finally granted Dowd her wish with a fifteen-minute interview that she quickly cranked into an article. The timing wasn't by accident. The next night, Geffen and his Dream Works SKG partners, Spielberg and Katzenberg, hosted a star-studded $1.3 million, three-hundred-person Obama fundraiser at the Beverly Hilton. After the event, Barack and Michelle Obama, Geffen, Spielberg, Katzenberg, former Disney and Fox studio head Joe Roth, movie producer Lynda Obst, Maureen Dowd, William Morris Agency chairman Jim Wiatt, and director James Mangold all headed back to David Geffen's compound.[16]

Toward the end of the shindig, Geffen slipped Obama a copy of Dowd's *New York Times* column, slated to run the next day. Obama read it as Geffen looked on. Geffen's comments quoted in the op-ed were heat-seeking missiles aimed at the Clintons. The piece quoted Geffen as saying that Bill Clinton was a "reckless guy who gave his enemies a lot of ammunition to hurt him," that "the Clintons were unwilling to stand for the things that they genuinely believe in," and that "everybody in politics lies, but they do it with such ease, it's troubling." Dowd's column made reference to the murderer Leonard Peltier having gone without a pardon, quoting Geffen as saying, "Yet another time when the Clintons were unwilling to stand for the things that they genuinely believe in." But Marc Rich landing one? "An oil-profiteer expatriate who left the country rather than pay taxes or face justice?" Geffen fumed.[17] The article set off DefCon 1 at Hillary headquarters. That morning they issued a press release with the screaming headline: "CLINTON CAMP TO OBAMA: CUT TIES & RETURN CASH AFTER TOP BOOSTER'S VICIOUS ATTACKS." The idea was to go on offense, but the ground had already shifted underneath Team Hillary. As reporters John Heilemann and Mark Halperin recount, the one-two punch of the Geffen-Dowd hit job was the Hillary Clinton campaign's "worst nightmare splashed across the screen in garish Technicolor. Two paragons of the bicoastal liberal Establishment, one from Hollywood and one from the *Times,* conspiring to take down Hillary."[18]

The rest is history. Not only was Geffen the tip of Obama's spear, but he has remained one of Obama's biggest fundraisers and driving forces. And all the cash, power, influence, and moviemaking marketing support Geffen has given Dear Leader continues to pay big dividends for the billionaire media mogul. In November 2009, Obama hosted his very first official state dinner for India's prime minister, Manmohan Singh. Prime Minister Singh sat at the head table sporting a killer turban. Beside him, ready to pounce on any nonorganic food items that might land on the prime minister's plate, sat Michelle "Never been proud of America until I got to take $350,000 Spanish vacations on your tax dollars" Obama. And you'll never guess who was seated right beside Michelle O. That's right, David Geffen.

To be sure, as the liberal Gawker.com notes, the sixty-eight-year-old Geffen was likely outshined at the event by his date that evening, twenty-six-year-old surfer boyfriend Jeremy Lingvall.[19]

From right to left: David Geffen, Food Witch, and Prime Minister Singh, wearing a sweet-ass turban.

Obama to Lingvall at the president's first official state dinner: "Keep your hands off him, pretty boy. Geffen is *my* man, not yours!"

Still, being Obama's right-hand man is not without its perks. And as my investigation into David Geffen will reveal, not without its hypocrisies, either.

What worked for Obama then will work for Obama now. The Hollywood image makers that marketed Obama like an iPad 2 are prepared to do it all over again. And they will.

"I have a dependency on President Obama," Katzenberg said at a Hollywood fund-raiser for the Messiah back in late 2011. "We must keep fighting for him so he can keep fighting for us." Celebs including Will Smith, Eva Longoria, Jack Black, Earvin "Magic" Johnson, Quincy Jones, Hilary Duff, and Danny DeVito gladly shelled out up to $35,800 a plate to hear BHO tell them how valuable they were.

"It's not going to be as sexy" as 2008, Obama warned the glitterati. "If things are just smooth the whole way through, not only is it a pretty dull movie, but it doesn't reflect our experience," he added in comparing his reelection bid to the arc of a film.[20] In fact, Obama is so convinced that the road to another four years in the Oval Office travels through Tinseltown that he held a secret meeting with high-level movie executives and talent producers who were identified as key people to "shape the national political conversation heading into a tough race in 2012."[21]

Some conservatives shrug off Hollywood's influence. *Oh, those are just a bunch of dumb Hollywood actors and musicians,* they say. *No one pays attention to them anyhow. No one is stupid enough to let media and celebrity culture influence how they vote.*

Um, yeah. That was the same thinking in 2008 that produced the largest electoral landslide in the youth voter demographic ever recorded. Among voters ages 18–29, Barack Obama won a jaw-dropping 66 percent of votes to John McCain's puny 32 percent.[22]

Anyone who believes that the same inanity among the youth

vote that produced these numbers won't rear its ugly head again clearly has not watched an episode of MTV's mind-expanding (imploding?) docudrama *Teen Mom* or the oh-so-wholesome and enlightening *Skins*.

The same Hollywood loons who got Obama elected will do so again. That is, unless we muzzle them.

How? Not the way the Left tries to do, by silencing dissent. But by putting their political stances and public statements under the microscope of scrutiny to analyze whether they live by the same policy prescriptions they seek to inflict on America. That means taking their views seriously enough to inspect and investigate them. Hollywood's media megaphone is powerful. Voters deserve to know whether progressives are the real deal or whether they are merely engaged in high-wattage hypocrisy. Better still, we must determine what radical progressive ideas will do to America.

The book you're about to read will piss you off. The hypocrisies my investigation uncovered on Obama's staunchest supporters are breathtaking in their sweep and astounding in their arrogance. But what makes them particularly egregious is not what they say about human failings, but rather what they say about the illogic of Obama's radical agenda against America. Not even *Obama's own staunchest Hollywood allies* live by the crap he seeks to foist on America. That's why it's high time we wake up America before the Hollywood goons hit the airwaves, Obama wins reelection, and it's too late.

It's time to recognize and unveil the marketing and fundraising power the Hollywood Left wields.

It's time to dig into the data and set the record straight.

It's time to turn the media spotlight back on the Hollywood imagemakers.

What I'm saying is . . . it's time for a Tinseltown takedown.

1 Hollywood Welfare

How Hollywood Idiots like Michael Moore Swipe $1,500,000,000
of Your Tax Dollars Each Year and Then Whine That You Should Pay
Higher Taxes

Hey, you know what? Studio executives? They would
shoot a movie on Mars if they could get a 25 percent tax
break.

—Director Michael Corrente[1]

No one watches the snoozefest Oscar awards anymore. But for a
second let's pretend they did. As the camera scans the audience of
Hollywood moguls, directors, producers, and movie stars, isn't your
heart struck by the extreme poverty on display? I mean, just look
at them all, sitting there being forced to wear last season's Gucci
and Prada collections, instead of owning the latest and greatest
runway fashions. The inhumanity! How can we, the American tax-

payers, sit idly by as Michael Moore is starving to death, withering away? And look at poor Alec Baldwin and Robert Redford. How can we, the most powerful nation on earth, look on with callous hearts as these two honorable men are forced to endure ever worse plastic surgery? After all, if Redford's facial skin gets pulled any tighter, the man will morph into a drum.

That's why something must be done. We, the American tax-payers, must take immediate and decisive action. And thankfully, in 2010 alone, hardworking Americans like you did just that. You spent less time with your family so you could work longer hours at your job so that $1,500,000,000 of your tax dollars could be con-fiscated from your paycheck and added to Rob Reiner's.

Indeed, the next time you see Obama's Hollywood foot sol-diers, two words should instantly pop into your mind: *welfare recipients.*

Since 1992, Hollywood has been involved in a heist that would make even Bonnie and Clyde jealous. Few Americans know about it. But so-called movie state tax credit programs, which exist in forty-three states, have become one of the silent budget killers in many states throughout the country. In an effort to attract their Hollywood pals to shoot in their states, Democrat lawmakers began offering tax subsidies. In places like Michael Moore's Michigan, the tax credit is as high as 42 percent. The argument was that by subsidizing film productions, states could experience massive job creation for their citizens, spur economic spending for their busi-nesses, and turn themselves into filmmaking Meccas. Furthermore, by featuring a state's scenery in a movie, proponents claim, you will want to travel and visit the state, thus bringing forth a tidal wave of tourism dollars.

Brilliant!

Take a movie like, oh, I don't know . . . *Texas Chainsaw Mas-*

sacre. See, right there you've got a piece of tourism gold, baby! Dismembered limbs, decapitated heads, and a homicidal maniac wielding a chainsaw all set against the bucolic Texas scenery?

"Honey, pack the bags, load up the kids, and board the dog. Lone Star State, here we come! I loves me some *Texas Chainsaw* tourism!"

Idiots.

Indeed, like most progressive policy prescriptions, the whole Hollywood welfare thing has been an unmitigated debacle. Worse, for a party that vehemently opposes tax cuts for the wealthy and demands higher taxes for everyone, Hollywood's welfare heist is yet one of many examples of the Left's breathtaking hypocrisy.

In fiscal year 2010, the forty-three states that offer film subsidies spent $1.5 billion of your tax dollars subsidizing film and TV production.[2] Let's put that in real terms. Hollywood's 2009 welfare payments would have been enough to pay the salaries of 23,500 middle school teachers, 26,600 firefighters, and 22,800 police patrol officers.[3]

But here's where it gets good. Are you ready for this? If a producer doesn't have a big enough tax liability to use up all of a refundable film tax credit, that state cuts him a big fat check anyway. That's right. Direct cash payment to a Hollywood welfare recipient. I mean, come on, people . . . how is James Cameron supposed to scrape by on a measly $210 million?! Seriously. He *needs* your money to survive, you stingy conservative mongrel!

But we're not done. It gets better. There's also something called a "transferable tax credit." These little doozeys are cash cows for producers and cow pies for taxpayers. Movie producers who are given transferable tax credits to come shoot their movie in that state can then sell their tax credits to companies that owe state taxes, no matter what kind of business it is. Generally, the businesses that snatch up these movie tax credits are one of liber-als' favorite corporate bogeymen—insurance companies. In Con-necticut, for example, big bank bailout winners Bank of America and Wachovia gobbled up a combined $7 million in film tax credits. And in Massachusetts, half of all transferrable credits were bought up by insurance companies.[4] What this means is that taxpayers get to spend more hours at work to ensure that Hollywood fat cats can cash in by selling credits to Obama's bailout buddies and the insurance companies.

As Sharon Carty, writing for *USA Today*, put it, the movie industry is a "gypsy-like" business that "roams from place to place to find the best locations—and the best deals."[5] Robert Tan-nenwald, writing for the Center on Budget and Policy Priorities, agrees. He notes that state film subsidy programs are a "wasteful, ineffective, and unfair instrument of economic development." He says that what lawmakers sell as a "quick fix" to boost jobs and bolster businesses within a state generally goes bust. The reason? "In reality they benefit mostly non-residents, especially well-paid non-resident film and TV professionals . . . The benefits to the few are highly visible; the costs to the majority are hidden because they are spread so widely and detached from the subsidies."[6] But perhaps those states should remain grateful, because, as the Tax Foundation reports, "In many states, today, movie producers actu-ally pay a negative tax."

Well, hell . . . no wonder Hollywood progressives think the rich should pay more in taxes! It's because they don't pay a single penny of the taxes they owe!

Now let's be clear. There's absolutely nothing wrong with busi-nesses trying to bring down their tax burden. But that's not what's at issue here. As the *Wall Street Journal* explains:

This is the same Hollywood film industry whose members fund causes and candidates that favor raising taxes on everyone else. The Motion Picture Production and Distribution industry last year gave $14 million in political contributions: 89 percent went to pro-tax Democrats. A few years ago, director Rob Reiner funded a successful California initiative to raise the state income tax rate to more than 10 percent. Unlike a film shoot, which can relocate on a moment's notice, your average small businessman in Encino is stuck paying the highest tax rate in the country—at least until he gives up and moves to Reno. . . . As a general principle, however, states shouldn't chase smoke stacks or film production crews with specific tax breaks. It makes much more sense for cities, states, and the federal government to lower tax rates for everyone.[7]

The liberal lunacy of it all is compounded when you stop and consider the fundamental truth that progressives chronically deny but their own economic behavior proves: tax cuts incentivize business decisions. Everywhere and always the Leftist cacophony remains: "Stick it to big business! U.S. corporate tax rates should be high! Companies won't up and leave the country if we raise taxes on business, so jack 'em up!" In one regard, they are right: it's way harder for a brick-and-mortar, mom-and-pop pizza shop to pick up and leave than it is for a motion picture filming crew. But that just goes to show how cynical and outrageous the Hollywood welfare boondoggle truly is. As the film tax incentive programs demonstrate, producers and directors can and do change their entire filming location based on a "lowest bidder" style of tax negotiations. The Hollywood Left wants lower tax rates for them and higher tax rates for the rest of us, including small business owners who don't have the lavish lifestyle and luxury of being able to hop in their private carbon-spewing jet and zip over to another state to do business to swipe handfuls of taxpayer cash. Must be nice.

But the sheer hypocrisy of it all is breathtaking. Take, for example, the case of Michael Moore. At the July 2008 Traverse City Film Festival event, director Moore participated in a panel discussion wherein he decried Hollywood welfare in the form of so-called state tax credit programs. "These are large multinational corporations—Viacom, GE, Rupert Murdoch—that own these studios," said Moore. "Why do they need our money from Michigan, from our taxpayers? We're already broke here. Why? I mean, they play one state against another and so they get all this free cash when they're making billions already in profits. What's the thinking behind that? . . . Giving free money to a bunch of billionaires."[8]

Flash forward to 2010.

Following the release of Moore's pro-socialism, anti-capitalism "documentary" film, *Capitalism: A Love Story*, a film that has grossed $17,436,509 in worldwide sales, Michael "I Hate America" Moore asked his cash-strapped home state of Michigan to fork over $1 million from the State of Michigan Film Office so he could get himself some of that taxpayer "free cash" he decried all those corporatist pigs getting just two years earlier.[9] The request was approved.

"The hypocrisy of Michael Moore is absolutely stunning," says Michigan state senator Nancy Cassis. "One day he criticized the film giveaways and then asked for a $1 million handout of his own. We are supposed to be spurring economic growth, but we're giving taxpayer money to a film that trashes our economic system. How responsible is this?"[10]

Not very.

Michigan has a $1.6 billion budget shortfall and some of the highest unemployment in America, thanks to the Obama economy. But is that enough to stop Hollywood's leading binge eater? Pshhh.

"Our small businesses in this state, that create 70 percent of all the jobs, have been hardest hit by the new Michigan business tax—and the surcharge of 22 percent on that tax—which is going to subsidize these giveaways and these handouts," said Senator Cassis. "Meanwhile, these small business employers are letting go of employees. . . . We simply can't afford this handout to one industry—Hollywood producers—over all others. Really, we're robbing Peter—the hardworking Michigan businessman—to pay Paul—the Hollywood tycoon."[11]

Michael LaFaive, fiscal policy director at the Mackinac Center, weighed in on Moore's brazen hypocrisy: "While we don't blame Mr. Moore and his production team for taking what is offered, it's striking that a movie focused on the inequities of granting taxpayer dollars to private enterprise would apply for and receive taxpayer-funded incentives."[12]

But given the state of Michigan's insane decision to up their Hollywood welfare rate to the highest level in the land, perhaps it's not as surprising after all. In 2007, spending on film productions in Michigan was $2 million. Yet after it decided to extend the jaw-dropping 42 percent Hollywood welfare rate, the state attracted more than one hundred movie and TV productions and exploded spending on movies to $224 million. Sounds great for the Michigan economy, right? Wrong. In September 2010, the

Michigan Senate's Fiscal Agency reported that, even under the rosiest economic assumptions, tax receipts generated by new economic activity barely recoup 10 percent of the cost to taxpayers. As Manhattan Institute fellow Josh Barro writes, the report "estimates that the $125 million Michigan will spend on film credits in FY10–11 will generate just $13.5 million in new tax receipts, for a net fiscal cost of $111.5 million." And as for private sector activity? "The report finds the credits will generate just $78.5 million . . . well below their fiscal cost."[13] How could they? As the report concludes, 47 percent of the qualified expenditures were found to not even affect the Michigan economy.

It's even worse than that, though. As Bureau of Labor Statistics data reveals, not only has Michigan's film subsidies program failed to produce the jobs boom supporters promised, but the state has actually *lost,* not gained, film and entertainment jobs. Since Michigan's Hollywood welfare program's inception, the number of Michigan film jobs has gone from 5,867 jobs to 5,290, a 9.8 percent drop.[14]

Michigan isn't the only state where taxpayers are taking it on the chin to fund Hollywood's welfare handouts. Indeed, a quick tour around the country reveals just how corrupt and hypocritical Obama's biggest supporters truly are.

Take Massachusetts, for example. For every film tax credit dollar that John "What Yacht Taxes?" Kerry pays in the few Massachusetts taxes he fails to dodge each year, the commonwealth gains a measly $0.16 in revenue, mostly in the form of income tax revenues withheld from film company employees. That means the remaining $0.84 has to come from budget cuts or from charging Barney Frank's prostitution ring roommates higher taxes on their—*ahem*—income (that's not a low blow, unfortunately . . . you could Google it).[15]

But it gets even more outrageous. Check out this little gem buried in the middle of the Massachusetts Department of Revenue report:

> We estimate that of the $395.4 million in total payroll expenses of feature films produced in Massachusetts since 2006, $62.9 million or 15.9 percent was paid to Massachusetts residents. Of the estimated $332.5 million paid to non-residents, $177.3 million was accounted for by wages and salaries of 36 individual actors, directors and producers who were paid more than $1 million per production.[16]

Excuse me? Come again? The salaries of thirty-six Hollywood wing nuts—morons who don't even live in Massachusetts—account for $177.3 million of the total payroll expenses?! And these overpaid, Obama-worshipping idiots expect you and me to foot the bill for the very crowd who lectures us that we working chumps need to pay more in taxes . . . and still buy your stinking ten-dollar movie tickets?!

Um, how about shove it in your Hollywood pie hole.

As the report makes clear, for all the arguments by the Democrat politicians who do the bidding for their Hollywood cronies about how bringing the film industry to a state will result in huge job creation for the state, the reality in Massachusetts is that 18 percent of all the wages paid went to residents. The remaining 82 percent went to nonresidents.[17]

Bottom line: in 2009, Massachusetts's Hollywood welfare program produced a paltry 473 full-time-equivalent (FTE) jobs for residents and shelled out more than $170,000 of taxpayer dollars for each $50,000 job. "The evidence is clear, and we face a choice," concludes Northeastern University law professor Peter Enrich: "will we continue to throw $100 million each year at the illusion of turning Boston into Hollywood East?"[18]

Next up, Connecticut. Whether a company owes Connecticut taxes or not, Connecticut foots 30 percent of a production company's costs.[19] In 2009, Connecticut's Office of Fiscal Analysis projected a $116 million revenue loss from film credits, "a loss that is *more than one-third* the projected revenue loss from *all* business tax credits *combined*."[20]

Obama's Hollywood cronies promised Connecticut voters that these tax credits would "pay for themselves." Instead, Connecticut is hemorrhaging tens of millions on this outrageous Hollywood welfare scheme and leaving citizens holding the tab. When you dig even deeper into the pungent heap of steaming Hollywood hypocrisy, what's even more amazing about the Connecticut case is that 89 percent of the production spending that amassed the $116 million in film production credits wasn't even real "Connecticut spending." What this means is that, even as Connecticut remains in a state of economic free fall and budget deficits as far as the eye can see, taxpayers are subsidizing entertainment production costs and expenses occurring *outside their own state!*[21]

As a Connecticut Voices for Children report reveals, Connecticut's tax giveaways to the entertainment industry far eclipse any tax incentives the state offers to other businesses or industries. For example, the $116 million loss in revenue to the entertainment industry is "equal to one-third of total corporation business tax revenues that had been projected for FY 09 ($722.0 million)" and "more than five times greater than the state's total investment through tax credits in research and development and research and experimentation and more than ten times Connecticut's investment in job creation tax credits."[22]

Unfair, you say? Come on! Stop being so greedy! Hollywood

luminaries *need* your money! They're suffering just like all the rest of us. I mean, how else are they going to afford their Beverly Hills mansions, fuel their private fleets of sports cars and SUVs, and buy their bling, bling? These are hard times for a good brother in this Obama economy!

Consider the case of Rhode Island. Rhode Island's Hollywood welfare headaches began in 2005 when Democrat leaders in the House and Senate introduced and rammed through the legislation for their liberal Hollywood comrades.[23] From there the boondoggle produced predictably abysmal results.

For example, when tax cheat Wesley Snipes and Cybill Shepherd filmed their straight-to-DVD thespian spectacular, *Hard Luck* (oh, the irony), Rhode Island taxpayers were on the hook for $2.6 million in Hollywood welfare for the production company, which spent a total of just twenty-six days in the state. That figure was just a quarter of the total $11 million the company reported spending in the state. However, upon closer examination of the company's cost report, only $1.9 million of the total $11 million was spent on the state's residents or vendors. The remainder was spent out of state. As the *Providence Journal* reported, "Even in the food arena . . . the producers paid more to out-of-state catering companies ($87,633) than they did to in-state caterers ($52,071)."[24]

If that pisses you off, just wait. Did you know that you are also buying Obama's pals Mercedes and Range Rovers?

Cut to the state of Iowa. Not surprisingly, with hundreds of millions of taxpayer dollars sloshing around, scandals and accounting hijinks can't be far behind. Just ask Iowans. In 2007, Iowa got on the Hollywood welfare train and offered a 25 percent credit for film investors and production companies. They also sweetened the welfare deal by exempting income and sales taxes to qualified service providers. As Thomas Wheeler, who then worked at the Iowa state film office, pitched it, Hollywood productions shooting in Iowa could enjoy "half-price filmmaking." Soon, Obama's entertainment industry pals began doing what liberals do best: snatching up taxpayers' money.

In 2009, under the weight of the Obama economy, and like most states in America, Iowa saw its tax revenues nosedive. So the Iowa Department of Economic Development capped the Hollywood welfare program to $50 million. But before the changes went into effect, a tsunami of applications totaling $363 million flooded in, a figure equal to roughly 6 percent of Iowa's *entire* $6 billion budget.

That's when Iowa officials took a closer look and uncovered the scandal. As Des Moines accountant Joe Kristan reports, an outside auditor's investigation revealed:

- A Mercedes and a Range Rover were purchased for producers to keep with film credit funds.
- Not a single film's expenses were adequately documented. Only two of eighteen even submitted receipts.
- Contracts were amended to increase credits after approval.
- Large payments were made to relatives of filmmakers with credit funds.
- Payments were made outside of Iowa, when only payments in Iowa qualified.[25]

In related news, Democrat tax-cheat congressman Charlie Rangel replied, "Taxpayer funded Mercedes and Range Rovers? Dude, I've always wanted to film a movie in Iowa!"

Seriously, though, isn't that just peachy? Hollywood welfare recipients get to roll on dubs in the new Range Rover and Mercedes that you and I bought them, hook up their relatives with fat welfare checks, and all without the hassle of doing the required paperwork. Shoot, most of us who actually work for a living can't even get a travel expense reimbursement without filling out a mountain of paper as big as Rosie O'Donnell's butt. But in the highfalutin world of Hollywood welfare, none of that's required. Just show up, flash your "I love socialism" pass, and head straight to the front of the taxpayer-funded welfare line.

Even as we working suckers foot the bill to subsidize the crap that Hollywood studios churn out every year (*Hot Tub Time Machine,* anyone?), Obama's biggest supporters also nab extra perks. One of these involves fee-free locations. For example, if your private organization or company wants a state or city government to stop traffic or provide police officers, in most states you must pay fees and taxes for these services. But in six states, if you're a liberal Hollywood loon, your taxes and fees get swallowed by the taxpayers.

It's astounding to see the lengths some states will go to fight for the chance to waste piles of your hard-earned money. In West Virginia, for example, the state has something they call—are you ready for this?—"River On Demand."™ Quoth the West Virginia Film Office website: "Ever wanted to control the flow of a river? River on Demand™ is your answer."[26]

Um . . . no, actually. I've never wanted to control the flow of a river. But apparently for control freak Left-wingers who want to micromanage every inch of your existence, speeding up and slowing down the flow of river currents is a real gas.

The website goes on to explain that this is "a complimentary service made possible by the drawdown of the Summersville Lake by the U.S. Army Corps of Engineers, Huntington District." Yep. That's right. West Virginians, some of the poorest folks in the country, are footing the bill so that Obama's Hollywood pals can crank up or slow down how fast the river runs. Funny, I don't recall Greenpeace protesting the man-made environmental degradation of treating a river current like a faucet so that liberal idiots can frolic around in the water while the rest of West Virginians are out busting their humps at work. But who cares? Obama's Left Coast cronies are getting the taxpayer-funded welfare hookup, yo. Woo-hoo![27]

Equally bizarre and annoying is the fact that even when the theme or title of a movie is location-specific, producers and directors will often shoot a film in a different state if they think they can nab a better tax deal. For example, the U.S. Naval Academy movie *Annapolis* was, naturally, going to be shot in Maryland. That is, until Pennsylvania wooed the producers to pack up their gear and hightail it up the interstate so they could pocket $10 million in taxes. Similarly, when filmmakers wanted to turn John Grisham's Mississippi-based book, *The Runaway Jury,* into a movie, the state of Louisiana undercut Mississippi by offering a more favorable tax incentive package.[28]

As the *Economist* magazine reported, the movie *Gran Torino,* which originally focused on Minnesota's Hmong immigrants, was moved to Michigan to score that state's insane filmmaker welfare program, which can equal up to 42 percent of production costs. Similarly, the movie *Battle: Los Angeles* was filmed mostly in Baton Rouge, Louisiana, to nab a slice of its generous taxpayer-funded movie welfare pie. As Michigan state senator Jud Gilbert points out, if you offered a 42 percent rebate on, say, car production, that industry wouldn't be in crisis, either; picking winners and losers in business based on ideological symmetry is wrong.[29]

The Hollywood graft racket knows no end. Take, for example, the fact that one of Obama's bailout buddies, Chrysler, still blew millions on movie cross-promotions, even as they held their hands out to you and me. "This spring, *Terminator 4* comes out and we will be one of the sponsors," Chrysler director of media Susan Thomson said in a presentation at the Automotive News World Congress, bragging about their role in the new Christian Bale movie at the time. "We have a following with the *Terminator* movies and we are going to continue with that." This means that Chrysler, to which Obama eventually gave $12.5 billion of our tax dollars, was so broke, so destitute, that they still had enough funds to help underwrite Obama's Hollywood pals for their next flick.[30]

Thankfully, with the new wave of Republican governors now in charge, some have begun to push back against the lunacy of making taxpayers line the pockets of the Hollywood hucksters. One GOP rock star who gets it is New Jersey governor Chris Christie. Amid his heroic effort to save his state from its $10 billion budget shortfall, Christie suspended New Jersey's Hollywood welfare program. Of course, Obama's Democrat buddies in the New Jersey legislature promptly launched into action to try and avert any savings to the taxpayers. Can't allow any of that. But the brawler Christie fights on.

But New Jersey's neighbor, my home state of New York, isn't so lucky. We have nothing even closely approximating leadership. And so dimwits like Alec Baldwin rule the roost. "I'm telling you right now," screamed dad of the year Baldwin, "if these tax breaks are not reinstated into the budget, film production in this town is going to collapse, and television is going to collapse and it's all going to go to California."[31] So far, no word yet on the Empire State glitterati packing up and heading for the Left Coast.

"But Jason," you say, "states need jobs! Isn't there at least marginal job growth as the result of taxpayers spending tens of millions to attract movie production crews to their towns? I mean, don't local businesses, hotels, and restaurants experience increased business that covers the 'investment' by taxpayers?"

Um, no!

The job creation myth is phonier than the boobies bouncing around on the set of *Jersey Shore*. As the Center on Budget and Policy Priorities 2010 report found, because workforces outside of Los Angeles and New York lack the specialized skills producers need to shoot a film (such as scoring enough weed to keep Woody Harrelson's head from exploding), producers import high-paid "talent" from other states.[32] They call this lacking "crew depth."

"Estimates of revenue gains range from $0.07 to $0.28 cents per dollar of awarded subsidy," writes Robert Tannenwald. "The only studies claiming that a state film subsidy pays for itself were financed by the Motion Picture Association of America and/or a state office of film and tourism."[33]

Shocker.

So there you have it. Despite the fact that tens of millions of Americans are out of work and struggling to make ends meet in the economic quagmire that is the Obama economy, a little-known but massively expensive Hollywood welfare system continues to suck taxpayers dry to the tune of $1,500,000,000 in 2010 alone. Meanwhile, progressives scream and preach that we should raise taxes on everyone else, even as they demand that they pay few or no taxes at all.

Again, there's nothing wrong with trying to lower your taxes, but government has no business picking which industries should win and which should lose. It should lower everyone's taxes. Unlike movie productions, mom-and-pop stores can't up and leave to hunt down the lowest tax burden.

Furthermore, don't preach to us about how it's "patriotic" to pay higher taxes, when you do everything in your power to dodge them. Worse, don't cry about cuts to "social programs" and "poverty programs" when it's *you* who are hogging $1.5 billion of taxpayer money that could be going elsewhere.

So next time you're clicking past the Oscars, pause and say a prayer for the poverty-stricken celebrities. These welfare recipients desperately need your hard-earned tax dollars. Furthermore, find it within your heart not to mope and whine when it costs you eighty dollars to take the family to the movies. It's your duty, your responsibility, to help a 90210 neighbor in need.

After all, Michael Moore needs a gut tuck.

Private Jets Against Global Warming

Why Hollywood Eco-Crites like Leonardo DiCaprio, Al Gore, and Madonna Need to Shut Their Pie Holes and Reduce Their Own Gargantuan Carbon Footprints

Support global warming, baby!

—Obama supporter and genius rapper Akon mistakenly
yelling an anti-environmental chant
at the "Live Earth" concert[1]

It was Barack's "Katrina."

History will record that the worst environmental disaster in American history took place on the watch of the Messiah who promised to heal the oceans. But when his chance came for strong, decisive environmental action, Obama played eight rounds of golf, attended rock concerts and a baseball game, took two vacations, and appeared on *The Tonight Show* as eleven men died, 1.84 million gallons of chemical dispersants sloshed into the sea, countless marine animals perished, and 200 million gallons of crude oil gushed into the ocean to create an oil slick the size of Kansas.[2] The same socialist who believes government can save our souls leads a government that couldn't even plug a hole. Still, just eighteen days before the environmental catastrophe, Obama could be heard telling a North Carolina audience, "It turns out, by the way, that oil rigs today generally don't cause spills. They are technologically very advanced. Even during Katrina, the spills didn't come from the oil rigs, they came from the refineries onshore."[3] My, my, my . . . what a difference eighteen days make.

And what was Leftist Hollywood's response to the biggest environmental catastrophe in the history of the United States?

Silence.

Hollywood progressives never miss out on a chance to wag their famous fingers in our faces and lecture the unwashed masses about the need to defend and protect Mother Earth, to become guardians of the planet, and to alter our entire way of living to combat the environmental Armageddon that is global warming. So naturally, you would have expected the Hollywood eco-crowd to have shamed Dear Leader into environmental obedience. Surely they scolded him for his inaction and bumbled handling of the eco-crisis, a performance so abysmal that it made President George W. Bush's management of Hurricane Katrina look stellar. Furthermore, you would have expected massive environmental rallies, concerts, and charity events broadcast on national television to raise money for the cleanup effort and to help the thousands of coastal residents whose property, jobs, and livelihoods were destroyed by Obama's negligence and inability to handle the catastrophe, let alone heal the oceans. But, of course, none of that happened. Instead Hollywood ran interference for their favorite Marxist. As New

York *Daily News* columnist Andrea Tantaros put it, "At a benefit concert in 2005, Kanye West proclaimed that Bush doesn't care about black people. If that logic is correct, I guess Obama doesn't care about pelicans. Or fishermen."[4]

To be sure, a few minor-league celebrities like Lenny Kravitz and Mos Def (like I said, minor-league) held a small benefit concert. And good for them. But those waiting for Leonardo DiCaprio, George Clooney, and Barbra Streisand to descend on the Gulf shore, hold a massive press conference highlighting the environmental destruction, and then spur massive fundraising while condemning Oilbama's incompetence were left waiting. "The celebrity effort in the wake of the gulf oil spill has been a D-plus, B-list effort at best," wrote Alyssa Giacobbe for AOL News. "So what gives? Where are the photos of Lady Gaga in waders? Does Clooney have something against tuna?"[5]

The answer is that Hollywood eco-crites didn't dare shine a harsh and negative spotlight on the Messiah. Indeed, with the help of Hollywood's buddies in the liberal media, progressives have all but erased Obama from his starring role as the lead character in the environmental horror show that was the Gulf oil spill. *Time* magazine did a one-year follow-up story on the environmental status in the Gulf, titled "The BP Oil Spill, One Year Later: How Healthy Is the Gulf Now?" Unbelievably, the article did not even mention Barack Obama's name a single time. Better still, amazingly the piece declared that "a year after the spill began, it seems clear that the worst-case scenario never came true," that the oil mysteriously "disappeared from the water," and that the "ecological doomsday many predicted clearly hasn't taken place."[6] Or how about the wonderful headline from ABC News that screamed: "BP Oil Spill: Clean-Up Crews Can't Find Crude in the Gulf," as if Mother Nature, sensing that the man in the Oval Office is a compassionate tree-hugger, decided to pitch in and make the oil magically disappear.[7]

Of course, the scientific reality, as Harvard University professor David Ropeik points out, is that "tens of millions of gallons of crude oil leak into the ocean every day. Naturally, from the sea floor." In fact, that evil, eco-hating punk known as "the ocean" is responsible for contributing "the highest amount of oil to the marine environment," according to those right-wing radicals over there at the U.S. National Academy of Sciences.[8] But why let science get in the way when eco-hype and scare tactics are so much more effective in grabbing media coverage and conning the young liberal masses? Indeed, as Ropeik notes, the psychology of risks makes humans believe that "risks that are natural aren't as upsetting as risks that are human-made."[9]

Can you even *imagine* what the progressive media and Leftist Hollywood's response would have been had the largest environmental disaster in American history happened on George W. Bush's watch? Ha! The spectacle would have made *Avatar* look like a low-budget production. Still, the environmental double standard is hardly surprising when you realize just how flush with eco-hypocrites Hollywood truly is. After all, as Matt Bellamy, lead singer of the rock band Muse, brilliantly put it, Hollywood's environmental lobby might better be known as "private jets for climate change."[10]

To wit: Sting and Trudie Styler. There's nothing quite as satisfying and refreshing as listening to two mega-wealthy nitwits hold forth on how the average Jack and Jill are terrorizing Mother Earth, only to then find out that the mega-wealthy nitwits in question own seven homes, zip between them on private jets, and in their squadron of vehicles, haul a 750-person crew with them around the globe, and have a personal carbon footprint thirty times bigger than the average person's. And that's why you just have to love Sting and his eco-princess, Trudie Styler, who co-founded the Rainforest Foundation. So environmentally evolved is Sir Sting that the man even has a species of Colombian tree frog (*Dendropsophus stingi*) named after him.[11]

But unfortunately for the Stingmeister, despite all his "fresh-as-a-rain-forest-mist" posturing, he and his bride have quickly become two of the biggest eco-crite Obama supporters to grace the public stage. In fact, in 2008, Sting and his band were named one of the world's worst polluting bands.[12] Predictably, Sting spun the stinging indictment from the environmental crowd he claims to champion.

"I think it's an amusing red herring for the media to blame celebrities for the global crisis we're in," groused Sting. "I've done a lot of work to try and safeguard vast amounts of equatorial rain-forests over the past 20 years. I think I've tried to ameliorate my carbon footprint which is admittedly large. . . . It's difficult to do my job and not have a carbon footprint."[13]

Really? You don't say! It's also difficult for us working-class slobs to do our jobs and not leave a carbon footprint, either, but thankfully our footprints don't equal one of yours, Sasquatch.

"I would like to think that we both work pretty hard for the rights of indigenous people and for the rights of conservation of the Amazon rainforest," said eco-crite Styler, "but we do need to get around. It's a difficult one."[14]

Actually, no, Trudie, it's not a "difficult one." It's a convenient one. Or, as your good buddy Al "Massage with a Happy Ending" Gore might say, an "inconvenient truth." No word yet on whether the building of Trudie's seven homes—castles, really—involved cutting down and using that natural resource known as "wood," or whether the massive carbon emissions from their lugging a

750-person crew around Mother Earth and flying private jets has negatively impacted the "indigenous people" they claim to save. But who cares? They are really, really compassionate and think that trees are super groovy.

Yet the Stingster and Mrs. Stingy don't stop there. Mrs. Stingy also enjoys lecturing the Wal-Mart shopping hordes on the importance of reducing "food miles" (eco-crite lingo for the amount of miles one wastes driving—*gasp!*—to the grocery store instead of growing organically at home). Instead, Styler says we should be more like her and eat more expensive, locally grown organic foods, like the vegetables she grows at her Italian estate that she sells for a profit . . . after having them *transported* to London.

Pause and let that one sink in for a second.

Or how about the time Mrs. Sting tried to force her then-pregnant chef to drive one hundred miles, as the cook alleged in a legal dispute, to make one of her kids soup and salad (a trip the chef made regularly via train and taxi)?[15]

But as clueless as all this seems, Mrs. Sting wants you to get her "message in a bottle" and send out yet another SOS to stupidity because, despite her eco-hypocrisy, Styler wants us to know that the real culprit isn't her and her husband, but those wicked oil companies that sneak all that fuel into the private jets she flies on.

"Yes, I do take planes. My life is to travel and my life is also to speak out about the horrors of an environment that is being abused at the hands of oil companies." And that, you see, perfectly explains why, in 2009, the Pollution Princess decided to fly a beauty expert on a private jet to fix her hair and makeup before Barack Obama's White House dinner. Later, Styler confessed that she and her entourage of eight flew a private jet to the White House Correspondents Association Dinner.[16] So, you see, it really wasn't eco-hypocrisy, because it was all in service of the Messiah Obama.

And there's the rub. Sting and Trudie Styler's real goal isn't environmental protection. It's Obama-style socialism. But don't take my word for it. Just listen to Sting's hair-raising interview with CNN reporter Don Lemon:

STING: *Well, you can see the enthusiasm out there. And people are here to really tell big government that we want big government to make big decisions about the most important problems we face. And also to pressure our corporations to behave properly, as consumers, but we're here to—we're asking for big government, basically.*

CNN: *You want big government?*

STING: *Of course we do. This is a huge problem, and only the government can solve it. You know, the man on the street can do a little bit, but big governments need to make decisions. We need to stop clear-cutting forests. We need to protect the forests. That's the simplest way of cutting greenhouse gases.*

CNN: *Yes.*

STING: *And prevent global warming.*[17]

There you have it, folks. Big government must seize control of your life in order to save your life. It's a level of brazenness that borders on delirium.

"The man on the street can do a *little* bit"?

Come again?! Did you really just say that?!

Newsflash: How about starting by not lecturing us about our lightbulbs and SUVs and instead SELL YOUR SEVEN FREAKING MANSIONS, STOP FLYING ON PRIVATE JETS, and QUIT GLOBETROTTING AROUND THE PLANET WITH YOUR 750-PERSON CREW IN TOW!

Nauseating? You bet. But again, the goal here is total state power to control and dictate every part of our lives. Besides, Obama Zombie eco-crites like Mr. and Mrs. Sting are simply following the dictates of the Godfather of Global Warming, the Sultan of Science, the Guru of Groin Massages, none other than Hollywood's ozone Oscar winner, Al Gore.

"Humanity is sitting on a ticking time bomb," screamed *An Inconvenient Truth*'s website. "We have just 10 years to avert a major catastrophe that could send our entire planet into a tailspin." Gore's award-winning "documentary" has since been discredited as scientifically shoddy and shot through with more holes than a block of Swiss cheese. Furthermore, in the wake of "Climate Gate," which exposed the University of East Anglia's Climate Center's emails between climate "scientists" attempting to cover up their own data's inconsistencies, it's now clear what kind of sham science these so-called "climate experts" produce. In thirty years we'll likely look at Gore's flick as this generation's *Reefer Madness* equivalent—pure hype-driven silliness. Still, for the time being, until we hit Gore's magical "ten years to global cataclysm" time marker, we're stuck with the eco-crowd's hyperbolic drivel. For example, you just have to love the opening description found on Amazon.com for the socialist redistributionist plot masquerading as science that is *An Inconvenient Truth*. "With the fate of our planet arguably hanging in the balance, *An Inconvenient Truth* may prove to be one of the most important and prescient documentaries of all time."

Puhleeze.

But what's not a joke, of course, is that Al Gore stands poised to become, as the *Telegraph* newspaper dubbed it, the world's "First Carbon Billionaire." [18] He's for "going green," all right—all the way to the bank. And cashing in, Mr. Gore is! When Gore left the White

House, his assets were estimated to be worth less than $2 million. In 2009, the *New York Times* inquired as to Gore's current net worth, but Gore's spokeswoman refused to cough up the figure. Still, as the *Times* notes, "the scale of his wealth is evident in a single investment of $35 million in Capricorn Investment Group, a private equity fund started by his friend Jeffrey Skoll, the first president of eBay."[19] But that's chump change for Mr. Ozone. Indeed, it appears that before the planet explodes from spontaneous combustion, by working in cahoots with Barack, Al "Massage My Groin" Gore is determined to loot taxpayers' dollars in an eco-heist unlike anything we've ever seen.

But don't take my word for it. As the *New York Times* has revealed, the investment firm where Gore is a partner, Kleiner Perkins Caufield & Byers, one of Silicon Valley's biggest venture capital groups, invested $75 million in Silver Spring Networks, a company that works with utilities that "install millions of so-called smart meters in homes and businesses." As the *Times* reported in November 2009, "the deal appeared to pay off in a big way last week, when the Energy Department announced $3.4 billion in smart grid grants. Of the total, more than $560 million went to utilities with which Silver Spring has contracts." As the article hilariously understates (it is the *Times*, after all), Mr. Gore and his carbon-conning chums could "recoup their investment many times over in coming years."

Gee, ya think? Turning $75 million into $560 million from taxpayers? Move over, Gordon Gekko! There's a new Wall Street raider in town!

The way this racket works is that Gore leverages his "star power" and name recognition to land appointments with the big-wigs in government and business, trades favor on his high-level contacts at places where his eco-disciples are firmly entrenched, such as the Department of Energy or the Environmental Protection Agency, and then gives a wink and a nod to governmental appropriators when it comes to cut the billions of government dollars (aka YOUR MONEY) when doling out the government contracts.

Cha-ching!

In any other business, this would be considered a crime, something akin to insider trading or influence-peddling. But if you're a progressive, global warming crusader like Al Gore, it's just another day at the office. "Do you think there is something wrong with being active in business in this country?" Gore said with less than a hint of irony during a congressional hearing. "I'm proud of it. I am proud of it," Gore said.[20]

Another massive moneymaker for Captain Ozone has been the "significant portion of the tens of millions of dollars he has earned since leaving government" in eco-energy and technology businesses, such as so-called carbon trading markets, solar cells, and urinals that don't require water when flushing.[21] Moreover, Gore banks fat bucks serving as an "adviser" to such tech giants as Google and serving on the board of directors of Apple. In April 2011, the conservative zealots at Greenpeace declared that Apple was the "least green" tech company because of its "dirty data centers" that rely on coal for 54.5 percent of their energy.[22]

Gore is also founder of the London-based Generation Investment Management, which is run by former Goldman Sachs head honcho David Blood. The firm is affectionately known as "Blood and Gore."[23] When Congresswoman Marsha Blackburn of Gore's home state of Tennessee called him out on the jaw-dropping hypocrisy of Gore bashing corporations for greed and profiteering while himself making tens of millions by leveraging his eco-hype scam to swipe taxpayer dollars, Gore incredulously replied, "Congresswoman, if you believe that the reason I have been working on this issue for 30 years is because of greed, you don't know me."[24]

Yeah, we don't know you, Al . . . just like your now ex-wife and your many horrified ex-masseurs!

Of course, when anyone points out Gore's bald-faced hypocrisy, both from his personal homes that suck up energy like a vampire or his blatant big business eco-profiteering, Gore gets his hemp-stitched britches in a bunch. For example, according to the Tennessee Center for Policy Research, Gore's Tennessee mansion consumed nearly 221,000 kilowatt-hours (kWh) of electricity annually (more than twenty times the average U.S. citizen).[25] But no sooner does someone point out Gore's blatant hypocrisy than he hides behind the skirt of one of his eco-princesses, like his "environmental adviser" Kalee Kreider. "You can attack the messenger but the message remains the same," says Kreider. She's right. The message *does* remain the same: Al Gore has foisted one of the biggest socialist redistributionist scams on the American people ever devised and is making massive profits in the process.[26]

One of Gore's leading Hollywood accomplices in the global warming scare scam has been his film producer, Laurie David. Like her hero, David has achieved the status of being a world-class Hollywood eco-crite as well.

"I'm not perfect," said Laurie David, producer of *An Inconvenient Truth*. "This is not about perfection. I don't expect anybody else to be perfect either. That's what hurts the environmental movement—holding people to a standard they cannot meet."[27]

No, Laurie, what hurts the environmental movement is total environmental hypocrites like yourself who create grossly misleading "documentaries" with Al "Massage My Lower Chakra" Gore, brag about using compact fluorescent lightbulbs and recycled toilet paper (you don't even want to know), only to then zip around on chartered Gulfstream jets that burn as much fuel on a transcontinental flight as a Hummer does over an entire year.[28] She bristles when anyone criticizes her or her main man, Gore. "What this lame attempt to discredit Al Gore tells me is that we are winning," said David. "This is comedy at its best—it's straight out of the David Letterman show."[29]

But for Laurie David, who used the personal fortune of her ex-husband, *Seinfeld* co-creator Larry David, to help finance Al Gore's error-filled "documentary," the hypocrisy goes much further. After all, it was Gore himself who said, "Laurie David has done more than any one person I know to raise awareness of the climate crisis." Indeed, prior to her divorce-inducing affair with her building contractor, Bart Thorpe, when she wasn't out condemning SUV owners as "terrorist enablers" or bragging that she forced her kids to take shorter showers, David could be found at her 25,000-square-foot house on Martha's Vineyard.[30] I mention the affair because it's relevant to the rest of the story. You see, David's Martha's Vineyard mansion has been cited as a serial violator of Massachusetts's Wetlands Protection Act. The eco-infractions occurred while erecting her tennis court and, previously, "when construction of a stone fire pit, barbecue grill area and wooden stage for a children's theatre with seating was begun in a wetland without a permit."[31] No need to worry, though, when your contractor doubles as your lover. "She's obviously a very busy person and she trusted the contractor," said Bart Thorpe to the *Martha's Vineyard Gazette*. "I inadvertently made a mistake. It's something she had no knowledge of and had nothing to do with, and it's a minor thing," said the chivalrous lothario.[32]

David's former neighbor, Jacqueline Mendez-Diez, is no fan of the eco-vixen:

Actually, Laurie David has been creating one HUGE carbon footprint here on Martha's Vineyard for the last 6 years. Her disgusting and ostentatious trophy building has been virtually ceaseless for about 6 years now. The trucks and pollution stop only when Mrs. Carbon Sasquatch is here for her summer vacation, making herself the center of everyone's attention.

And I'd say the fact that I saw Laurie and her hottie but dumb building contractor, Bart Thorpe, holding hands while walking on a secluded dock to a boat yesterday, has a lot more to do with her marriage breaking up than the scratchy toilet paper she's forced on her family. . . .

I met Laurie David 6 years ago. I didn't like her then. I don't like her now. She is the prime example of a spoiled, selfish, rich girl who says, "do what I say, not what I do." She is a narcissist and a hypocrite to the nth degree.[33]

Ouch. That's definitely going to leave a mark.

"I normally wouldn't care," Mendez-Diez told Fox News, "but this woman was going around the country telling everyone to reduce their carbon footprint. . . . She built this reputation on confronting people about their lifestyle—about what kind of car they drive, about everything they do—and in her personal life she took 75 acres of undeveloped wetlands and developed swimming pools during a six-year construction project. It's ridiculous!"[34]

It may be ridiculous but it's hardly surprising. Hollywood's eco-idiots know no limits. Take, for example, the vice chair of Conservation International, Harrison Ford. "We all know that our planet is at a critical juncture," said an aging Indiana Jones. "Humanity needs a healthy planet to survive."

To demonstrate just how dire saving the planet is, Ford, sixty-eight, decided to take one for the team by cutting a commercial for Conservation International that involved the earring-wearing near septuagenarian demonstrating the horrors of deforestation by—I crap you not—having his *chest waxed*. In this video he declares, "When rainforests get slashed and burned, it releases tons of carbon into the air we breathe. It changes our climate. It hurts." Then some babe at a beauty parlor proceeds to rip a chunk of Ford's chest follicles out on camera to show the world just how much of an eco-warrior he really is.[35] What a *badass*.

(Side note: for those seeking a low-cost, fast way to lose weight, simply pull up the YouTube of this visual atrocity and let the purging begin.)

Yet far from being just your typical environmental whack job, Harrison Ford, friend of forests and foe of hair follicles, is also a raving aviator. In an interview with Britain's *Live* magazine, Ford, who has been flying since he was fifty-two years old and is the proud owner of *seven* aircraft, told the publication, "Learning to fly was a work of art. I'm so passionate about flying I often fly up the coast for a cheeseburger."[36]

Crickets chirping.

Homeboy flies a jet to grab a Big Mac?! Can you say pollution pimpin'?

When confronted about the blatant hypocrisy of the chairman of a global conservation group using one of his seven carbon-spewing airplanes to go grab a *cheeseburger*, Ford mounted a stirring defense. "I only fly one of them at a time," said Indiana Jones. Of his critics, Ford said, "They're quite right. I'll start walking everywhere when they start walking everywhere."

Testy, testy, Indiana!

Ford, who in 2010 spoke on Capitol Hill about general aviation at an event sponsored by the Aircraft Owners and Pilots Association, came ready to spit out statistics like his jet engines spit carbon: "The contribution of general aviation to the greenhouse gas emissions is less than two percent—and all of aviation, less than two percent of greenhouse gas emissions. And private, or general aviation, is less than that."[37]

It's quite comical how Hollywood's loudest environmental advocates are among the most egregious offenders. I guess this explains why Leonardo DiCaprio gets so annoyed when he gets called out on his eco-hypocrisy. "I've been driving a hybrid car for five, six years now. My house is built green, I have solar panels," brags DiCaprio.[38] In fact, DiCaprio, like most other eco-crites, wears his environmentally evolved snobbery on his sleeve. So eager for us to know what a green guy he is, DiCaprio even showed up at the Oscars in a hybrid car and blathered endlessly about worldwide access to clean water.[39]

One can imagine, therefore, how irritating it must be for someone as enlightened as DiCaprio to have to be subjected to scrutiny instead of met with fawning genuflection. For example, following the Cannes Film Festival premiere of the maudlin eco-documentary DiCaprio produced, *The 11th Hour*, a British journalist asked whether Leo had taken a carbon-belching jet to the French Riviera. "No," DiCaprio huffed sarcastically, "I took a train across the Atlantic." One of Leo's representatives, Ken Sunshine, has rushed to Leo's defense: "No star at his level flies commercial planes more than he does."[40] Indeed, at the press conference, DiCaprio clarified that he had, in fact, taken a commercial flight from New York and declared proudly, "I try to travel commercial as much as I can."[41]

"As much as I can"? What the hell does that even mean? As in, "as much as I can stomach being among you lower forms of human existence"? Are there not commercial flights that fly to every spot the thirty-eight-year-old eco-freak could ever wish to jet? Or is he worried that his mere presence aboard a commercial flight might cause pandemonium and the trampling of innocents by hormone-flushed tweens? Hate to break it to you, bro, but *Titanic* was almost a *decade and a half* ago (1997). On the teenage estrogen-o-meter, you hardly move the needle anymore. You've long been outfoxed by those vampire *Twilight* kids and that Canadian brother, Justin Bieber. Sorry to say, Leo, but you will be just fine among us common folk.

But none of this seems to have put a dent in DiCaprio's environmental self-righteousness and piousness. "Global warming is not only the No. 1 environmental challenge we face today," declares the genius climate scientist, "but one of the most important issues facing all of humanity."[42]

The eco-warrior's total disconnect with reality can sometimes be staggering. Without even a hint of ironic self-awareness, the *Titanic* star actually said these words out loud: "I was on a *plane* with Al [Gore] [emphasis mine] and I asked him, 'Don't you get disillusioned and think we're not doing enough?' Al answered, 'It wakes me up in the night, it terrifies me that we're too late and haven't done enough. But I can't have that attitude, I can't give up.' That's inspiring. Al still believes we can change."[43]

You can't make this stuff up, folks. The dude describes himself having a conversation with Al Gore *on a freaking plane* and doesn't even cringe in embarrassment. Even as he and Gore puff themselves up with self-importance and gush about saving the planet, the clouds are whizzing by the windows of their carbon-pooping plane. *Unreal!* But it doesn't stop DiCaprio from flacking for his hero, Gore.

"We're all trying the best we can, truly, we really are," said DiCaprio at Cannes. "Attacks on Al Gore, for example, I think are misdirected. Don't shoot the messenger, you know what I'm saying?"

Uh, no, Leo, we don't know what you are saying. What *are* you saying?

The climate expert DiCaprio continued: "If you're going to attack somebody on the way they conduct their life, let's talk about the big picture, let's see what big oil companies are doing."

Well, let's see . . . they are making the fuel that just powered the private jet you took to Cannes, and before that the commercial jet you took from New York. And, of course, there's the fact that your entire industry—remember, the word *industry* often involves carbon-producing enterprise—was cited in a two-year study by the University of California at Los Angeles's Institute of the Environment as producing more pollution than either aerospace manufacturing, apparel, hotels, or semiconductor manufacturing, second only to your nemeses in petroleum manufacturing. Yep, that's right, Hollywood is Los Angeles's second-largest air polluter, what with its pollution-puking diesel generators used to power movie sets and the massive emissions that result from the gargantuan electricity sucked up by studio lots and the trailers, camera vehicles, and equipment trucks that run endlessly.[44] The entertainment industry lecturing anyone about environmental destruction is like Pamela Anderson lecturing about the evils of plastic surgery. Consider the source!

Here's a request for the eco-princesses: stand up and raise your hand if you want to go back to those golden days of horse and buggy, where a one-way trip from New York to Los Angeles would take six months. C'mon, don't be bashful now. It's not easy being "green," as that noted philosopher and Jim Henson creation, Kermit the Frog, was fond of saying. Heck, not only have carbon-spitting cars and airplanes made traveling more convenient and efficient, but they have also purged us of the days of having to inhale piles and piles of horse manure. Yes, Lefties, horses took craps back then, too, and thus the towns were filled with its putrid odor, not to mention deadly diseases contracted by the inhabitants for being around animal shinola all day.

In any event, "global warming" shouldn't get us all hot and bothered. The evidence that man's actions are warming the planet are crumbling down like a game of Jenga.

First off, carbon dioxide itself makes up a tiny percentage of the earth's atmosphere. Just how tiny? I'll let geologist Dudley Hughes explain: "For simplicity, let us picture a football stadium with about 10,000 people in the stands. Assume each person represents a small volume of one type of gas. . . . Carbon dioxide is represented as only about 4 parts in 10,000, the smallest volume of any major atmospheric gas." In other words, CO_2 makes up less than 1 percent of the atmosphere.[45] And if you're still confused that CO_2 is a pollutant, here's your friendly reminder of the day: You exhale it and plant life feeds off it. You know, the whole "the circle of life" thing.

In reality, if man were truly culpable of destroying the planet with fossil fuels, the patchouli brigade wouldn't be relegated to falsifying data to help their cause. By now you've probably heard some sanctimonious professor or *New York Times* columnist tell us that the polar bears are dying, that the white furry creatures are on the verge of extinction. Except not really. In 2006, government scientists Charles Monnett and Jeffrey Gleason wrote an article for the journal *Polar Biology* in which they suggested that the death of a handful of polar bears may be the result of shrinking ice caps. The global warming lobby jumped on this news to scream, "You see, climate change is real. Polar bears are dying. Stop pollution now!" and all their usual hysteria. This conclusion was repeated in

Al Gore's faux-documentary *An Inconvenient Truth* and polar bears were even slapped on the endangered species list as a result.

Fast-forward to today: Gleason has since told federal investigators, "We never mentioned global warming in the paper." He went on to admit that their research was "sloppy." Indeed, the research was so "sloppy" that Gleason's partner, Monnett, was put on administrative leave at the Interior Department. It turns out the duo were studying whale migration, not polar bears, and that their "study," they now claim, was blown way out of control. "I think these sorts of things tend to mushroom, and the interpretation gets popularized," Gleason said. "Something very small turns into this big snowball coming down the mountain, and that's, I think, what happened with this paper."[46]

I could go on and on poking holes into the Left's sacred religion of global warming. But I won't. Instead I'll leave you with this quote from esteemed physicist, self-described liberal, and Princeton professor Freeman Dyson: "all the fuss about global warming is grossly exaggerated."[47]

Now let's go back to our favorite Hollywood hypocrite. Unlike most progressive Hollywood eco-crites who are satisfied to merely destroy Mother Earth from the rarefied air inside their private jets, Leonardo DiCaprio is a dual threat, dropping carbon bombs from the air but also wrecking coastal beaches by sea. In fact, Leo's environmental invasions are so epic that not even a Hollywood screenwriter could make up something this incredible. Here's the dirty inside story.

Hollywood producer Andrew Macdonald and director Danny Boyle decided to shoot the movie *The Beach* on the island of Phi Phi Le, just off the coast of the Thai mainland.[48] The island is uninhabited, unsupervised, a designated national park, and at the time had no enforceable restrictions on the use of the island. Eco-warrior Leonardo DiCaprio was the star of *The Beach*. "Preservation of the environment has always been of utmost concern to me," Leo assured the nearby Thai locals, "and I would never be part of any project that did anything to harm nature. I have seen extraordinary measures being taken to protect the island. And I pledge to remain vigilant and tolerate nothing less than these maximum efforts," DiCaprio told Thailand's environmentally worried citizens.[49]

What resulted, say Thailand's environmental protestors, was nothing short of a pillaging of the beach. Coconut trees were ripped up, dunes were bulldozed, coral reefs were damaged, and vegetation was yanked out. Protestors camped out on the beach, several hundred miles southwest of Bangkok, and watched as DiCaprio's eco-pillaging took place. When a dozen villagers tried to peacefully stage a sit-in on the beach—something you would think Hollywood-types would support—a group of "thugs" who villagers say were led by government officials forced them to leave, sparking anticorruption officials to investigate the head of the Royal Forestry Department's decision to let the studio infiltrate the island.[50] The indigenous people resisted, as residents of the island joined with twenty-nine nongovernmental organizations to protest after Twentieth Century Fox successfully gained permission to shoot after posting a $139,000 bond against environmental damage. "This [Fox's actions] is actually a well-known method of forest encroachment by developers," said the official statement from the protestors. "It turns natural, ecologically varied sites into coconut plantations. This is not making a movie. It's an abuse of power."[51]

DiCaprio got his little feelings hurt. To hear Leo tell the story, it seems that a big, powerful group of bullies, Thailand's environmentalists, decided to use him and his Hollywood comrades to gain media attention. "I'm a little bitter, just because it is a lie and people's perception may be a little tainted," DiCaprio whined in an interview in Hawaii. "It had a lot to do with the political propaganda that was going on in the country," said the excuse-making star.[52]

DiCaprio might have well been describing the fearmongering global warming hysteria that Hollywood hypocrite hucksters like him and Gore have beat like a drum. But the legal case brought by the concerned Thai citizens took a circuitous seven-year route that ended at the Thai Supreme Court. In 2006, the high court upheld a verdict of the appeal court and ruled that DiCaprio's movie, *The Beach,* did, in fact, destroy part of the environment. But for Di-Caprio, the whole thing was just a bunch of wild-eyed environmentalists exploiting the media to score environmental points.

Gee . . . I wonder where they learned that trick?!

"We were used as a test case over the ability of the forestry department to rent out islands to movies or for anything else," groused DiCaprio. "We were targeted as this big Hollywood machine that came in and disrespected this island. A lie started and all of a sudden it just grew and grew and became something else and became widespread. That became the story, no matter what we said about it. There was no way we could contradict it."[53]

Nothing worse than a Hollywood eco-crite feigning victim-hood.

But progressive Hollywood honestly must think we're too stupid to notice their hypocrisy. For example, how is it that someone as environmentally obnoxious as Robert Redford, whom *Time* has listed as one of environmentalism's "superheroes," could drone on endlessly about the evils of environmental destruction and carbon emissions, even as he has, as recently as 2008, done ten voiceovers for commercials by *United Airlines*?[54] Seriously? Does he think just because we can't see his seventy-four-year-old visage that we don't know that it's his voice trying to get us to board those carbon cannons called jets?

Redford's environmental hypocrisy runs much deeper. As Irish director Phelim McAleer, who co-created a short film on Redford's environmental two-stepping, points out, Redford recently sold a dozen pieces of land near his Sundance ski resort in Utah, which is home to ninety-five guest cottages, 180 private homes, and a ski area.[55] Redford sold the plots to developers who want to build luxury homes there in undisturbed wilderness near an undeveloped ridge. The motive for destroying the once-pristine mountain peaks? Redford's dozen plots of land went for $2 million a pop.[56]

But it gets better. Redford recently lobbied against a similar project in California's Napa Valley, where he has owned a home for eight years. The proposed plan for the Angwin Ecovillage would create 275 eco-friendly homes that utilize solar energy, wastewater reuse, and organic farm co-ops. But unlike his lucrative Utah land deal, Redford didn't have anything to gain financially from the Angwin Ecovillage. And so Redford issued the following statement opposing the eco-friendly housing development: "I believe that the citizens of Napa Valley, from American Canyon to Calistoga, care about preserving our beautiful agricultural and rural heritage. That is why I am happy to join the Advisory Council of Save Rural Angwin in its efforts to preserve this naturally carved land-basin from development."[57]

"It's the hypocrisy that gets me," says McAleer. "He's taking a lovely virgin ridge and building McMansions on it. Granted, they're nice, lefty, eco-McMansions. But they're McMansions all the same. At the same time, he's trying to stop other people from building houses in a nice spot."[58]

Robert Redford's profit-fueled hypocrisy is matched by Barbra

Streisand's hypocritical eco-hectoring, which ignores her glaring global warming inconsistencies. "Everyone has the power to make a difference by making simple, conscious decisions in their everyday lives," Streisand wrote on her website. She then included an oh-so-helpful list of things we can do to save the planet from intergalactic catastrophe. Among the "Simple Things We Can All Do To Help Stop Global Warming," Babs recommended using the lovely CFL lightbulbs, which are filled with that environmentally friendly substance known as *mercury*, cleaning the condenser coil on your refrigerator, and waiting to start your dishwasher until it's full.[59]

Of course, all this stands in sharp contrast to Streisand's own behavior when she's out on tour. In her contract, for example, she demands that she be supplied with "120 bath-sized towels immediately upon arrival." Perhaps she needs all these towels to handwash the army of vehicles she requires for her tour. Among the fleet are thirteen fifty-three-foot semi-trailers, four rental vans, fourteen crew and band buses, and, of course, the requisite limo befitting any limousine liberal. This doesn't include the numerous private jets she hops aboard frequently.[60] And, when Streisand isn't on the road touring America, leaving a cloud of carbon in her dirty wake, she's busy declaring a "Global Warming Emergency" and spending $22,000 a year watering her lawns and gardens.[61]

When you really start researching the actions versus the words of Hollywood progressives, what you uncover is borderline environmental schizophrenia. Consider the following:

- Paul McCartney fancies himself an environmental activist. But the former Beatle stirred up a hornet's nest among environmentalists when it was revealed that he had his new Lexus 600h flown into England from Japan using a cargo plane, instead of sent by ship alongside hundreds of other cars. "It's like driving the car 300 times around the world," said Gary Rumbold of co2-balance, an international company that helps people reduce carbon emissions.[62]

- Green advocate Brad Pitt jets around the globe. According to Fox News, a few of Pitt's trips include "Los Angeles to New York round trip (carbon footprint: 1.814 tons). Chicago to Los Angeles one-way (carbon footprint: .798 tons) and from Los Angeles to Namibia (carbon footprint: 3.569 tons)." But it's all okay, of course, because Pitt is building environmentally friendly houses in New Orleans's Lower Ninth Ward.[63]

- Natalie Portman wants you to believe she's a dyed-in-the-wool greenie. But her allegedly vegan line of shoes uses synthetic materials. Still, when you're hot and politically correct, people like Debbie Levin, president of the Environmental Media Association, stand ready to line up in your defense. "What Natalie Portman is doing with her shoes, even if they're not as green enough as they could be, she's saying she's concerned enough to try and maybe other people will try too. Nobody's perfect. If you have to be perfect, you have an environmental crowd of like three people."[64] Agreed. So enough with the high-horse Hollywood hectoring from people who run circles around the average American's carbon output.

- Jennifer Lopez's personal brand has been revived, thanks to her spot on *American Idol.* J-Lo is also the proud owner of the obligatory Hollywood eco-crite vehicle of choice, a Toyota Prius. But for Jenny from the block to make up for even a single one of her private jet trips from Los Angeles to New York she would have to drive her ugly Prius around planet earth—twice![65]

- Supermodel Gisele Bundchen is smokin' hot and a United Nations goodwill ambassador. And I want to go on record as saying that, if she ever wants to turn from her evil eco-crite ways and dump that Tom Brady chump, I will boldly and courageously offer my assistance and support. (Hey, what can I say? I'm a classy gentleman.) That said, for now she's a straight-up hypocrite. That's not me saying that. It's Philip Dowds, a Massachusetts Sierra Club official. Upon learning about the massive mansion with a six-car garage that Gisele and Brady were building, Dowds said to the *Boston Herald*, "How big a space do two people need? A 20,000 square-foot house—the resources that it takes to put it together and the land that it needs, this just can't happen anymore." Dowd pointed out that the house was big enough to provide shelter for twelve or thirteen average-sized American families. But that doesn't stop Gisele from lecturing to all of us on her website about how to live green.[66]

- George Clooney wants you to know he drives what may be possibly the world's ugliest, most ridiculous-looking vehicle (if you can call it that), a Tango electric car. The thing looks like a squished golf cart but it gets 135 miles to the charge. It turns out, however, that all the eco-goodwill Clooney builds up by suffering the public humiliation of driving that thing is all for naught. Clooney, who flies private jets, uses 7,000 gallons of jet fuel when he flies private from Los Angeles to Tokyo. That means he would have to drive over fifty-seven Pacific Oceans to make up for his wicked carbon-barfing ways. When he was called out on his environmental hypocrisy, in typical snooty "I'm so much better than you" Clooney fashion, the star's publicist, Stan Rosenfield, replied, "You clearly have no understanding of certain people's need for private transport," adding that Clooney has "no control" over where and when he travels. Yep. Uh-huh.[67]

- Jann Wenner, the founder and publisher of the legendary *Rolling Stone* magazine, uses his magazine as an environmental bludgeon to nag readers to be eco-friendly and "go green." In fact, the magazine does a special "green" issue for this very purpose. Worse, *Rolling Stone* is the very magazine that tied the 9/11 terrorist attacks to Bush's environmental policies. (In 2003, the magazine published a letter by Robert F. Kennedy Jr. insanely alleging that "our addiction to fossil fuels" made us a "target for terrorist attacks.") But if ever there was a person who needed a stern green lecture, it's Wenner. He has a chauffeur drive him in his Mercedes the fifteen blocks between his apartment and office, owns a GMC Yukon Denali, has a pair of snowmobiles at his Sun Valley, Idaho, retreat, doesn't recycle, and travels aboard his Gulfstream jet. "Lending out the jet is a huge part of Jann's starf**king," one insider told *Radar* magazine. "It's half the reason he has the plane." Wenner loaned out the private jet to his good pal and fellow eco-crite John Kerry during the 2004 presidential campaign. Birds of a feather.[68]

- Julia Roberts is hot, no doubt about it. But she's adding more heat to the global warming epidemic with each hypocritical move the Pretty Woman makes. As is required for any Hollywood eco-crite, Roberts owns a Prius. But beyond her feeling all warm and fuzzy for being such a stalwart defender of the planet, Roberts's self-congratulatory car purchase is instantly negated when you learn that she flew a private jet with Rupert Everett 1,749 miles from Chicago to Los Angeles during the filming of *My Best Friend's Wedding*. That's 2,750 gallons of jet fuel. Julia's "Prius penance," as TMZ notes, would mean that she would have to drive 30,000 miles, over the distance around the planet, just to "even out her consumption in the air." Doh![69]

- And then there's James Cameron, producer and director of *Avatar,* a movie about blue people who are used and exploited by those murderers of Mother Earth: corporations and the military. Cameron has no problem ramming his environmental agenda down the throats of the moviegoers who have made him mega-wealthy. But it seems he has some trouble when it comes to practicing what he preaches. Cameron doesn't just have a carbon footprint—his lifestyle creates a carbon crater. According to documentary filmmakers Ann McElhinney and Phelim McAleer, the progressive Cameron owns three—count them, *three*—houses in Malibu for a combined 24,000 square feet. That's ten times the average American home. The billionaire filmmaker also has a one-hundred-acre ranch in Santa Barbara, a JetRanger helicopter, three Harley-Davidson motorcycles, a Corvette, a Ducati, a Ford GT, collection of dirt bikes, a yacht, a Humvee fire truck, and even a squadron of private submarines![70] In fact, in the wake of

Oilbama's bungling of the gulf oil spill, Barack reached out to James Cameron before even talking with BP CEO Tony Hayward because Cameron has filmed movies underwater.[71] Few people have dared to call Cameron out on his laughable hypocrisy, however. According to *New York* magazine, this dude has an explosive temper. "Here's what James Cameron says to studio suits who impede his vision," reports *NY* magazine: "'Tell your friend he's getting f**ked in the ass, and if he would stop squirming it wouldn't hurt so much.'"[72] Ah yes . . . just the kind of man we want our president consulting in the midst of eco-catastrophes and teaching eco-morals to America's youth—and all from the comfort of his asteroid-sized carbon crater.

It's hardly surprising that Hollywood hypocrites behave the way they do and trash the very environment they claim to protect; they are merely following in the footsteps of Dear Leader. Hilariously, in April 2011, as Barack declared the forty-first annual Earth Day, he capped a three-day campaign-style journey that racked up 10,666 miles on Air Force One, burned 53,300 gallons of fuel, and cost you and me the taxpayer $180,000. And as *U.S. News* reports, those figures don't even include the gas needed to fuel his helicopter, presidential limousine, or the twenty-nine vehicles that travel with the president's limo. But who cares? It's just your normal "do as I say, not as I do" progressivism. Indeed, during a question-and-answer session following the president's speech in Pennsylvania, Obama lectured a father of ten that he should buy a hybrid van (which are not sold in the United States) and said, "If you're complaining about the price of gas and you're only getting 8 miles a gallon, you know, you might want to think about a trade-in." Of course, what the hypocrite president failed to realize is that his own vehicle, the presidential limo, gets—you guessed it—8 to 10 miles a gallon.[73] So it's little wonder Hollywood's eco-crites constantly embarrass themselves. They're just following the lead of their radical hero in the Oval Office.

Next, you almost have to admire the gall of a guy who can lecture the unwashed masses about "doing their bit" to preserve the planet and why it's critical that we develop alternative sources of fuel, even as he has a Boeing 707 aircraft parked in his backyard—literally.[74] Flying enthusiast John Travolta is a licensed pilot. He's also the proud owner of five private planes, including a Boeing 707, three Gulfstreams, and a Learjet that he flies all from the comfort of his very own private runway. "You know what they say," Travolta has been quoted as saying, "'If it ain't Boeing, I ain't going.'"[75]

"I'm probably not the best candidate to ask about global warming because I fly jets," said Captain Obvious. He added that global warming is "a very valid issue," before musing that he is "wondering if we need to think about other planets and dome cities."[76] Cue the *Jetsons* theme song and move over, NASA director, there's a new king in town! And, despite the fact that the typical 707 can carry 150 passengers, Travolta has been known to fly solo.[77]

But at least Travolta seems in on the joke and at least recognizes the apparent contradiction. The same cannot be said, however, for Madonna. Indeed, the Material Girl lives up to her name. Madonna headlined the London leg of the historic 2007 Live Earth concert, a breathtaking fact given that her investment portfolio has included more than $1.3 million in oil exploration and mining stocks.[78] When she was still married to Guy Ritchie, she flew her son and five friends aboard a private jet for New Year's. Her carbon footprint has been estimated at more than one hundred times a person's average. But there's nothing to see here, folks. At least, not according to her spokesperson, who, in answer to public criticisms, issued the following PR spin boilerplate: "She is educating herself and her family and has begun to make changes around her that reflect her awareness and concern for the future of the planet."[79]

Lame.

Luckily for eco-crites like Madonna, celebrities can now turn to so-called carbon coaches (what was that P. T. Barnum said about suckers . . . there's one born every minute?) who can help teach them new and exciting ways to wag their fingers in our faces as they consume enough energy to power the northeast quadrant of the United States. Celebrities like rocker KT Tunstall have already been snookered . . . er . . . um . . . I mean have hired a carbon coach. If you don't know who KT Tunstall is, don't worry about it—neither does the rest of the country.[80]

Perhaps we should be grateful for Madonna's Live Earth indiscretions, though. Madonna's Confessions tour produced 440 tons of CO_2 in just four months, and that figure omits the tens of thousands of fans' vehicles driving to and from the events, the truckloads of equipment, and the power needed for the stage riggings, reported John Buckley, managing director of CarbonFootprint.com. "It's great for the celebrities to come out and support the cause," said Buckley, "but they have to then follow it up in their own lifestyles. . . . Perhaps [Madonna's] next world tour will be performed in one venue, but broadcast to billions over the Internet."[81] Ha! Don't hold your carbon dioxide on that one, carbon boy. In the immortal words of that renowned world philosopher, P. Diddy, "it's all about the Benjamins, baby!"

But it's hard to reason with the irrational. Indeed, Madonna has given us such sweet odes to presidential leadership as "Just go to Texas and suck George Bush's d**k" and "f**k George Bush."[82]

Ah, yes . . . the harmonious sounds of a Nobel Peace Prize in the making.

But when she's not busy fashioning the Democrat Party's campaign slogans or headlining concerts dedicated to averting environmental devastation, Madonna can be found tooling around in one of the myriad automobiles in her personal fleet of eco-wreckers, which include a Mercedes Maybach, two Range Rovers, an Audi A8, and a Mini Cooper S.[83]

Everyone on planet earth wants clean water and air. But the idea that the planet is on the brink of global annihilation and that man-made carbon is the culprit is a bunch of hot air. You don't even need to believe the mountain of scientific evidence that makes a mockery of the radical environmentalists' phony claims (despite Al Gore's bloviating, Greenland is not even close to shrinking rapidly, reports the *New York Times*[!]).[84] Nor do you even need to realize that "green is the new red" (as in socialist/communist wealth redistribution masquerading as environmentalism). No, all you need to look at is the very behavior of the Hollywood eco-crites.

If the world were truly about to blow up because of carbon emissions, would Oscar winner Al Gore and his producer, Laurie David, really be flying around the world on private jets? If Mother Earth were truly just years from Armageddon-like consequences, would Barbra Streisand and Mr. and Mrs. Sting be traipsing around the globe with an army of equipment trucks and concert trailers, and taking more trips on jets than you and I could ever hope to have in a lifetime? If our day of environmental reckoning were fast upon us, would Leonardo DiCaprio be going around the world trashing beaches? Or Barack Obama be celebrating Earth Day by sucker-punching the planet with carbon emissions?

No.

And so, how about we start with the proposition that we, the unwashed, stupid, dumb, ignorant, Wal-Mart shopping, gun-owning, God-fearing dum-dums, will begin altering our lifestyles just as soon as Obama's Hollywood followers stop flying on private jets, lugging huge crews around the earth, living in energy-sucking mansions, driving SUVs, and working in an industry that is second only to petroleum refineries in pollution output.

Sound like a deal? Good.

Now, if you'll excuse me, I'm going to go spray aerosol cans into the air to catch up to Leonardo DiCaprio and Al Gore on my carbon footprint.

3 Working-Class ~~Heroes~~ Zeroes

*How Bruce Springsteen and Jon Bon Jovi Dodge Taxes While
Pretending to Be Farmers—and Other Financial Feats of
Do-Gooder Greed*

We granted tax cuts to the richest one percent . . .
increasing the division of wealth that threatens to
destroy our social contract with one another.

—Bruce Springsteen[1]

The reason I'm running for president is because I can't be
Bruce Springsteen.

—Barack Obama[2]

Bruce Springsteen is a man of the people. He stands up for the
little guy. A regular blue-collar Joe. A union man. A bona fide
working-class hero.

And, when he's not busy being all that . . . he's a tax-dodging, union-busting, liberal hypocrite worth over $200 million who pretends to be a farmer to save hundreds of thousands of dollars on his property taxes that would have otherwise funded the welfare programs he pretends to care about.

That's right. Mr. "Union Man, Blue Collar" Springsteen is a total fraud.

You've got to hand it to "the Boss," though. He's mastered the common man pose perfectly. As the *New York Times* breathlessly writes, "He still comes across as a working-class guy from New Jersey, invoking a populism as he sings about jobs, families, and everyday life."[3] But when he's not busy pretending to be Average Joe, Springsteen can be found counting his riches, jetting back and forth between his concerts and his New Jersey estate, convincing voters that he's just a nonpartisan dude with no political axe to grind.

"Personally, for the last 25 years I have always stayed one step away from partisan politics," the aging rocker said. "Why is it that the wealthiest nation in the world finds it so hard to keep its promise and faith with its weakest citizens?"[4]

Well, Bruce, perhaps part of the answer involves poseur progressives like you who claim to want to "help the poor" through big-government programs yet do everything in your power to avoid paying your taxes.

Yet despite his protestations to the contrary, before he threw his weight behind Barack Obama, the Boss spent 2004 raising $44 million for presidential loser John Kerry. "I've got 25 years of credibility built up, and this isn't something I've moved into lightly," Springsteen said. "But this is the one where you spend some of that credibility. It's an emergency intervention. We need to get an administration that is more attentive to the needs of all its citizens."[5]

When Bruce's efforts to elect the tax-dodging Kerry went bust, Springsteen took his faux "everyman" act on the road in service of his favorite socialist, Obama.

Indeed, Springsteen is no stranger to politicizing his music. His song "Born in the U.S.A." is a critique of LBJ's Vietnam War. He even saw fit to exploit the Amadou Diallo tragedy, which left the West African immigrant dead when police mistook him for a criminal suspect, with his song "American Skin." Four officers in the Bronx shot Diallo to death at night, confusing his wallet for a gun. The officers were eventually acquitted of all charges by a racially mixed jury, which led some in the community to cry foul and organize mass demonstrations. It wasn't a pretty time for New Yorkers, and the Boss decided to cash in on the distress. That led Patrolmen's Benevolent Association president Pat Lynch to condemn Springsteen's attempt to score political points off the tragedy. "I consider it an outrage that he [Springsteen] would be trying to fatten his wallet by reopening the wounds of this tragic case at a time when police officers and community members are in a healing period," Lynch said.[6]

By 2008, however, Bruce was ready to move beyond profiting off of tragedy and had set his sights on electing a fellow phony to the Oval Office. Springsteen's song "The Rising" became a campaign staple for Obama's speech venues and culminated in him playing for Obama's inauguration. But it is the Boss's bogus blue-collar, factory worker, union man shtick leading up to the election and following that qualifies him as a grade-A Hollywood hypocrite.

"We granted tax cuts to the richest one percent . . . increasing the division of wealth that threatens to destroy our social contract with one another and render mute the promise of 'one nation indivisible.'"[7]

This is an incredible statement on so many levels that I don't quite know where to begin. First of all—and I want all the progressive, Obama-worshipping Hollywood hypocrites to listen up once and for all—if you are against the so-called Bush tax cuts (which weren't "cuts" but instead holding taxes at the same rate they used to be), and if you sincerely believe in your bleeding Marxist heart that higher taxes are the answer to all that ails America, then here's my suggestion:

SELF-IMPOSE THE HIGHER TAX RATE YOU WISH TO PAY!

Thanks to something called the "Gifts to the United States Government Fund," any citizen who wants to fork over their hard-earned money so that Barack Obama can waste it on useless crap is free to do so. Created in 1843 for citizens who wanted to donate gifts or bequests "from individuals wishing to express their patriotism to the United States," the Department of the Treasury's special fund allows Bruce Springsteen and every other liberal you've ever heard blather about the need for higher taxes to send a check or money order directly to Uncle Sam. I mean, you want to do like your main man Barack says and "spread the wealth around," right, Bruce? In fact, let's make it even easier on the Boss. Bruce, here's the exact mailing address you need to send your $200 million check to:

Gifts to the United States
U.S. Department of the Treasury
Credit Accounting Branch
3700 East-West Highway, Room 622D
Hyattsville, MD 20782

In fact, we need to have this address printed on business cards, so that every time you hear a rich limousine liberal claim to be "standing up for the little guy" by declaring that rich people like them should be paying higher taxes, your response will be "So what's stopping you? Here's how you can," and you can hand them the above address.

Imagine the billions of dollars that will instantly begin flowing into the public coffers. George Soros, Barbra Streisand, George Clooney, David Geffen, Steven Spielberg, Matt Damon, Jon Bon Jovi, Whoopi Goldberg, Bruce Springsteen will all magically and cheerfully begin self-imposing a higher tax rate on themselves. After all, why would any progressive ever take any deductions? Seriously. If their argument is that progressive taxation is fair and preferable, why in the world would they ever do anything to lower their own taxes? Doesn't "social justice" and "equality" require that they pay the full rate? Thankfully, with the implementation of the "Let Them Pay Higher Taxes" plan—henceforth to be referred to as the "Hollywood Hypocrite Tax"—the national deficit crisis will be solved in no time.

Yeah, right . . . and Pamela Anderson doesn't have hepatitis C.

Why is that? (Not the part about Pammy having hep-C, but liberals not self-imposing higher taxes on themselves when it is perfectly lawful for them to do so.) Answer: Because Hollywood is filled with a bunch of photo-op-hungry Lefty frauds who would rather feign compassion for the poor than actually put their money where their progressive mouths are. If they were really interested in helping the underclass enjoy economic uplift they would realize that it's impossible to be "for" jobs and against those who create them. Better still, they would learn a thing or two about how lower taxes help, not hurt, the poor.

But perhaps the second reason Bruce Springsteen's poverty

poseur antics are so appalling is that the man is a first-rate tax dodger. Consider the following. In 2011, perhaps wanting some local free press, Springsteen decided to write a letter to the editor of his town's newspaper. In response to an article about tax cuts and aid to entitlement programs, the Boss wrote in to praise the piece for being "one of the few that highlights the contradictions between a policy of large tax cuts, on the one hand, and cuts in services to those in the most dire conditions, on the other." Furthermore, Springsteen wrote, "your article shows that the cuts are eating away at the lower edges of the middle class, not just those already classified as in poverty, and are likely to continue to get worse over the next few years." Then, with his well-honed "everyman" touch, he signed the letter along with his oh-so-common-man-sounding town name, "Colts Neck."

Now, all this would be just fine and dandy. But there's one small problem with Springsteen's anti-tax-cut posturing: the man is a first-rate tax evader.

Bruce Springsteen pays over $138,000 a year in taxes for his three-acre home in Colts Neck, New Jersey. He owns another 200 adjoining acres. But because he has a part-time farmer come and grow a few tomatoes (organic, of course) and has horses, his tax bill on the remaining 200 acres is just $4,639 bucks. Do the math. By being a fake farmer, the working-class zero Springsteen is making a mint by robbing New Jersey of the antipoverty program funds he says they desperately need.

"I think it is unfair to our other property taxpayers that if you are a fake farmer, and that you don't legitimately farm, that you are getting a property tax break and forcing your neighbor to pick up your tab," said state senator Jennifer Beck. "That was not the intent of the law. It's a violation of the public trust."[8] When Fox 5 New York reporter Barbara Nevins Taylor asked a lawyer for the trust that owns Springsteen's land to comment on the Boss's lucrative fake-farming tax breaks, predictably, the lawyer had no comment.[9]

The tax loophole comes from the New Jersey's Farmland Assessment Act of 1964. Originally the provision was created to help preserve agriculture in New Jersey. To qualify for the tax break, landowners must own at least five acres of land and produce just $500 a year in goods in order to qualify. Anyone who can meet those minimum standards can reduce their farmland tax bills by an astounding 98 percent.[10]

Now, here again, no conservative begrudges anyone—not even a die-hard Obama Zombie like Bruce Springsteen—from lowering their tax burden by taking full advantage of every tax break available to them. That's legal and fine. But for a guy who makes hundreds of millions pretending to be a guardian of the working class, and who advocates taxing the rich at higher rates, to then turn around and utilize obscure tax loopholes to pocket hundreds of thousands of dollars that would otherwise go to his beloved social programs . . . well, that's just flat-out Hollywood hypocrisy.

Bruce Springsteen's neighbor who lives on the property that backs up right against his says that she thinks the Boss's tax loophole is unfair. She lives so close to him that she says she can sometimes hear the band practicing. "It's unfair that I have to pay, for an acre and a half, $6,000 and then they are paying, for hundreds of acres, $200."[11] But apparently the equality crusader Springsteen sees it differently. And in fact, his tax-evading ways seem to have rubbed off on his bandmates.

E Street Band drummer Max Weinberg lives on McClees Road in Middletown, New Jersey. In addition to being the drummer for Springsteen's band, he is the former bandleader for Conan O'Brien on the former shows *Late Night with Conan O'Brien* and *The Tonight*

Show with Conan O'Brien. Weinberg's home sits on two acres. For his home and residential land, Weinberg pays $49,000 in property taxes. But on the additional thirty-four acres Weinberg owns, he pays a paltry $122. The reason? Weinberg sells wood.

In 2004, Max Weinberg campaigned for another "tax them but not me" progressive, John Kerry, for president. Weinberg's hypocrisy is well noted. In 2002, Weinberg won a conservation award for his work as a member of the board of trustees for the Monmouth Conservation Foundation. The next year, however, Weinberg decided to cash in by selling twenty-two acres of his massive estate in Middletown Township, New Jersey, so they could be sold as new home lots, a move many of his neighbors protested as bringing on environmental degradation for profits. One *Newark Star-Ledger* columnist labeled Weinberg a "symbol of hypocrisy," and Weinberg told the *Wall Street Journal* he's been branded an "arrogant rock star." But, as it turns out, Weinberg, who played at Bill Clinton's 1993 inauguration, is just a capitalist pig when it comes to real estate.

"If you ask somebody, 'Give me the stereotypical description of a rock star,'" says Weinberger's friend and attorney, Jerry Zaro, "they would not say meticulous due diligence. It's nothing for Max to go down to city hall and spend a day mired in their arcane regulations." Weinberg did his first real estate deal over thirty years ago and never looked back. "When I was out on tour, I had a lot of time on my hands," Weinberg says. "And all I did was read books about architecture and how to build houses."[12] Apparently, he also picked up a thing or two on how to cut his property taxes by 98 percent, thereby depriving more welfare recipients from getting their hands on his hard-earned money. The shamelessness and inhumanity of it all.

But you see, Bruce Springsteen's solution to all this wealth accumulation by the richest Americans was Barack Hussein Obama. And that's why, standing in front of eighty thousand Obama Zombies on a stage at Philadelphia's Vote for Change rally, the "everyman" profitmonger took to the stage to flack for the most unqualified presidential candidate in American history.

"In my job, I travel the world, and occasionally play to big stadiums, just like Senator Obama," Springsteen said during the 2008 election. "I've continued to find, wherever I go, America remains a repository of people's hopes, possibilities and desires, and that, despite the terrible erosion to our standing around the world, accomplished by our recent administration, we remain, for many, a house of dreams."

Oh, how poetic, Boss. Preach on.

"One thousand George Bushes and one thousand Dick Cheneys will never be able to tear that house down. Our sacred house of dreams has been abused, looted and left in a terrible state of disrepair."

Setting aside for a moment the obligatory swipe at Bush and Cheney, you gotta love the fact that the guy chooses a *housing* metaphor when he's a first-rate tax dodger on, well, property taxes. But I digress.

The swan song of justice continued: "It needs care, it needs saving, it needs defending against those who would sell it down the river for power or a quick buck. It needs strong arms, hearts and minds. It needs someone with Senator Obama's understanding, temperateness, deliberativeness, maturity, compassion, toughness and faith to help us rebuild our house once again."

Gag.

Not surprisingly, after Barack won the White House, Springsteen was invited to play at the One's inaugural. Never one to miss an opportunity to leverage his "blue-collar, union man" hokum shtick, Springsteen decided to cross-pollinate his brand with Obama's by titling the album—get your barf bag ready for this—*Working On a Dream.* Better still, in an effort to cash in and ride the marketing wave of progressive O-basms exploding across America, Springsteen shrewdly decided to "bookend" the Obama inaugural by releasing one album one week *before* the event (January 13, 2009) and another one week to the day *after* Obama's inauguration (January 27).[13]

Cha-ching!

Springsteen has a seven-album contract with Columbia Records that the *New York Times* estimates to be worth $110 million.[14] On January 13, just one week before he would play at Obama's inaugural, Bruce Springsteen fans saw the arrival of the Boss's ten-dollar collection of Bruce Springsteen and the E Street Band's *Greatest Hits,* which is a compilation of eleven songs from his 1995 anthology, as well as "Radio Nowhere" from *Magic.* But there was just one problem with Mr. Union Man's new album: Springsteen had cut an exclusive deal to sell the greatest-hits record at that champion of all things union . . . *Wal-Mart* . . . the same Wal-Mart that endlessly draws the ire of left-wing labor groups for blocking the unionization of its employees. Yeah, *that* Wal-Mart.

The backlash went viral immediately. "Doing a deal with Wal-Mart goes against his principles that he has said he has stood for," said Springsteen biographer Charles Cross, author of *Backstreets: Springsteen, The Man and His Music.* Fans agreed. "Bruce is doing biz with Wal-Mart?" one fan wrote on a fan site. "Kind of goes against everything he stands for."[15]

Yep. That's sorta what hypocrites do.

Team Springsteen immediately went into damage control. In an interview with *Billboard,* Jon Landau, Springsteen's manager, tried to spin the public relations disaster by pointing out that the artist's records are already for sale in Wal-Mart. Gee, that really takes the sting out of it for union hacks. ("Nothing to see here, fellas. We've actually been screwing you for years. No worries!") But Landau dug the grave deeper by adding that a full 15 percent of all of Springsteen's total sales came from Wal-Mart, one of progressivism's most treasured targets. The backpedaling was in full whirl. "We're not doing any advertising for Wal-Mart," Landau said. "We haven't endorsed Wal-Mart or anybody else."

No, you don't endorse them, you just use them to deliver you massive profits from a company that, to hear you tell it, enforces slave wages and violates labor laws. How noble.

But even better than Landau's flaccid attempts to fight back against Springsteen's anti-union business deal were the ridiculous talking points from the Boss himself. Check out this piece of pure Springsteen spin:

"We were in the middle of doing a lot of things, it kind of came down and, really, we didn't vet it the way we usually do. We just dropped the ball on it. Given its [Wal-Mart's] labor history, it was something that if we'd thought about it a little longer, we'd have done something different. It was a mistake. Our batting average is usually very good, but we missed that one. Fans will call you on that stuff, as it should be."[16]

Wow. Wow. And more wow.

There is something Obama-esque in Springsteen's nonapology apology. It's so absurd that it doesn't just strain credulity, it snaps it in half. Are we really to believe that Springsteen's army of advisers and lawyers were just too gosh darn busy to realize that *Wal-Mart*—one of the Left's favorite punching bags—is no fan of unions? Does he seriously believe that his fans are so stupid as to think that a man who has sold upwards of 120 million records worldwide, and who sells 15 percent of all of his albums through Wal-Mart, just "let it slip through the cracks" that he was giving an exclusive deal to a company that stands at odds with his self-proclaimed support for unions? Or could it instead be that Team Springsteen well understood that having the ten-dollar record appear on the shelves of the biggest retail chain on planet earth just one week before the rocker would be performing in one of the most-watched venues on planet earth—a presidential inaugural— might stand to make Springsteen a pile of cash? And all from those working-class dolts he knows didn't vote for Obama but who nonetheless love shopping and spending their hard-earned money at the wicked Wal-Mart.

In fact, the closer you study Springsteen's words and deeds the more you realize how plastic and practiced his common man pose truly is. Check out this excerpt from an interview he granted to London's *Sunday Times:*

> There's a widespread political consciousness that's per-haps deeper in Europe than it is in the States. . . . The climate [in America] is very, very ugly for getting things done. The moderate reforms President Obama fought to make are called Marxist, socialist. I mean, the most ex-treme language is put into play to describe the most mod-est reforms that would move the economy back towards serving a majority of its citizens. . . . The biggest problem we have now is almost 10 percent unemployment, but we also have the disparity of wealth. You can't have an American civilization with the kind of disparity of wealth we have. It will eat away at the country's heart and soul and spirit.[17]

What eats away at the "heart and soul and spirit" of America is progressive phonies like Springsteen who pretend to loathe profits and scream for higher taxes on the rich only to then, in typical Leftist hypocrite fashion, make massive profits while clawing to pinch every penny of savings on their taxes. But like a Method actor who refuses to break character, nothing seems to stop this fraud from playing the role of a lunch-pail-carrying factory worker instead of a capitalist pig who, according to *Forbes* magazine, banked $70 million last year alone.[18]

"Our economy has oriented itself away from the mass of US citizens and oriented itself to be at the service of the folks at the top, the plutocracy. [It] has to be oriented back to where it serves the health and purposes of a majority of American citizens," said Springsteen.

Plutocracy, eh? Mighty fancy word there ain't it, Bruce? Be careful. Your everyman poseur panties are showing.

The dude's complete detachment from reality, combined with the Orwellian manner in which he condemns the wealthy as being greedy even as he sidesteps property taxes, is arresting in its lack of self-awareness. But at least the New Jersey huckster understands one truth: "Most people don't want to be taking their political direction from guys that are shaking their ass in front of 60,000 people. That's understandable."[19]

Agreed. So shut your Obama-worshipping socialist yap and go count the mountains of money that evil capitalism and that union-busting Wal-Mart have made you.

THERE REALLY MUST be something in the water over there in New Jersey, because the Garden State sure cranks out some of progressivism's finest rock star hypocrites. In fact, just down the road from Springsteen's drummer's mansion is eighties hair band rocker turned Obama appointee to the "White House Council on Community Solutions" (whatever the hell that is) Jon Bon Jovi. With as many czars as Obama has appointed, it was only a matter of time before he created a Cheesiness Czar.

Still, Bon Jovi's support for progressive causes and liberal Democrats is well established. In 2004, he subjected unwitting Democrats to the agony of listening to him and Richie Sambora playing acoustic sets at rallies for John Kerry and John "Love Child" Edwards throughout America. In 2008, Bon Jovi held a private fundraiser at his mansion for Obama. In 2009, he helped Hillary pay back her campaign debt by playing a Manhattan fundraiser for her and also performed for New Jersey's then governor Jon Corzine before my homeboy Chris Christie pulverized him at the polls. And of course who could forget the epic Bon Jovi performance at Obama's inauguration concert, wherein the cheesy rocker, standing on the steps of the Lincoln Memorial, managed to crucify the Sam Cooke classic "A Change Is Gonna Come." Dogs throughout the D.C. area haven't been the same since.

Like Bruce Springsteen, Jon Bon Jovi has amassed incredible wealth using the same carefully crafted "factory worker turned rocker" ruse. But with an average concert ticket price of $105 for a nightly gross of $3,800,000, it's unclear how many factory workers can afford to attend his concerts. Indeed, in 2010, Bon Jovi scored $200 million in gross concert receipts.[20] To date, Bon Jovi has sold more than 130 million records worldwide. And like every hardworking blue-collar worker, Bon Jovi retires nightly to his quaint fifteen-acre, $22.25 million mansion estate on the Navesink River in Middletown, New Jersey.

Being a good Obama Zombie Democrat, Bon Jovi is eager to

pay his $295,689 a year in property taxes on his castle-sized estate. But it's the remaining 6.85 acres of his land he's not so excited about paying taxes on. Instead of cheerfully funding the kind of poverty programs and social welfare programs that he's so keen on garnering publicity and photo ops for, the blue-collar multimillionaire would rather slash his property taxes on his remaining acres all the way down to $104. That's less than the dude spends to highlight his hair! After all, why fork over your hard-earned cash to the state of New Jersey to fund big-government programs when you can instead claim to be not a rock star but a *bee farmer*?[21]

And to think that all this time you thought Jon Bon Jovi was just a washed-up cheeseball eighties rocker. Little did you know that he's a hardworking farmer of bees. Heck, the only thing that resembles a beehive on or near Bon Jovi is the brother's haircut. (There are hairdos and there are hairdon'ts. He habitually violates the latter.)

Bon Jovi's spokesman spun the honeybee farm tax cut this way: "Jon is scrupulous about paying his fair share of taxes. The exemption for raising honeybees existed long before he purchased that land, and he continues to employ a beekeeper and raise honeybees."[22]

What the hell does that have to do with anything? Look, if tax-and-spend liberals believe the rich should pay more in the form of a progressive tax system, then why in the world would they take an exemption on anything? Seriously. Why not just multiply his income by the federal and state rates, cut a check, and send it to the New Jersey state house and Dear Leader in D.C.? If progressive Democrats believe the wealthy should "pay their fair share" in the form of far higher tax rates, why not double the rate they currently pay? Come on, you greedy progressives. Where's all that liberal "compassion," "generosity," and eagerness to "give back to the society that made you rich"?

The answer, of course, is that while they may believe all that crap in theory, in practice they believe that they should keep what they've earned. Furthermore, because of the multiple charities and foundations they are a part of, they also believe that private organizations are more effective and efficient in delivering services and support than their government counterparts. If they didn't believe this, they wouldn't establish private charitable interests. But to say all that wouldn't help their Leftist cause, so they can't say those things. After all, Barack Obama is counting on them to sell the "big government is great" myth.

But it's not enough for Jon Bon Jovi. When he's not busy suiting up for a hard day of bee farming, Bon Jovi can be found whining and crying about how that big ol' meany, "technology," is robbing him and his fellow progressive rock stars of even more cash to stuff in their capitalist coffers. Of course, he doesn't put it quite that way. Instead he prefers to camouflage his beef with digitally downloadable music in longing for a bygone era.

In an interview with Britain's *Sunday Times Magazine,* the fifty-year-old Bon Jovi waxed nostalgic about the glory days (sorry, Bruce) when kids could plunk down their allowance on an entire album without knowing its contents and thereby enrich the musician more ably, rather than having the ability to cherry-pick the one or two kernels of corn from the poo pile that is a Jon Bon Jovi album.

"Kids today have missed the whole experience of putting the headphones on, turning it up to 10, holding the jacket, closing their eyes and getting lost in an album; and the beauty of taking your allowance money and making a decision based on the jacket, not knowing what the record sounded like, and looking at a couple of still pictures and imagining it. God, it was a magical, magical time," said Grandpa Jovi. "I hate to sound like an old man now, but I am, and you mark my words, in a generation from now people are going to say: 'What happened?' Steve Jobs is personally responsible for killing the music business." [23]

Come again? Steve Jobs was responsible for "killing the music business" because he gave consumers more choices? Far be it from me to get between two progressives locked in a tussle. But I'm siding with the late Steve Jobs on this one. I think Kyle Buchanan put it best when he responded, "That's right: Steve Jobs, who presented an online system that actually got artists paid and staunched [sic] the illegal downloading that had previously gripped the music industry, has *personally* thwarted the most important criteria you could use when deciding whether to buy a record: the ability to discern for yourself just how feathery Jon Bon Jovi's chunky Meg Ryan do is on the album jacket." [24]

Look, hating taxes is as American as it gets. (Boston Tea Party, anyone?) Furthermore, we know that letting people keep more of the money they earn yields bigger federal revenue in the end. John F. Kennedy and Ronald Reagan proved that. But big-government, tax-and-spend progressives don't believe that. They believe increasing taxes on citizens, particularly those who earn the most, is a sacrosanct act of patriotism. That's fine. Then let them self-impose higher tax rates on themselves. After all, aren't liberals the ones always talking about the importance of "sacrificing for the good of the community" and the importance of "spreading the wealth around"? Then let them.

But they don't. And they won't. Instead, like tax evaders Bruce Springsteen and Jon Bon Jovi, they, like the rest of humanity, will do everything in their power to scrape and claw to keep every last penny of their hard-earned money. Furthermore, the reason they give exclusive record deals to retail behemoth and union foe Wal-Mart, and lament the decline of high-profit record sales lost to iTunes, is that they are first-class capitalists. And good for them! That's the American way.

It's only when they rail against the evil rich, stoke the flames of class warfare, and push their phony populist pablum that their actions morph into straight-up Hollywood hypocrisy, the kind that makes a mockery of their progressive message and lays to waste the idea that high tax rates produce growth and economic flourishing. If that were the case, they would gladly fork over their mountains of money without claiming a single deduction. Furthermore, they wouldn't hunt for every loophole in the monstrosity that is the tax code.

The Boss and the Cheesiness Czar need to give up the faux populist ruse and get back to what they do best: farming organic tomatoes and raising bees.

The Priestess of Pigs
(Capitalist, That Is)

How Arianna Huffington Amassed a Corporate Empire by
Denouncing . . . Well, Corporate Empires

The litany of sins committed by the high priests of profit
is a study in venality, deceit, theft, treachery, pride, and
most of all, greed, greed, and more greed.

—Arianna Huffington, author of *Pigs at the Trough: How Corporate*
Greed and Political Corruption Are Undermining America[1]

Arianna Huffington is one *scary* broad.

She also happens to be the darling—or *daaahling,* as she
would say in her Greek, aristocratic drawl—of the Hollywood Left.
Huffington pulled off what few progressives thought possible: she
created the *Huffington Post* blog, the liberal counterweight to the
conservative-leaning *Drudge Report* news website. The *Huffington*

Post—HuffPo as progressives affectionately call it—can go toe-to-toe with the *New York Times* on Web traffic. And it does so without all the additional brick-and-mortar costs that come with running a traditional print paper, such as delivery, ink, and paper.[2] That means it's profitable. In the age of the dying dinosaur that is the traditional newspaper, that makes *HuffPo* a long-term media platform for progressive influence.

Arianna Huffington's genius lay in her decision to attract high-profile celebrities and give them a massive media megaphone from which to spout off about anything they wanted. Specifically, by leveraging her socialite connections, she turned 250 celebrities into bloggers. She corralled Sean Penn, Ellen DeGeneres, Barack Obama, Larry David, Diane Keaton, Walter Cronkite, Desmond Tutu, King Abdullah of Jordan, Alec Baldwin—and all for zilch in pay.[3] All they received was the satisfaction of knowing they could weigh in on news and current events. Sometimes, busy celebrities just call Arianna Huffington on the phone and begin ranting their blog screeds so she can transcribe and post them. Other times the celebrities dash off opinion-editorials themselves or have their publicists do it for them. But either way, Arianna Huffington gives celebrities the one thing they crave but lack: political credibility.

The celebrity articles are magnets for Web traffic. But to kick the website into overdrive, Huffington has enlisted thousands—nine thousand, to be exact—bloggers to write articles on a whole lot of nothing. In exchange, these "citizen journalists" (yes, that's really what she calls them and, yes, the bloggers really fell for it) crank out truckloads of article content and are paid absolutely nothing. Instead of money, these citizen journalists have the satisfaction and pride of knowing that their Leftist rants are worthy enough to appear on the *Huffington Post* alongside articles by mega-celebrities. That, along with the visibility of being one of thousands of writer bees buzzing away on blog entries blathering about the evil George W. Bush or that nightmarish economic system known as "capitalism," is thought to be payment enough.

What the bloggers and Hollywood A-listers may or may not have understood but that Arianna Huffington clearly did was the way search engine optimization (SEO) works. SEO is how you get your website ranked higher on Google or other search engines. The more content you have, and the more keywords your site contains, the higher it climbs on Google search results. With nine thousand people blogging on everything from food to fashion to fascism, the *Huffington Post*'s search results and subsequent traffic rose like a rocket. The higher a website ranks in the search engines, the more traffic it receives. And the more clicks a website receives the more it can charge for—drum roll, please—advertising!

Cha-ching!

"[Arianna Huffington] doesn't apologize for things," said Jason Keath, the president of the social media firm Social Fresh. "She's paid attention to technology more. She's paid attention to SEO [search engine optimization] more."[4] Indeed, as one Associated Press profile on Huffington put it, Huffington quickly realized that Web links and so-called back links fuel "steroidal" Web traffic.[5]

And therein lies the business brilliance of capitalist extraordinaire Arianna Huffington. By enlisting everyone from Hollywood A-listers to presidents to her hordes of progressive bloggers (with a few token moderates and conservatives thrown in for cover), Huffington created a digital empire of content that quickly dominated search results, garnered 25 million unique visitors monthly, and sent advertising rates soaring. With just $1 million in seed money, within a year Arianna Huffington and her business partner Kenny Lerer had turned the website into a revenue-generating advertising platform.

Fast-forward six years. In 2011, the princess of pixilated progressivism did what her legions of Lefty followers thought was the unthinkable: she made a massive profit—*gasp!*—and sold the *Huffington Post* to corporate behemoth AOL for a reported $315 million, with Huffington receiving an undisclosed but huge portion of that figure in cash and shares. In typical progressive fashion, the fallout has been hysterical and filled with emotionally over-the-top rhetoric.

"We made HuffPost and we are being abandoned," groused one *HuffPo* blogger.[6] Another disgruntled sucker . . . er, I mean "*HuffPo* citizen journalist," R. B. Stuart, said he regrets publishing an estimated $25,000 worth of content. Then, in a slap in the face to all *real* victims of slavery, he said, "Arianna not only sold her soul as well as her ship of slaves, but sowed the seeds of her demise with this act of greed and exploitation."[7]

Then came the denunciations from the professional groups. America's Newspaper Guild, the so-called journalists' union, has launched a campaign designed to convince Arianna Huffington to donate a portion of her AOL profits to pay journalists. "After building a media empire based on unpaid writers and republishing the works of others," said guild president Bernie Lunzer, "we are calling on Arianna Huffington to invest in quality journalism by sharing a portion of this fortune."[8]

Other voices from the Left rained down derision and invoked— shocker of all shockers—even more slavery imagery. As *Los Angeles Times* columnist Tim Rutten put it: "To grasp its [the *Huffington Post*'s] business model . . . you need to picture a galley rowed by slaves and commanded by pirates. . . . The fact is that AOL and the Huffington Post simply recapitulate in the new media many of the worst abuses of the old economy's industrial capitalism—the sweatshop, the speedup and piecework; huge profits for the owners; desperation, drudgery and exploitation for the workers. No child labor, yet, but if there were more page views in it . . ."[9]

Wowzers.

Indeed, when you see just how pissed off she's made her own Lefty followers, it can be tempting to want to like the woman; you almost don't know whether to high-five her or shove her.

But the real Arianna Huffington is no one anyone should cheer. Indeed, she is deserving of not just progressive contempt but conservative repulsion as well. She's derisively been called "the most upwardly mobile Greek since Icarus."[10] When you unmask the hidden history of the woman who gave Leftist Hollywood one of its most successful media ventures ever, what you find goes beyond hypocrisy. It's downright haunting.

Arianna Stassinopoulos was born in Athens, Greece. In 1972, she graduated with a master's in economics from Cambridge University. "I was lucky that I got my degree in economics at Cambridge where I inhaled a healthy skepticism of the power of the free market to bring about the good society," writes Huffington. "After all, Cambridge was the home of John Maynard Keynes. I well remember a lecture in my freshman year in which free-market guru Milton Friedman was dismissed in one sentence as someone who did not understand Keynesian Economics."[11]

By all accounts, Stassinopoulos was a talented student who harbored a burning drive. She was the first female president of the prestigious debating society the Cambridge Union, and her Cambridge classmates remember her as being "ambitious beyond measure."[12] To wit: one year after graduation, she published what would be the first of her thirteen books, this one titled *The Female*

Woman. In 1980, at the dawn of the Age of Reagan, she immigrated to New York. Then, in 1986, she married oil baron turned California GOP congressman Michael Huffington and launched her career as a then-conservative pundit and author. For a time, Michael Huffington was even considered a possible contender for the Republican presidential nomination.

Behind the scenes, however, those who knew the couple best quickly realized that it was Arianna who was running the show. To many, the congressman, who later ran unsuccessfully for U.S. Senate, was merely a ventriloquist dummy being controlled by Arianna. As one of his former congressional staffers explained, "On any big decision you'd go in and talk to him and leave, and then you'd see his phone light go on, and he'd call Arianna to ask her. Walking from his desk to your own, you could [count] 3, 2, 1 and Arianna was on the line."[13]

Arianna Huffington's former literary agent, Peter Matson, remembered Arianna's control over her then-husband as being complete. "If anyone thinks she hasn't seen herself in the White House yet, then you don't know Arianna Stassinopoulos Huffington. Michael was searching for himself, and Arianna found him. My illustration for them is 'Driving Michael Huffington': Arianna wearing a cap behind the wheel and Michael sitting in the backseat looking perfectly bewildered."[14]

In 1994, *Vanity Fair* journalist Maureen Orth, who was the wife of the late NBC News reporter Tim Russert, published a lengthy, devastating exposé that unmasked Arianna Huffington. The feature piece ran the gamut and even alluded to her husband's alleged bisexual tendencies, allegations that, as it turned out, were later confirmed when, in 1998, Michael Huffington publicly announced he was bisexual, following the couple's divorce. But it was Orth's investigative historical work into the secret life of the Greek-born social climber that would ultimately spark a long-standing feud of Orth and her husband, Tim Russert, against Arianna Huffington.

First, there were the abusive practices against the dozen staff members the couple employed to work in their $4.3 million mansion in Montecito, California, and their swank digs in Washington. Arianna hired the former servants of ambassador Pamela Harriman. Many workers didn't last long and quit after being treated "like slaves." Others said the Greek goddess would throw temper tantrums, scream commands over the speakerphone from her bathtub, make her children's bodyguards fetch her tampons from grocery stores, and would even keep a lock on her refrigerator—and that was on good days. "We were joking about making a t-shirt that said 'I quit the bitch,'" remembers one former researcher. "Arianna was so cruel—mean and nasty to everyone in the house." When she wasn't busy barking orders, she would complain about her "lazy and stupid" Mexican servants, one of whom turned out to have been hired illegally.[15]

Then there was her faux philanthropy and volunteerism. When Maureen Orth interviewed Arianna, she asked the wealthy diva when she volunteered, which was a frequent theme Huffington stressed in her speeches and books. "Very regularly," Huffington responded. Yet when Orth went to meet with the directors of the charities Huffington claimed involvement in, the reporter says she was "hardly prepared for the reaction" she got from the charity director. "No, she has never volunteered here. In three years, no one has ever seen Arianna but twice, and both times she brought a TV crew with her. It was self-promotion, nothing more. She's never given a penny to us and never even worked with the children. . . . We don't want our name used in connection with her. . . . It's using needy children in a needy situation for political gain and it's really disgusting."[16]

Before the days of berating her squadron of servants or using charities as photo ops (complete with a film crew in tow), Huffington, who has authored thirteen books, was busy plagiarizing the life's work of others to create a profit for herself.

"What she did was steal 20 years of my work," said the late Lydia Gasman, who was a University of Virginia art historian. Gasman was widely regarded as a leading expert on Pablo Picasso. In 1988, Arianna published a book called *Picasso: Creator and Destroyer*. The book, which was written with the help of Picasso's former mistress Françoise Gilot, infuriated many in the art world. It painted Picasso as a misogynistic sex addict who used his creative brilliance to raze the lives of the women who worshipped him. But Huffington's book "systematically cannibalizes" the epic four-volume Ph.D. thesis that Gasman had not formally published but was available on file in typescript, says John Richardson, Picasso's principal biographer.[17]

Gasman confronted Arianna. "I told her she was an intellectual kleptomaniac," said Gasman. "She started to cry and said, 'I didn't mean it. I think like you.' She proposed 'Entre nous, a secret arrangement if I can make it up to you.'" Arianna then had her then-husband Michael join Gasman at a Manhattan hotel for dinner, wherein Michael Huffington put the question to Gasman: "How much money do you think your work is worth?" Gasman replied, "One million dollars. I worked all my life on it." Not surprisingly, Arianna and Michael Huffington remembered the ugly ordeal differently and claim it was Gasman, not Michael, who broached the buyout. After Gasman had her lawyer file a complaint with Simon & Schuster, publisher of Huffington's Picasso book, the cash-strapped academic ultimately decided against pursuing a legal battle with the multimillionaire Huffington. In fact, Arianna and Michael even threatened to sue her for extortion.[18] With no

settlement inside or outside the courtroom, the "intellectual kleptomaniac" got away scot-free.

Plagiarizing epic works on Picasso and turning them into
profit centers, however, was just one of Arianna Huffington's acts
of literary legerdemain. In 1993 she published *The Gods of Greece,*
which was cribbed from psychologist James Hillman. "The basic
ideas running through the book are mine—that's what they're for.
I just find her method not decent, not scholarly," Hillman told
Orth. "I praise her for her 'mercurial' gifts. As you know, Mercury
was the god of thieves."[19]

Of course, using the ideas and writings of others to make a
profit would later become the entire framework for her creation
of the *Huffington Post,* albeit in a more legal way that relied less
on blatant plagiarism. Far less known, however, is the mistress of
manipulation's long-standing involvement and priestess status in
a cult known for financial and sexual exploitation.

Between 1990 and 1993 Arianna Huffington gave $35,000 to
something called the Foundation for Individual and World Peace.[20]
The organization was run by Roger Hinkins, a schoolteacher who,
in the 1970s, transformed himself into "John-Roger," the head of
a California-based New Age cult known as the Church of the Movement of Spiritual Awareness, or Movement of the Spiritual Inner
Awareness (MSIA), which its members pronounce "Messiah." The
path Stassinopoulos Huffington took to get enmeshed in the cult,
reports Orth in *Vanity Fair,* is as bizarre as it is frightening:

> In Paris in the late 70s, Arianna Stassinopoulos was
> ordained a minister in the Church of the Movement of
> Spiritual Inner Awareness. In 1984 she was baptized in
> the river Jordan. In her ordination, Arianna, who at-
> tained the highest level of secret initiation, "Soul Initi-

ate," swore devotion to a curious divinity. The document of ordination reads: "We do this through the order of the Melchizedek Priesthood, the Office of the Christ, the Mystical Traveler, Preceptor Consciousness, and into God. This delineates for you the divine line of authority" . . . They believe that the Preceptor Consciousness, which is embodied on the planet only every 25,000 years and is therefore higher than Christ, is personified by John-Roger. Soul Initiates such as Arianna are required to pray by chanting the secret names of God that John-Roger gives them. . . . Arianna Huffington, who has followed the diminutive John-Roger all over the world for two decades [as of 1994], has never renounced her ministry. . . . When I asked Arianna if she still chants the names of God that John-Roger gave her—a dead-bang giveaway, according to ex-M.S.I.A. members, as to whether or not someone still believes—she replied, "These are sacred questions . . . I pray. I'm not going to discuss how I pray." [21]

That's right. The creator of the most influential progressive media platform in existence and the "digital gathering grounds" for Hollywood celebrities and like-minded liberals is the brainchild of a cult priestess—and a gold digger to boot. One former MSIA member, Susan Roberts, recalls Arianna Huffington standing up at a MSIA retreat in upstate New York in 1987 and declaring, "'Dahlings, if you want to marry a rich man like I did, then tithe!' Everyone whooped and hollered." Indeed, cult leader John-Roger "guided her every step in her pursuit of Michael Huffington." She would call John-Roger following every date she had with Huffington to get advice on what her next moves should be. [22]

Since Orth's reportage in 1994, not surprisingly, Huffington has taken great efforts to publicly distance and shield herself from scrutiny of her cult membership. What's more, before his untimely death, Tim Russert, the husband of Maureen Orth, became a frequent target of Huffington's scorn. Arianna even kept a running "Russert Watch" column on the *Huffington Post*. Russert remained unfazed. "I've been attacked by Arianna the right-wing radical *and* Arianna the left-wing revolutionary," he said. "I guess the only constant in her life is she keeps watching *Meet the Press*."[23]

Following her divorce from her bisexual oil baron husband, the once-card-carrying conservative pundit morphed herself into a hard-core progressive. She became known as a one-woman battering ram bashing capitalists and businesses as profit-seeking pigs feeding at the trough of greed. "I called myself a conservative," Huffington told reporter John Stossel. "The main reason was because how I saw the role of government. I actually believed that the private sector would be able to address a lot of the issues that I believed were very important, like taking care of those in need. And then I saw firsthand how difficult it was."[24] Huffington says that after seeing poor people in the inner city, she realized that her advocating free market capitalism—the kind that lifts people out of poverty—had made her "the mouthpiece for such hypocrisy."[25]

Even some on the Left, however, saw through Huffington's shtick. "I used to debate Arianna on [CNN's] *Crossfire*," said Democrat political strategist Bob Shrum. "She was about as conservative as you can get, and suddenly she's for activism and social conscience. I think she's just blown on the winds of fads."[26]

Whatever the case, for the next decade, Arianna Huffington, the onetime advocate for free markets and capitalism, turned her guns on so-called greed and corruption created at the hands of those evil people who work hard to make money to feed their families. Here's a taste from the Huffington hit parade of her best-selling, profit-making books:

Pigs at the Trough

- "The general public is up in arms—and rightly so—about the kind of corporate greed that leads to massive shareholder rip-offs."
- "Who filled the trough? Who laid the table at the banquet of greed? Who made it possible for the pigs to gorge themselves on ludicrous quantities of stock options, grossly inflated pay packages, and a dazzling array of perks so indulgent they make Donald Trump look puritanical?"
- "Just as communists had promised a utopia in which the state would wither away, the free-market ideologues in control in the nineties promised us that we would reach Nirvana when all government intervention would, well, just wither away. We would then find ourselves in a glorious Brave New World. Marxists and CNBC stock analysts together at last, holding hands and feverishly chanting: 'From each according to his culpability, to each according to his greed.'"
- "We've seen the results of capitalism without conscience. . . . All in pursuit of ever-greater profits."

Third-World America

- "So we look at the suffering all around us, at the shuttered factories and stores, and worry that it is just the tip of the iceberg—or the tip of the tip of the iceberg. We try to fight off the fear that if things don't change—and in a big way—we may find ourselves working at Wal-Mart or McDonald's or Dunkin' Donuts for minimum wage."

- "We have to ask ourselves what this remade world will look like. Will it be a place where economic opportunity is once again real for everyone, not just the economic elite? Will it be a place where greed and selfishness are no longer rewarded and 'the least among us' are given a helping hand, rather than the back of it? . . . Will it be a place where transparency reigns and backroom deals are banished from the halls of power? . . . Will it be a place where Main Street replaces Wall Street as the center of the economic universe?"

Right Is Wrong
- "Psychologists say that cognitive dissonance, the belief in conflicting ideas, is resolved through rationalization and, as rationalizations go, the virtue of self-interest—greed is good—is a very powerful one."

The cumulative effect of Huffington's progressive rhetoric was to position herself as the Left's leading crusader against corporate greed and those who would exploit workers to make massive profits. Where others were dirty, Huffington, the "Minister of Light," was pure. Where others had sold out their progressive calling for profits, Arianna Huffington had turned from her wicked capitalistic ways and had "given back" to the progressive community by way of creating the *Huffington Post* blog, the celebrity-studded liberal counterweight to conservatives' *Drudge Report*.

What ideological purity . . .

What progressive purposefulness . . .

What a heaping pile of steaming donkey poop!

Cult leader Rev. John-Roger (left) and his most successful M.S.I.A. (pronounced "Messiah") disciple, Priestess Arianna Huffington (right) at her 2004 book launch party. Say what you will about these two space cadets: I bet they throw a freaking awesome Halloween party!

Just as she had conned Christian conservatives into believing that the cultic pig princess was one of them, so, too, did she hoodwink Leftist dupes into believing that she was an anti-corporate, anti-profit, anti-exploiter of labor. Chief among the Democrat dummies were the nine thousand progressive bloggers—or, as Stalin reportedly called American liberals, "useful idiots"—and 250 celebrities who agreed to create content for Arianna Huffington for zero pay.

But Stassinopoulos Huffington wasn't content just to leverage liberal blogger idiots and her celebrity pals to build her profit machine. She also poached Web traffic by piggybacking off the labor of real reporters by posting so-called real journalistic articles and placing advertising next to them. As former *Washington Post* editor Len Downie Jr. explains, Huffington's news aggregator website and those like it are "parasites living off journalism produced by others," a strategy the *Wall Street Journal*'s editor in chief Robert Thomson deems "tech tapeworms."[27] As the Associated Press points out, even as the "mainstream" news media were tinkering with paid versus unpaid subscription models for their websites, along came Arianna Huffington, who "upended their business models."[28] To this day, media outlets are trying to figure out how to monetize their online content. To wit, the *New York Times* allows free access to online users, but there's a limit. Readers are required to purchase a digital subscription if they exceed a certain number of articles on the website.

In 2011, as we saw earlier, Huffington and AOL issued an announcement that made progressive jaws drop. Arianna Huffington, Hollywood's high priestess of anti-profit, anti-greed, and anti-capitalism, cashed in to the tune of a $315 million AOL buyout. Immediately, many on the Left labeled Huffington a sellout.

"Given the fact that its founder, Huffington, reportedly will walk away from this acquisition with a personal profit of as much as $100 million, it makes all the Post's raging against Wall Street plutocrats, crony capitalism and the Bush and Obama administrations' insensitivities to the middle class and the unemployed a bit much."[29]

Adding insult to the injury for progressives has been Huffington's breathtaking contention that the Left versus Right journalistic paradigm is outmoded and unhelpful. "It's time for all of us in journalism to move beyond left and right," said Huffington. "Truly, it is an obsolete way of looking at the problems America is facing."[30]

As writer Mayhill Fowler, the former *HuffPo* "citizen journalist" who recorded Obama at that San Francisco fundraiser lamenting that we Americans "cling" to guns and God, wrote on her personal blog, the AOL merger "gives the lie to [Huffington's] frequent assertion this past year that she is pro Main and con Wall Street. Of course, the hypocrisy of her 'let's hear it for the little people' mantra has already been undercut by her refusal to pay bloggers like me." Fowler has quit blogging for the *Huffington Post* and says leading Democrat figures must understand that they can't "say one thing and do another: to talk sympathy for working people and yet blog at a site that treats its writers badly."[31]

One reservoir of Huffington's useful idiots, the anti-consumerism anti-capitalists over at the magazine *Adbusters*, decided to rise up, pixilated pitchforks in hand, and mount a digital posse to lash back at the Princess of Pigs. You just have to love the screed they posted. It's one part whine, one part temper tantrum, topped off with a splash of pure cluelessness at how a ruthless corporate raider like Huffington actually operates. It begins with a lament that "socialite" Arianna Huffington "exploited" their idealism (read: stupidity) and "let us labor under the illusion that the

Huffington Post was different, independent and leftist." But then the wicked witch did a dastardly thing. She waved her corporate wand and—poof!—made a pile of money and left thousands of bloggers "working for a megacorp."[32]

To which I respond: Bahahahahahaha!

But the "pat-them-on-the-head" idiocy of it all comes full circle in the call to action:

> The Huffington Post is not Arianna's to sell. It is ours: the lefty writers and readers, environmentalism activists and anti-corporate organizers who flooded the site with 25 million visits a month. So we're going to take it back. We'll stop going to her site. And we'll stop blogging for her too. Then we'll give birth to an alternative to AOL's HuffPo. . . . We're the ones who built the Huffington Post. And now we will be the ones who will huff & puff it down.[33]

In response, Arianna cackled her witch laugh and said, "Cute. Now pass me that bucket of money over there next to my platinum bathtub."

"The backlash is well deserved," says Jack Lule, a Lehigh University journalism professor. "She has made a fortune on the back of freelance writers working for nothing, but there is a political betrayal too. She betrayed the ideals of a lot of people who were happy to work for nothing because they thought it was for a cause."[34]

One journalist and organizer, Jonathan Tasini, has since filed a class-action lawsuit for $105 million and vowed to make Arianna Huffington "a pariah in the progressive community."[35] "Anybody blogging for the Huffington Post now is a scab. They're a strike breaker. They're producing content for somebody who is attacking workers," says Tasini.[36] But of course, the savvy Huffington has whisked aside the case as "utterly without merit." Only time will tell if she's correct. She likely is.

As for her involvement in her cult, Huffington was seen in 2004 with her "Jesus" John-Roger at her book launch party (see photo on page 94). Furthermore, according to Gawker, she has all but forced some of her *HuffPo* employees to attend John-Roger–related seminars. A 2008 *New Yorker* profile on Huffington cited the socialite turned socialist turned corporatist as being "less defensive" about her relationship with the creepy cult leader than in the past. But some of Huffington's relationships, such as the one with her former bridesmaid, Barbara Walters, suffered from her dealings with her higher than Jesus cult hero, John-Roger. When Huffington introduced Walters to John-Roger in the eighties, Walters said, "I did not take to him the same way that she had. That caused a pause in our relationship, and, I think, of some others."[37]

As for conservatives, while they recognize her power and influence, there is a little satisfaction in the irony of her double-crossing of both the right and the left. She pretended to be a conservative who supported capitalism, then pretended to be a progressive who hated capitalism, then proved to be a master of capitalism who laughed all the way to the bank. "Whatever happens, you have to admire Huffington's chutzpah," wrote syndicated columnist Debra J. Saunders. "Having played the left-wing card to attract like-minded readers, Huffington and her venture capitalist pals will have made millions off a website that doesn't pay most of its writers. . . . I wonder if the next batch of citizen journalists can spell the word 'sucker.'"[38] But mostly, conservatives shrug off her criticisms of figureheads like Rush Limbaugh and Bill O'Reilly. As ever, Rush had the best line on the saga that is Arianna Huffington: "She was just as mixed up then as she is now," said Limbaugh. "She is a silly woman. Fortunately, no one can understand what she's saying."[39] Indeed, even some on the Left were already on to Huffington's ruse even before her AOL switcheroo. "Nobody bamboozles Arianna Stassinopoulos Huffington," said *Washington Post* liberal columnist Dana Milbank. "If anybody was fooled, it was those who believed she would be a more enduring progressive than she was a conservative."[40]

Having successfully duped conservatives and Hollywood progressives, Arianna Huffington's anti-greed, anti-capitalism hypocrisy reaches a level that's hard to beat. The Priestess of Pigs is a profile in the dark arts of manipulation and ideological dexterity.

"I expect this to be my last job," Huffington says of her new AOL editor position. "I expect this to be my last act."[41]

Let's hope.

(I think . . . maybe . . . hell, who can be sure . . . it's Arianna Huffington, for crying out loud.)

5 Hollywood Hatemongers

Spike Lee, Oliver Stone, Whoopi Goldberg, Ted Danson, and Hollywood's Racist, Race-Baiting Progressives

When I was there [South Africa] I seriously wanted to pick up a gun and shoot whites. The only way to resolve matters is by bloodshed.

—Spike Lee[1]

As the 2008 election of Barack Obama taught us, Democrats are more compassionate, more just, more racially color-blind than those evil, racist, nasty Republicans. After all, the only reason anyone could dare to oppose electing the Messiah to the presidency is that they're a bigot. As everyone knows, the Democrat Party is the party of civil rights, equality, and justice for all. The Republican Party is the party of the KKK, lynching, and obstructing passage of all of America's major civil rights amendments and laws.

Oh, wait a minute . . . my bad . . . I got that exactly backward.

Heck, even Representative Jesse Jackson Jr. has, in a rare moment of bold candor, admitted what almost every Obama Zombie denies:

> There is no doubt that the Democratic Party is the party of the Confederacy, historically, that the Democratic Party's flag is the Confederate flag. It was our party's flag. That Jefferson Davis was a Democrat; that Stonewall Jackson strongly identified with the Democratic Party; that secessionists in the South saw themselves as Democrats and were Democrats; that so much of the Democratic Party's history, since it is our nation's oldest political party, has its root in slavery.[2]

As Pulitzer Prize–winning historian James A. McPherson said in an interview with Fox News analyst and author Angela McGlowan, "I think that the general public awareness of the nineteenth-century American history and maybe even the first half of the twentieth century is sort of blotted out or eclipsed. . . . I find that all the time in my students, even here at Princeton, that sometimes they are a little bit surprised to find out that on many issues, and especially on the race issue, the Republican Party was, for a long time, the far more liberal party."[3]

But it's far worse than that, which is why on the Democrat Party's website, they deftly skip over huge swaths of their party's history. As University of North Carolina emeritus professor of history Allen W. Trelease wrote, "The Klan became in effect a terrorist arm of the Democratic Party."[4] As even the progressive Columbia

University professor Eric Foner has conceded, "Founded as a Tennessee social club, the Ku Klux Klan spread into nearly every Southern state, launching a 'reign of terror' against Republican leaders—black and white."[5] The liberal historian goes on to say, "In effect, the Klan was a military force serving the interests of the Democratic Party, the planter class, and all those who desired the restoration of white supremacy. It aimed to destroy the Republican Party's infrastructure, undermine the Reconstruction state, reestablish control of the black labor force, and restore racial subordination in every aspect of Southern life."[6]

So maybe it should not be terribly surprising that some of Obama's loudest and most vocal supporters in Hollywood—celebrity Democrats who claim to support racial equality and unity every chance they get—turn out to be some of the biggest hypocritical bigots in America. Even as they preach the phony liberal line of peace and love and hippy goodness and kumbaya bullcrap, these race-hustling hatemongers reveal the Democrat Party for what it has always been: home to those who view life through the prism of race and reject the color-blind America that the antislavery Republican Party was founded on creating.

First up, director and Obama worshipper Spike Lee. In 2008, Spike Lee campaigned hard for Barack Obama on the grounds that the community organizer would bring racial unity and spark a sense of togetherness heretofore unseen in American history. Proving that the man never met a slavery metaphor he didn't like, Lee saw Obama's triumph in the Democrat primary as a chance to move beyond "massuh Clinton." As Spike put it, "The Clintons, man, they would lie on a stack of Bibles. Snipers? That's not misspeaking; that's some pure bullshit. I voted for Clinton twice, but that's over with. These old black politicians say, 'Ooh, Massuh Clinton was good to us, massuh hired a lot of us, massuh was good!' Hoo!

Charlie Rangel, David Dinkins—they have to understand this is a new day. People ain't feelin' that stuff. It's like a tide, and the people who get in the way are just gonna get swept out into the ocean."[7]

Obama and Spike are tight. According to Lee, Obama told him that the first movie he ever took Michelle Obama to see was Spike Lee's movie *Do the Right Thing*. "I'm riding my man Obama. I think he's a visionary. Actually, Barack told me the first date he took Michelle to was *Do the Right Thing*. I said, 'Thank God I made it. Otherwise you would have taken her to *Soul Man*.' Michelle would have been like, 'What's wrong with this brother?'"[8] I guess Malia and Sasha Obama have Uncle Spike to thank for their existence.

But Lee, who fancies himself a champion of black folk, makes it clear that he believes black identity and radical progressive politics are twinned. Spike has no use for the historic contributions and achievements of black Americans like General Colin Powell and Justice Clarence Thomas. "They think like whites," says the racist director. "There's a difference between having a black skin and black thinking."[9]

The bigotry of such rhetoric is striking. According to Lee, to be black and conservative is to be a sellout, an "Uncle Tom," a traitor to the race. The idea that a black American might think independently, vote his or her conscience, and see policy through rational eyes that are unclouded by Lee's "I hate whitey" mantra never seems to have occurred to the bigot director.

In an astoundingly self-unaware statement of total hypocrisy, Spike Lee has blasted those who would use the word *racist* like a smoke screen to obfuscate the real issues under consideration in any debate. You know, sort of like the way *all his films and public statements do*! "Anyone who disagrees with my outlook on the world calls me a racist, in the hope that they'll draw attention away from their own beliefs." You see, for Spike Lee, like most race-obsessed progressives, it's all about uncovering the "structural," hidden, latent forces of oppression and racism that are invisibly lurking like the boogeyman around every corner of American life. "I've been described in the press as an angry black man . . . the angry black man is an image they can use." When the reporter asked whom "they" referred to, Lee replied "the media, the studios. The infrastructure." In other words, everyone—The Man! "Even if I was angry, I think African-Americans are more than justified in feeling that way, considering the situation that's been forced upon us for centuries."[10]

Ah yes . . . the good ol' "wicked whitey made me do it" defense. Yes, well, Mr. Lee, as you're busy shoveling hundred-dollar bills into the fireplace at your mansion, perhaps you would do well to ask yourself: What in the hell am I doing fiercely supporting the very political party who "forced" the "situation" of slavery upon us "for centuries"? What an unthinking bigot you are! Are you not aware that the Republican Party—the ANTI-SLAVERY PARTY!—was freaking *created* to end the very thing you sit inside your multimillion-dollar home fuming about—slavery? Hey, Spike, how about you do a film on, oh, I don't know, say, the Thirteenth Amendment, the Fourteenth Amendment, the Fifteenth Amendment, the anti–Ku Klux Klan acts of the 1800s, Reconstruction, the 1957 Civil Rights Act, the 1960 Civil Rights Act, the 1964 Civil Rights Act. Why? Because every single one of them was made victorious because of the REPUBLICAN PARTY! Wake up from your case of historical amnesia, bro. Put down the "I hate whitey" CliffsNotes and crack open a history book. Your ignorance is breathtaking. It's also an embarrassment to the movement, my brother.

Lee apparently sucked in history, because time and again his comments and movies reveal a disturbing lack of historical knowledge. For example, Lee made a movie about one of his black radical heroes, Malcolm X, the high school dropout criminal who preached a venomous doctrine of hate against "white devils," as he called Caucasians. Indeed, any time "leaders" of black Islam pop off and spew their usual racist bilge, Lee remains tight-lipped. "The media always tries to pit black people against black people, so they want me to go onstage and blast Mr. Farrakhan or Mr. Muhammad," said Lee. "I'm not going to do it."[11] Of course, the person he really ought to have been "blasting" is Malcolm X. As a *New York Times* letter to the editor pointed out, "at the height of civil rights protest Malcolm traveled to the South, not to partake in civil rights protest, but to negotiate with leaders of the Ku Klux Klan on how to thwart the struggle for civil rights. This scene is omitted from Spike Lee's film . . . on Malcolm X."[12]

That's right, the thug Malcolm X met with the Ku Klux Klan to torpedo civil rights, all because Spike Lee's beloved patron saint preferred blacks and whites to remain separate, not integrated. And if that meant working with Klansmen to disrupt Dr. Martin Luther King Jr.'s efforts in the early 1960s, so be it. Either Spike Lee is ignorant of this fact (highly unlikely) or he is such a committed racist and hatemonger apologist that he wants to cover it up. Or maybe he's just such a money-hungry Hollywood hypocrite cash whore that he thought including such historically accurate scenes would dampen Malcolm X merchandising sales—sales he split with Malcolm X's widow (how gracious of Lee to allow X's widow to keep half the profits from the death of her husband) for all X-related merchandise.[13]

To be sure, not all African Americans were enamored with Spike Lee's revisionist history on the life and racist legacy of Malcolm X. Some black radicals thought Lee's depiction was too sanitized or, dare I say it, "whitewashed." "We will not let Malcolm X's life be trashed to make middle class negroes sleep easier," said poet and race-thug America-hater Amiri Baraka. Writer Yusuf Salaam agreed. "His male characters have been buffoons, broken and distorted. He should leave Malcolm alone."[14]

But in fairness, perhaps making an accurate portrayal of the black radical Nation of Islam "religion" would make selling movie tickets to largely black Christian audiences nearly impossible. After all, it is one of the most hysterically absurd fringe cults filled with racist lunatics. For example, the Nation of Islam "preaches that white people are the vile spawn of a Satanic laboratory experiment performed by a mad scientist Yacoub, and that they will all be destroyed by the arrival of miraculous machines from outer space, after which the rule of true black people will begin," explained the late liberal writer Christopher Hitchens.[15] You can see why Spike Lee would be impressed with folks of such ilk. But for the "prophet of anger," as one European journalist dubbed Lee, the world is full of racialist targets.[16]

Spike Lee has lashed out at director Woody Allen for failing to include black characters in his Manhattan-based movies, saying it is "unbelievable, in a city that's half black and Hispanic."[17]

Spike Lee has lashed out at Eddie Murphy and Whoopi Goldberg, calling them race traitors and Uncle Toms for selling out to a movie business dominated by white interests, as well as African American actors Ving Rhames and Cuba Gooding Jr. for behaving in a "servile" way.[18]

Spike Lee has lashed out at those who believe or engage in interracial marriage, a stance that must have been a source for considerable embarrassment when his dad, jazz musician Bill Lee, wed a Jewish white woman.[19] Doh! Consequently, Spike and his pops experienced a falling-out.

Spike Lee lashed out at the Cannes Film Festival and Steven Soderbergh when Lee, ever the sore loser, had his overrated film *Do the Right Thing* passed over for the Palme d'Or for Soderbergh's *Sex, Lies, and Videotape*. True to form, Spike played the tired, worn-out race card. "They're always looking for their white golden boy," said the Obama-loving race-baiter.[20]

Spike Lee lashed out at five-time Oscar-winning director Clint Eastwood for not rewriting history (like Lee does in his films) by including more black actors in Eastwood's two Iwo Jima movies, *Flags of Our Fathers,* and *Letters from Iwo Jima.* The first movie was about the U.S. Marines who raised the American flag at Mount Suribachi, none of whom were black. And the second film was told from the perspective of the Japanese forces, a military that wasn't made up of black soldiers. In characteristic badass style, Eastwood said Lee should just "shut his face." In characteristic ass clown style, Lee played—you guessed it—the race card. "The man [Eastwood] is not my father, and we're not on a plantation. . . . He sounds like an angry old man." The quintessential angry black man using "ageist" discriminatory language (as our PC language police would deem it) against Dirty Harry. Ain't that rich. But Eastwood wasn't having it and punched back harder. He defended himself and his past films as being historically accurate. For example, Eastwood's movie *Bird,* a biopic about jazz great Charlie Parker: "He was complaining when I did *Bird.* Why would a white guy be doing that? I was the only guy who made it, that's why. He could have gone ahead and made it. Instead he was making something else."[21] Then, in relation to Clint Eastwood's movie *Invictus,* about Nelson Mandela's efforts to unite post-apartheid South Africa, much to Spike Lee's chagrin, Eastwood clarified, "I'm not going to make Nelson Mandela a white guy."[22]

Spike Lee has lashed out at black movie director Tyler Perry for doing something Lee has seemed incapable of doing over the last decade—creating movies that actually make *money* and draw a *crowd*. Actually, Lee's beef with Tyler Perry involves—and I know you're never going to guess this—race! Shocker! Yes, it seems that Spike Lee, the man who condemns any black person who does not conform to his racist vision as inauthentic, seems a little more than upset that another black director makes movies that sell *way* more tickets than Lee's do:

> We shouldn't think that Tyler Perry is going to make the same film that I am going to make, or that John Singleton or my cousin Malcolm Lee [would make]. As African-Americans, we're not one monolithic group, so there is room for all of that. But at the same time, for me, the imaging is troubling and it harkens back to 'Amos 'n' Andy.' There is a lot of stuff out today that is coonery and buffoonery. I know it's making a lot of money and break- ing records, but we can do better. . . . I see these two ads for these two shows (Tyler Perry's *Meet the Browns* and *House of Payne*), and I am scratching my head. We got a black president, and we going back to Mantan Moreland and Sleep 'n' Eat?[23]

To his credit, director Tyler Perry came back with the perfect response to Lee's jealous sniping: "I'm so sick of hearing about damn Spike Lee. Spike can go straight to hell! You can print that. I am sick of him talking about me, I am sick of him saying, 'this is a coon, this is a buffoon.' I am sick of him talking about black people going to see movies. This is what he said: 'you vote by what you see,' as if black people don't know what they want to see." Indeed, in the last six years, Perry's films have raked in over half a billion dollars ($520 million), giving Lee something to be jealous about.[24]

Let's be honest: the only people who should be insulted by Perry's movies are transvestites. Madea, anyone?

Yet the idea that Spike Lee would criticize *anyone* for exploiting the black American demographic for profit-making is breathtakingly hypocritical. When Spike Lee released his movie *Bamboozled,* he caused a furor when he decided to launch a racially provocative ad campaign designed to play off racist black stereotypes—precisely the kind of "coonery and buffoonery" he blasts others for using. The newspaper ads for *Bamboozled* featured a "child with frizzy hair eating watermelon, which of course evokes an old stereotype so insulting that no non-black filmmaker, or ad man, would dare get near it," reported the *Gazette.* In fact, the *New York Times* found Spike Lee's ads so distasteful that they refused to print them. Others, like Najee Ali of a group called Project Islamic HOPE, blasted the ads as exploiting racism to make a buck. "I'm shocked and appalled that Spike Lee would have to resort to exploiting such negative images in order to promote the kind of controversy that translates into commercial profits."[25]

Tyler Perry, call your office.

But for all Lee's railing and ranting about "coonery and buffoonery," evil whitey, and the oppression of a capitalist system (aka "The Man") that holds a good brother like Spike down and forces him to make millions and live in freedom (the horror of it all!), Lee sure is quick to sell his soul to the commercial devil. No sooner did the mega-successful 1990s Nike Air Jordan commercials begin shooting than did Spike change his racially divisive tune—at least when The Man was willing to cut him a fat paycheck for both appearing in and directing the Nike spots. In one commercial,

Spike Lee appears on an outdoor basketball court called "Spike's Urban Jungle Gym." The ad features a black and a white basketball player making excuses for why they can't play together. That's when the great racial healer Spike Lee steps in and says, "If we're going to live together, we've got to play together."[26]

Cha-ching!

Nothing like selling racial harmony for fat coin, when every other word out of your mouth is some racial separatist screed against The Man!

In fact, some believe Lee's choice of sponsorships has fueled precisely the kind of negative stereotypes and self-defeating impulses that mire the black underclass in poverty. Take, for example, the aforementioned endorsement deals with Nike for Air Jordans. They were a sensational success for Nike. And yet, according to police estimates at the time, the city of Chicago alone experienced fifty apparel-related crimes a month. "While Spike Lee watches Michael Jordan dunk all over the world," said *New York Post* sports columnist Phil Mushnick, "parents around the country are watching their kids get mugged, or even killed, over the same sneakers Lee and Jordan are promoting. . . . It's murder, gentlemen."[27] There is also the issue of Reverend Jesse "Love Child" Jackson having called for blacks to boycott Nike because, according to Jackson, they did not hire enough blacks. At the time, Nike responded that 8.5 percent of its 4,500 employees were black, numbers that were relatively close to the black presence in the overall population.[28]

More recently, in 2010, Spike Lee teamed up with Absolut vodka to design a limited-edition bottle for Absolut Brooklyn. The one-liter bottle even showcases a brownstone building with the same number—165—that corresponds to Spike's Cobble Hill childhood house. The ad campaign was then plastered all throughout my hometown of Brooklyn and the Bedford-Stuyvesant neighborhood Spike is known to feature in his films. Even young teens saw the incredible hypocrisy and took offense. Frank Moore, nineteen, said that if he could speak directly to Lee he would say, "Do you understand what you're doing . . . that you're putting up an ad for liquor and you know there's an alcoholism problem here? My thing with Spike Lee is you should use your prestige and position of power to help the problem, not add on to it." Shenel Gunnis, seventeen, agreed. "I've seen his movies. I was a really big fan. But he lost respect from me. You're not supposed to be promoting stuff like that in areas that can barely afford food." Krystal Chapman, seventeen, was a student at the High School for Public Service in Crown Heights, Brooklyn. She felt Spike Lee leveraged his sway on the demographic his movies speak to. "He was targeting us . . . I think it is hypocritical."[29]

But none of Lee's racist hypocrisies seem to have fazed the filmmaker. "I have no conflicts at all, about my success. None," says Lee. "Black people should be the recipients of the money that is being generated by black culture. In the past we were getting flimflammed, bamboozled. Having talent is not enough. You have to know about royalties. You have to have some business know-how. . . . When black people start thinking more like entrepreneurs instead of just consumers, then we will have a whole lot more empowerment. Instead of 'Please Mr. White Man, can you do so and so for me,' we will call the shots."[30]

And yet, everywhere you turn, Lee is a walking contradiction. Take, for example, the stunning case of Spike Lee decrying America's violence and proliferation of guns even as he, in the same breath, called for the assassination of the former president of the National Rifle Association, Charlton Heston. Then days later he was out and about promoting five documentary-style television commercials he shot for the U.S. Navy (you know, those folks with weapons).

Here's how it went down: While standing fifty yards from an amphibious assault ship with "elaborate-looking guns" at Pier 88 on the Hudson River, Spike Lee was interviewed about those advertisements he directed for the Navy's advertising agency, BBDO.[31] No telling how much of your and my taxpayer dollars Lee banked for the gig, but while he was being interviewed he said, "The reason the United States is the most violent country in the history of civilization is the proliferation of guns." That's hypocritical enough. Now add to the mix that a few days prior to Lee damning America as the most bloodthirsty nation on earth, he had gone to the Cannes Film Festival and "jokingly" said that someone should "shoot him [Charlton Heston] with a .44 bulldog,"[32] and what do we get?

A real riot, that Spike Lee. A real riot indeed.

Of course, when the Obama-worshipping bigot isn't cracking hilarious jokes about assassinating Hollywood legends, he can be found wrongfully labeling Republicans as members of the Ku Klux Klan, while ignoring the *real* members of the Klan that belong to his Democrat Party. In 2002, Lee demonized Senator Trent Lott, saying, "The man is a card-carrying member of the Klan. I know he has that hood in the closet." Lott was never a member of the Klan, of course. But the irony is that the Democrat Party's then-leader in the U.S. Senate, the late Robert Byrd, was, indeed, a former member of the Ku Klux Klan![33]

Lest one think that Hollywood haters are solely into the black-white race card game, Academy Award–winning director Oliver Stone provides Hollywood's hatemongers with some much-needed, shall we say, "diversity." Instead of hating evil whitey, Oliver Stone saves his strongest venom for Jews.

In 2008, Oliver Stone strongly supported Barack Obama. Stone even helped create a MoveOn.org pro-Obama ad.[34] But in a July 2010 interview with the *Sunday Times,* anti-America, anti-Semite director Oliver Stone showed his true progressive colors. Stone trivialized the Holocaust and claimed that America's fixation with the annihilation of 6 million Jews was merely the end result of the "Jewish domination of the media." From there, the bigot shined up Adolf Hitler. "Hitler was a Frankenstein but there was also a Dr. Frankenstein. German industrialists, the Americans and the British. He had a lot of support," said Stone. "Hitler did far more damage to the Russians than the Jewish people, 25 or 30 [million killed]," explained the Hollywood Jew hater.[35] "There's a major [Jewish] lobby in the United States. They are *hard* workers. They stay on top of every comment, the most powerful lobby in Washington. Israel has fucked up United States foreign policy for years," explained the foreign policy expert.[36]

The response from Jewish leaders was swift and condemnatory. "When a man of Stone's stature says such things, it could lead to a new wave of anti-Semitism and anti-Israelism, and it may even cause real harm to Jewish communities and individuals," said Israel's diaspora affairs and public diplomacy minister, Yuli Edelstein.[37]

Likewise, the Anti-Defamation League condemned Stone's anti-Semitic remarks and demanded an apology. When Oliver Stone offered up a lame, halfhearted retraction, the ADL hit back. "Oliver Stone's apology stops short and is therefore insufficient," said Abraham H. Foxman, ADL national director. "While he now admits that Jews do not control Hollywood, the media, and other industries, he ignores his assertion that Jews are '. . . the most powerful lobby in Washington' and that 'Israel has fucked up United States foreign policy.' This is another anti-Semitic canard that Mr. Stone needs to repudiate."[38]

Under the weight of public pressure, Oliver Stone finally caved and issued a second apology, which the ADL accepted. "I do agree that it was wrong of me to say that Israel or the pro-Israel lobby is to blame for America's flawed foreign policy. Of course that's not true and I apologize that my inappropriately glib remark has played into that negative stereotype. I want you to know that I am categorically opposed to anti-Semitism—and all other racist ideologies."[39]

What a crock of communism! To begin with, Oliver Stone has made boatloads of cash distorting history and planting conspiratorial seeds in the minds of American kids who've already been brainwashed and primed by their liberal teachers and professors to believe only the worst about America. But even in his public statements, Stone never seems to miss a chance to blur the lines of history to serve his radical progressive agenda—and to make tons of cold, hard cash.

Take, for example, the KKK snow job he did during a 2010 interview with his fellow Lefty Hollywood pal Joy Behar. During the interview, Stone let this brain fart rip on air: "We have parties of Know Nothings for all our tradition. It goes way back, all kinds of rebellions. In 1923 in Washington, I believe, like, 100,000 Ku Klux Klan people dressed in white sheets walked down Main Street in Washington D.C., 100,000. The Ku Klux Klan was popular after World War I. That's in the heart of the country with white sheets, right, on horses. That's why The *Birth of the* [sic] *Nation* was such a popular film."[40]

Newsflash, homey: One of the reasons that the racist movie *Birth of a Nation,* based on the bestselling book *The Clansman,* gained significant steam was that Democrat bigot President Woodrow Wilson screened the movie INSIDE THE WHITE HOUSE. After watching the pro-KKK film, President Woodrow "I'm a Democrat and therefore hate black people" Wilson infamously declared that the movie "is like writing history with lightning, and my only regret is that it is all so terribly true." The movie then became a recruiting tool that sent KKK Democrat membership soaring by the millions—literally. As Pulitzer Prize–winning Princeton history professor James McPherson put it in an interview with Angela McGlowan, Wilson "did see that film—it was screened in the White House for him and he did endorse it. . . . I think his impact on the revival of the Klan and on the popularity of that movement, no matter what he later said, was important."[41]

But to anti-American, pro-communism conspiracy theorists like Oliver Stone, the hard facts of history are merely impediments, speed bumps on the way to reaching their illogical, insane ends. While on Behar's excuse for a show, Stone reiterated his support for Barack Obama. "I like Obama," said Stone. "I think he's moderate and he's smart and he's trying to reform a system which is essentially glued up. And he's got tremendous enemies, so I'm trying to, I'm rooting for him."[42] To be sure, when you look at the way Barack has played nicey-nice with thugs like Mahmoud Ahmadinejad and Hugo Chavez, it becomes clear why a communist like Oliver Stone would be rooting for a socialist like Obama.

In 2009, Stone made a glowing movie about Venezuela's socialist thug Hugo Chavez. Chavez, according to Stone, is a "brave, blunt, earthy" leader who supports freedom of expression by not censoring the Internet, except, of course, for the times that he censors the Internet. "The Internet cannot be something open where anything is said and done. Every country has to apply its own rules and norms," the Latin American despot proclaimed in remarks on how best to deal with his political opponents. "We have to act."[43] When ABC's *Good Morning America* anchor George Stephanopoulos asked Stone whether he thinks Venezuelan dictator Hugo Chavez is a "good person," the *Platoon* director said that he "absolutely" believes Chavez is a good person. And of course, Chavez believes Obama is a good person, too, since he finds common cause with the dictator's power-grabbing ways.

During a live television broadcast in 2010, Chavez said, "Hey, Obama has just nationalized nothing more and nothing less than General Motors. Comrade Obama! Fidel, careful or we are going to end up to his right."[44] When Stone was asked if he agreed with his good buddy Chavez's tongue-in-cheek suggestion that Obama may be veering further Left than Chavez, Stone said, "No, not at all. I think Obama's very much a centrist at a time of great change."[45] Chavez has even kidded that he hopes President Obama will consider appointing Oliver Stone or Sean Penn—two of Hollywood's favorite progressives—as the next U.S. ambassador to Caracas. "I hope they name Oliver Stone . . . Sean Penn," joked Chavez. "We have many friends there."[46]

In 2003, Stone made a glowing documentary about his good pal Fidel Castro. He has also met with Jew-hating, America-attacking, terrorist-sponsoring Iranian president Ahmadinejad. "Iran isn't necessarily the good guy," said Stone. "But we don't know the full story!"[47] As the tyrant-worshipping Stone explained, the United States' policy toward Iran has been "horrible."

During a panel discussion, Stone spewed his views about the 9/11 terrorist attacks. "I think the revolt of Sept. 11th was about 'Fuck you! Fuck your order.'" Even progressive writer Christopher Hitchens blasted the inanity of the statement. "Excuse me?" responded Hitchens. "Revolt? It was state-sponsored mass murder, using civilians as missiles. To say that this attack in any way resembles the French Revolution means you are a moral idiot, as well as an intellectual idiot. The man [Stone] has completely lost it."[48]

Straight down the line, if there is a dictator, communist, America-hater, or rogue enemy of the United States, Oliver Stone will find and hug him tight. And if they happen to already be dead, he will exhume their rotten and racist corpses and attempt to resuscitate and foist their hateful legacy upon an unwitting and impressionable army of Obama Zombies, young people who have been preternaturally wired to believe that anything and everything wrong in the world must necessarily be the fault of the evil, nefarious United States of America.

Indeed, Stone's greatest passion is reserved for some of history's most gruesome mass murderers. "Hitler is an easy scapegoat throughout history and it's been used cheaply," said Stone. "He's the product of a series of actions. It's cause and effect." To correct the negative PR that his mass-murdering heroes—Adolf Hitler, Joseph Stalin, and Mao Zedong—have received, Stone says that his forthcoming Showtime documentary series *Secret History of America* will place the monsters of human history "in context."[49] The only "context" we need is this fact: between Mao, Hitler, and Stalin, these three murderous dictators are responsible for, conservatively, 100 *million* deaths. But you see it is George W. Bush and those evil Jews who are the *real* tyrants.

Disgusting.

Simon Wiesenthal Center director Rabbi Marvin Hier says that "to talk about 'placing Adolf Hitler in context' is like placing cancer in context, instead of recognizing cancer for what it really is—a horrible disease, just as we must recognize Hitler as the ultimate expression of evil."[50] But according to Stone, mass murderers like Stalin and Mao have been "vilified thoroughly by history" and therefore need "a more factual representation" that allows viewers to "walk in Stalin's shoes and Hitler's shoes to understand their point of view."[51] Stone believes that his Showtime mockumentary will represent "the deepest contribution I could ever make in film to my children and the next generation." He adds, "Rush Limbaugh is not going to like this history." But it's all part of the process of engendering the essential "empathy for the person you may hate," says Stone.[52]

In this Hollywood radical's worldview, only capitalists who create jobs for people and presidents who fight to protect innocents are evil. As for *actual* villains who slaughter tens of millions, well, that's all just part of the messy business of creating heaven on earth—the stated goal of socialist/communist enterprises. After all, this is a Democrat who, in an interview with *Variety* columnist Army Archerd, said he can empathize with Palestinian suicide bombers because he "understands why they feel the way they do."[53]

You just can't make this crap up.

It's not just Hollywood movie directors, though, who are among the ranks of Obama's racist supporters. Actors have gotten in on the racial hypocrisy game, too. Two leading progressive Hollywood loons who take the cake for blatant racial double standards are former boyfriend and girlfriend Whoopi Goldberg and Ted Danson. In 2011, amid the furor over Donald Trump's urging that Barack finally release his long-form birth certificate to put the so-called "birther" issue behind the nation, Whoopi Goldberg took great offense that Trump would push the president to do what many thought he should have done years prior. When Trump appeared with Goldberg on *The View* to discuss the issue, Whoopi got heated and stopped short of calling the Donald a racist for daring to challenge the Messiah. Later, as Trump continued to press the issue, Whoopi Goldberg went on *The View* again and exploded:

"I'm getting tired of trying to find reasons not to think of stuff as being slightly racist," said the deeply offended Goldberg. "It is very difficult, on a daily basis, to see this stuff and not say, you know, this is what it is. I have been raised to think, 'Well, maybe that's not what they mean. Let me figure it out.' But, being black, when you say, 'Y'know, this is racist,' 9,000 people say, 'Oh, you're just playing the race card.' Well, you know, I'm playing the damn card now!" Goldberg added: "You know how Donald always says, 'People are laughing at us, thinking we don't have it'? Here's one of the reasons they're laughing at us, Donald. When you show such insane disrespect to the president of your country, other countries think we're idiots." [54]

Funny, I don't recall Whoopi Goldberg rising up in protest at the "disrespect to the president" when her pals were calling George W. Bush Hitler (apparently a compliment in Oliver Stone's book). Indeed, for a comedienne who has bragged that she is "the woman who made m.f. a house word" and has said, "I am no saint. I've always been known as the other side of tasteful," Goldberg's manufactured outrage at the mere questioning of the Almighty Obama seems a bit overly sensitive and precious. [55] Indeed, in the past, Goldberg has proven impervious to racial offense—even in the face of, well, blackface and the use of the N-word.

It all happened at the 1993 Friars Club Roast in honor of long-time Lefty actress and comedienne Whoopi Goldberg. The Friars Club roasts are private events for celebrities and comedians and are known for their bawdy, X-rated content. Back then, Goldberg was dating *Cheers* actor turned annoying progressive blowhard Ted Danson. The two appeared in a forgettable movie together, *Made in America*. According to Goldberg's retelling, she helped Danson develop his roastmaster routine and even went so far as to secure the makeup artist who did Danson's blackface and massive white lips, reminiscent of the Al Jolson routines that have become for many an icon of racism. As for the private performance itself, audience members recounted that Danson relayed explicit details about his and Whoopi's sex life as well as graphic descriptions about Goldberg's privates. That alone should have been enough to send the puke-o-meter redlining. But Danson's vulgar bit also included sex jokes that invoked black stereotypes and dropped the N-bomb more than a dozen times.[56]

Once the slow-motion train wreck was over, the condemnations came fast and furious. Montel Williams was so deeply offended that he resigned from the Friars Club. "I was confused as to whether or not I was at a Friars event or at a rally for the KKK and Aryan Nation," said Williams. He took particular offense at Danson's jokes about interracial children. "When Ted made the jokes about the racially mixed kids, and everyone knows my wife is white and just gave birth to our child, I could see my wife start to cry. If that's what Whoopi and Ted find funny in their bedroom, it's not funny to the outside world."[57] In his official statement on the matter, Montel made it clear that he found nothing funny or humorous about Goldberg and Danson's routine:

> As a society, we must explore our collective conscience and begin thinking about the consequences of these kinds of unintentional racial remarks. Some may find this brand of so-called humor funny. I do not. Some may think blackface is funny. I do not. Some may think sexually explicit jokes prefaced by and followed by racial epithets are funny. I do not, roast or otherwise. While I do not believe Ted Danson is a racist and I don't believe he or Whoopi Goldberg meant to be offensive to anyone, if I had known that their intent was to go that far, I would not have at-

tended the Friars Club Roast. In leaving, I simply followed my conscience.[58]

The *Los Angeles Times* printed an editorial slamming the Danson-Goldberg routine. "Race is no laughing matter," the piece said. "At a time when America's nerves are on edge over race relations, certain things just aren't funny. The 'N-word'—no matter the context or who speaks it—is not something to joke about."[59]

The national firestorm over Whoopi Goldberg and Ted Danson's racist performance spread far and wide. Singer Dionne Warwick, who was a member of the National Congress of Black Women, sent a letter to the organization's then-president, C. Delores Tucker. "Whoopi Goldberg has become a true disappointment. . . . With regard to Ted Danson, I will not give my brain the task of dignifying stupidity. . . . What could Whoopi have been thinking? . . . Obviously, not much!"

The controversy played out intensely on Main Street, U.S.A., as well. For example, one south Los Angeles video store owner took a hammer and smashed all of the movie videos featuring Goldberg and Danson and said he would not carry any of their films until they issue a full public apology.[60] Likewise, a *New York Times* article reported on how the Goldberg and Danson racist routine was playing out in African American beauty salons. The owner of a Manhattan hair salon, Richard Greene, told the *Times* that Danson and Goldberg's "little stunt" had been the talk of his shop among his largely black female customers. "A lot of people feel she's just covering up for Ted and not looking at it as an insult to a race of people," said Greene. "She may say, or think, that comedy has no limits. In reality it does, and what they did exceeded those limits."[61]

As syndicated columnist Carl Rowan put it, "The overriding

issue here is Goldberg's obvious lack of concern about her impact upon America's young people, especially Black girls who are being enslaved every day by illicit or promiscuous sex. Goldberg's foul mouth wounds Black women who are being cheated and humiliated by leaders of this society who disrespect and abuse them. . . . So Goldberg told Danson to show up in blackface? That only tells us how grossly insensitive she is."[62]

Actually, Whoopi Goldberg is *very* sensitive to discussions of race—at least when it's someone else making a statement that is not even remotely racial. But when she has her boyfriend show up in blackface with huge white lips, talk about sex using racial stereotypes, and start carpet bombing a two-thousand-person audience with the N-bomb . . . well, that's just playing around, no big deal, and nothing to get uptight about. Donald Trump's comments and actions weren't even in the same *galaxy* as Goldberg and Danson's antics. Still, Goldberg used Trump's critique of her hero Obama as a chance to, as Whoopi herself openly confessed, "play the race card."

As for Ted Danson, Whoopi said he was "hurt and upset that people are taking the whole matter in such a negative way." Danson's official statement was pure progressive hypocrisy: "Words by themselves are not racist. Racism is a matter of intent. My intent was to amuse my dear friend, Whoopi, in what I thought was the privacy of the Friars Club."[63]

How convenient.

WHAT HOLLYWOOD HYPOCRITES like Spike Lee, Oliver Stone, Whoopi Goldberg, and Ted Danson demonstrate is just how much Hollywood needs to preach its pro-diversity, anti-hate message not to us the general public, but to itself. In fact, the more closely you scrutinize the entertainment industry, the more you realize just what a bunch of flaming diversity hypocrites they truly are. For all its "multicultural finger waving" and affirmative action–loving rhetoric, progressive Hollywood remains one of the least culturally diverse industries in America.

One need only look at the 2011 Oscar nominees to realize the blatant hypocrisy Hollywood practices when it comes to "embracing diversity," as the liberal mantra goes. Every single one of the major category nominees for the 2011 Academy Awards was white! We should respond as the Left does.

Racists! Bigots! Haters! It's all Bush's fault!

You know things are bad when even liberal CNN International asks, "Where's the diversity at the Oscars?"[64] Out of ninety-three nominees announced in the major categories, ethnic representation accounted for just 3 percent. And for the most prestigious award category—the Best Picture segment—the ten nominations contained twenty-four producer nominees, yet not a single one was a producer of color.[65]

Haters! Hitler lovers! It must be global warming! It's all Bush's fault!

And don't even bring up the nonexistence of Asian American representation! If it ain't a Jackie Chan flick, fuhgetaboutit! Same goes for the dearth of disabled citizens being cast in roles for movies and TV, despite the fact that 20 percent of the U.S. population has a disability.[66]

Hey, hey, ho, ho, Hollywood wheelchair haters have got to go! Bush lied, Asian representation died!

Indeed, when you consider the writer and director categories, you realize just what a white spectacle virtually every Oscar awards ceremony truly has been. Hell, it wasn't until the year *2010* that Hollywood saw its first black winner of a screenplay Oscar

(Geoffrey Fletcher for *Precious*). And in 2010, Lee Daniels became only the second African American director ever to receive a directing nomination at the Oscars, as well as the first black *ever* to be nominated for the Best Director category by the Directors Guild Association.[67]

Klan members, the whole lot of them! Hollywood white boys club! Bush . . . er . . . uh . . . Obama hates black people!?

And when Hollywood isn't holding a good brother down, it's busy holding a good sister down! In 2010, according to a study by Martha Lauzen, the executive director of the Center for the Study of Women in Television and Film at San Diego State University, women accounted for a laughable 7 percent of all director spots.[68] And out of the ninety-three nominees announced in the major categories for the 2011 Academy Awards, women made up a paltry 15 percent.

Even that progressive must-see TV, *The Daily Show,* has been skewered for its dearth of female writers, with one reporter for Jezebel.com calling Jon Stewart's program "a boys' club where women's contributions are often ignored and dismissed."[69] *The Daily Show* responded fairly aggressively to the accusation. The women on staff wrote an open letter titled "Dear People Who Don't Work Here," arguing that *The Daily Show* "isn't a place where women quietly suffer on the sidelines as barely tolerated tokens." Yet as the *Huffington Post* noted, out of all the women who signed the letter, only two of them were writers and only one was a full-time female correspondent,[70] which sort of kind of proved Jezebel .com's original accusation.

We are woman, hear us write! A woman needs an Oscar like a fish needs an . . . um . . . Oscar!

In 2009, UCLA professor Darnell Hunt completed a report analyzing the hiring and income data for Hollywood writers. Hunt found that female writers "remain stuck at 28% of TV employment and 18% in features while the minority share has been frozen at 6% since 1999." Hunt added: "These findings are clearly out of step with a nation that elected its first African American president in 2008, a nation in which more than half of the population is female and nearly a third is non-white."[71]

Fight the Power! Hollywood is The Man! Down with The Man!

And when it comes to wage disparities—something Obama Zombies live to drone on about, despite all evidence that proves the numbers skew based on experience level, not race or gender—the numbers prove once and for all that Hollywood progressives all wear white sheets and beat women. Between 2003 and 2007, female writers' wages remained relatively unchanged ($82,604 in 2007 and $82,000 in 2003). But for male writers, overall wages increased by more than $4,000, moving from $84,300 in 2003 all the way up to $87,984 in 2007. The wage discrepancy for minority writers in film was especially racist in 2007 (no doubt because Bush was the president!). In 2007, minority earnings for film were $61,912. But for whitey, earnings stood at that towering $98,875.[72]

What do we want? Justice! When do we want it? Now!

It can be hilarious to listen to Hollywood elite and the dependably liberal media try to explain the lack of diversity found within the entertainment industry. If you listen to them long enough, before too long you will think you are at a rally for meritocracy and free markets, because inevitably that's the route their arguments take.

"Where are the diverse faces both in front of and behind the cameras?" asks CNN reporter Lisa Respers France. "It's a complex issue that involves both supply and demand."[73]

Oh . . . we see. It's one of those "supply and demand," "free market" thingamajiggers all those bigot economists and hate-spewing capitalists are always yapping about! Got it.

The *Hollywood Reporter*'s film editor, Gregg Kilday, similarly reverts to all that bigoted "economics" and "market forces" blather to cover up Hollywood's racist roots. "It's not the academy's fault," said Kilday. "It speaks to a larger issue in the industry in that it is still difficult for black filmmakers to do movies about black film matter."

What the hell "black film matter" is exactly, I nor anyone on planet earth has a clue. But I digress.

"A kind of mainstream commercial movie like a commercial comedy," continues Kilday, "is never going to show up on the academy list. . . . And serious African-American movies are probably even harder to get financed."[74]

IN A *PSYCHOLOGY TODAY* article titled "Whitewash: Is Hollywood Really Racist?" Dr. Rodolfo Mendoza-Denton discussed the issue of Hollywood's racial hypocrisy this way:

> Is Hollywood blatantly racist for not including a more diverse set of actors, actresses, and movies among the Oscar nominees? My strong guess is that privately, people are fuming at the suggestion. *Are we supposed to nominate lesser performances for the sake of keeping up appearances? Do we give up our standards of fine acting for the sake of being politically correct?* How is *that* being fair? It kind of begins to echo arguments against affirmative action.[75]

Bingo! And there's the rub.

Obama's hordes of Hollywood hypocrites are the first in line to tell us the progressive virtues of affirmative action, of quotas in college admissions, and that it is a moral imperative that we reject merit-based hiring and instead "embrace diversity," regardless of the economic consequences or impact on efficiency and performance. Yet when the question of race-based hiring and affirmative action quotas gets thrown back at them, Obama's "Yes, we can" coalition says, "No we don't, we won't, and we never have. It isn't about black or white. It's about green. This is a business! We hire those who draw the biggest crowds! Period."

Racist, capitalist pigs! Merit-worshipping bigots! Bush lied, hiring quotas died!

And the beat goes on.

6

Hollywood Leftist Loon Lifetime Achievement Award

And the Winner Is . . . Alec Baldwin!

There are many immutable truths in the universe. But the greatest of these is this: Alec Baldwin is a major-league butt hole.

After all, what other descriptor is there for a man who calls up his daughter and leaves the following on her voice mail:

> *Once again, I have made an ass of myself trying to get to a phone to call you at a specific time. . . . When the time comes for me to make the phone call, I stop whatever I'm doing, and I go and I make that phone call . . . and you don't even have the goddamn phone turned on! I'm tired of playing this game with you. I'm leaving this message for you to tell you that you have insulted me for the last time. You have insulted me. You don't have the brains or*

*the decency as a human being. . . . I don't give a damn
that you're 12 years old or 11 years old, or that you're
a child . . . or that your mother is a thoughtless pain in
the ass who doesn't care about what you do as far as I'm
concerned. . . . I'm gonna let you know just how angry I
am. . . . I'm gonna get on a plane, and I'm gonna come out
there for the day, and I'm gonna straighten your ass out
when I see you. . . . I'm gonna really make sure you get
it, about what a rotten little pig you really are. You are a
rude, thoughtless little pig.*[1]

And this year's Father of the Year Award goes to . . . Alec
"Little Pig" Baldwin!

Set aside for a moment the fact that Baldwin's rant seems to
suggest that he doesn't even know how old his own *child* is. But if
that alone doesn't qualify Baldwin for a Ph.D. in child rearing, how
about the fact that Baldwin, one of the Left's most reliable and
heralded progressive heroes, had the audacity to then go write a
book about . . . parenting! I crap you not. In the wake of Baldwin's
PR meltdown, his book, *A Promise to Ourselves: A Journey Through
Fatherhood and Divorce,* hit bookstores nationwide. And by "bookstores" I mean the dollar bargain bin at Goodwill.

According to Baldwin, the whole "daughter pig" public relations disaster and its concomitant effects on his acting career were
enough to make him suicidal.

"I had not made any preparations, but I thought how I would
do it," claimed the Father of the Year. "I was going to put the hose
in the most noxious of the cars I own, a Jeep, take some sleeping
pills, and take a nice nap in the front of my car in the garage."
Thankfully, his follow-through on his dark thoughts was as empty
as his acting. Yet it seems Baldwin has a habit of issuing false sui-

cide threats. As if the psychological damage he'd already done to his "pig" daughter weren't enough, in October 2010, in the wake of an argument with Baldwin, daughter Ireland called 911 and reported that her father had threatened to swallow pills. Can you say "add insult to injury"?

Through it all, Baldwin's primary concern with the public relations nightmare seemed to be how the public backlash might affect his flagging movie career and how he might resurrect his reputation, such as it was.

"If people wake up and go, 'You know something? He left that message for his daughter, and I thought he was a selfish, horrible man, but, damn, that show is funny,' if they are in the mood to forgive—never forget, but forgive—then you move on and survive. It means I'm funny enough for people to overlook something they don't care for."[2]

Despite his being in the cast of the successful TV show *30 Rock*, Baldwin's movie career has been a complete failure. Those aren't my words, they're Papa Pig's.

"I'll say this to you, and it's a difficult thing to say, but I believe it: I consider my entire movie career a complete failure."[3]

Alas, the joys of bipartisan agreement.

During his epic custody battle with Kim Basinger, Alec Baldwin had to attend a dozen anger-management classes. "I was Mr. Telephone Thrower. The holes where I put my fist in the wall dictated where we hung pictures." But Baldwin shrugs off the notion that he's still the same angry little man he's always been. "There are other people who have done what I've done. There's not one thing I've done that other people haven't done. I mean, I didn't hit somebody in the face with a baseball bat in road rage. I didn't boil a cauldron of dogs."[4]

Well, now . . . I guess the guy has a point after all.

But for a guy who claims to be sorry for calling his own child swine, Baldwin, one of Obama's strongest Hollywood backers, sure enjoys shifting blame. Even Lefty reporter Morley Safer seemed surprised by Baldwin's dissembling.

SAFER: *I've got to ask you about that notorious phone call you made. How could you do that?*

BALDWIN: *You get so frustrated. And you realize, number one—and it's wrong, it's totally wrong—that I was really speaking to somebody else when I left that message. I mean, I was pissed. I'd been putting up with this for six years.*

SAFER: *But you weren't talking to another person. You were talking to your daughter, to a kid. And you said, "You thoughtless little pig." I mean, I find it hard to utter those words.*

BALDWIN: *Did you ever lose your temper with your kids?*

SAFER: *Yeah, but nothing like that.*

BALDWIN: *If you're asking me do I feel bad about leaving that message, I think that goes without saying. At the same time, I'm pretty overwhelmed by the sanctimoniousness of people who say that, I mean, I got so many phone calls from people. . . .*

SAFER: *Well . . .* [5]

And there you have it, folks.

When Baldwin's not busy being "overwhelmed" by those "sanctimonious" folks who think calling one's offspring Porky Pig is a bad idea, the chief Obama backer is busy blaming his woes on—you guessed it—"the vast right-wing conspiracy." As Baldwin explained to Safer, "They hate liberals who can throw a punch." When Safer asked him who exactly "they" was, Baldwin replied, "They, the vast right-wing conspiracy that's after me."[6] Paranoia, Alec Baldwin is thy name.

Baldwin may be a progressive hero to the Hollywood Left, but to the rest of America he's an unhinged lunatic. During the impeachment trial of Bill "Cigar" Clinton, Baldwin went on *Late Night with Conan O'Brien* to call for the murder of representative Henry Hyde and his children.

"If we were in other countries, we would all right now . . . go down to Washington and we would stone Henry Hyde to death! We would stone him to death!" the peace-loving Baldwin shouted as he jumped to his feet and pumped his fist in the air. "Then we would go to their homes and we'd kill their wives and their children. We would kill their families."[7]

In the wake of Baldwin's public fantasizing about the assassination of a sitting member of Congress, the Capitol Police called the television network to explain that Baldwin's insane and radical ravings might constitute the issuing of a threat to the now-deceased congressman Hyde. Not surprisingly, Baldwin initially hid behind the skirt of his representative, Lisa Kasteler, who said he was merely offering up a heaping helping of hilarity. Incredibly, Team Baldwin chose to take a swipe at conservatives rather than offer an apology. "It was a parody," said Baldwin's lackey. "It was a parody of the hysteria in this country coming from right-wing fanatics."[8]

But for Hyde, a father and a man who had himself received prior death threats, Baldwin's sick rant was anything but funny. "I heard about it, and I'm sickened by it," said Congressman Hyde. "You have someone like that, talking in those terms, about killing your family? To kill my family because you disagree with me? To laugh about that? There are people out there, sick people, who are just waiting for a push. Excuse me for not laughing. He wants my family stoned to death by a mob. Imagine if a Republican said such a thing. I don't find any humor in it."[9]

Regardless, the classless Baldwin, the man who called his own eleven-year-old daughter a "rude, thoughtless little pig," continued to shrug off public condemnation and said Congressman Hyde needed to "lighten up."[10] Indeed, it wasn't until the then president of the Motion Picture Association of America, Jack Valenti, wrote Baldwin a note to express his "dismay and sorrow" for Baldwin's "over the top" rant that was "so off base as to boggle the mind" that Baldwin finally wrote a letter to Hyde and his family apologizing for his disgusting remarks aimed at the congressman, who Valenti said members of Congress "on both sides of the aisle think is the finest man to have mediating a dispute."[11]

In true Hollywood hypocrite fashion, however, Alec Baldwin doesn't take harsh words directed toward *him* as a laughing matter. After receiving a "constant and steady stream of offensive material that has been posted here on my Guestbook," wrote Baldwin on his official website, "regretfully we are closing the Guestbook indefinitely." Baldwin went on to explain that "most of the offensive material has been political in nature" and that "nearly all of the information . . . is misinformation or disinformation, fueled by political extremists whose only goal is to harass and disrupt."[12] Threaten to stone a sitting member of Congress and his family? No big deal, just free speech. Leave objectionable commentary on Alec Baldwin's website guestbook? Treason! This is how this Hollywood hypocrite thinks.

But for those who deny the existence of God, undeniable proof can be found in the fact that, thus far, Alec Baldwin has yet to make good on his threat to someday run for elected office. Still, that has not stopped him from dumping truckloads of cash in Democrats' direction. He's donated $10,000 to Senator Chuck Schumer. He gave former representative Patrick Kennedy, the late senator Ted Kennedy, Representative Timothy Bishop, and former senator Hillary Clinton each $5,000. He's donated $500 or more to thirty federal candidates. He's cut $30,500 in checks to the Democrat Party of New York. He's sent $22,500 to the Democrat Senatorial Campaign Committee. He's given $20,100 to the Democrat National Committee. In total, Baldwin has contributed over $152,000 to Democrats (the only exception being Senator Jim "Turncoat" Jeffords, who ditched the GOP).[13]

Indeed, in addition to being a big-time fundraiser for Leftist causes, Baldwin fancies himself somewhat of a policy wonk, ergo his continued flirtation with a foray into the political arena. From nuclear power to monetary policy to animal rights to taxation, you name it, he is a self-appointed policy expert on it.

In an October 2008 *Huffington Post* piece titled "To Hell with Wall Street," Baldwin unleashed a torrent against the $700 billion in Wall Street bailouts.

"If you give them the $700 billion, make them issue stock," writes Baldwin. "Make every recipient of the bailout issue stock in return for our 'investment.' Don't give them the dough. Make them sell a stake in their companies. Banks, investment firms, insurance companies, you name it. . . . Or . . . only give the money to small, local banks. . . . To Hell with Wall Street. . . . Don't give them the money. Don't loan it. Make them sell us a piece of the action."[14]

Fast-forward three years. Having blasted the bailouts under Bush, as soon as Baldwin's favorite socialist seized control of the White House, the Hollywood hypocrite turned into—brace yourself—*a pitchman for the very banks he blasted*!

"I'm going to do a series of commercials for them, Capital One," said Baldwin. "Capital One was so great in cooperating with me to set up a source for people to contribute online. Capital One will match to give to the Americans for the Arts."[15] Baldwin continued: "With Capital One, the point isn't me getting money and then giving it to charity. It's about Capital One partnering with me. They're joining me with this online component and this is something I want to build with them."[16]

So let's get this straight: Baldwin rails against the evils of big banks raiding the taxpayers for big money bailouts. He then links arms with the bank that got $3.56 billion—with a freaking *b*—of taxpayers' dollars so that they can give away the very money that *we* the taxpayers gave them for Baldwin's favorite charities, in this case some "save the arts" crap.[17]

Capital One—What's in your wallet? Taxpayers' money, that's what!

Oh, there's more. Baldwin was quick to show solidarity with the violent, Marxist, and health-code-violating movement known as Occupy Wall Street. After his visit to the dingy tents in lower Manhattan, Baldwin wrote an article for the *Huffington Post* titled "What Occupy Wall Street Has Taught Me." While he didn't acknowledge that a ratio of only three Porta-Potties per 1,000 people probably doesn't create the cleanest living conditions, the bothered actor did drone on and on about "excessive" bank fees, "predatory lending," "war for oil," and "high speed rails." Baldwin even found room to claim that Republicans in Congress fight against "long term interests of the middle class" and instead show allegiance to "corporate profitability."[18] You know, all those mindless Lefty buzzwords we're taught in college.

Forget for a moment that Baldwin is getting a fat paycheck from one of those banks he's decrying. Here's a dude who works for freaking General Electric, the very same company that employed legions of accountants who aggresively scoured every inch of the tax code to find obscure loopholes in order to bring its effective American tax rate in 2010 down to . . . zero. Hey, Alec, here's an idea: How about you quit your gig with GE in protest and demand that your employer start cutting a tax check to Uncle Sam in an effort to end the singular focus of "corporate profitability" that you tell us plagues our political system? Of course we know he won't do that. After all, the self-appointed warrior for the "middle class" would see that $65 million net worth of his erode faster than his marriage to Kim Basinger.[19]

Then there's the fact that Baldwin himself serves on the advisory board of the Carol Baldwin Breast Cancer Research Fund, which is named in honor of his mother, who is a breast cancer survivor. As it turns out, this admirable charity is funded by the investment bank Merrill Lynch as well as Exxon Mobil, the oil giant. As columnist Jeffrey Lord put it, "Alec Baldwin is a board member of a family charitable fund which partners with and takes money from a veritable who's who of that famous trifecta of liberal enemies: Wall Street, Big Oil and Corporations."[20]

See, as long as the banks are willing to pony up *your* tax dollars to fund *his* favorite charities, which then gives *him* a fat tax write-off for having "donated" his "time and talents" to the cause, then Baldwin is cool with it. But as soon as you and I call for less government and less spending of our tax dollars, well, we're greedy, evil racists who hate the poor and club baby seals.

Hypocrisy? What hypocrisy? Nothing to see here, folks!

Indeed, Baldwin's buffoonery knows no bounds. In April 2011, he emerged from a press conference on Capitol Hill with his good progressive pals Senator Dick Durbin and Representative John Larson. When a reporter asked Baldwin whether he believed Dear Leader had lived up to his expectations, the Lefty actor opened his yap and let this genius diarrhea flow: "Well, I mean, I think so because I think that when you come into office and you want to put your mark on things . . . you want to be able to spend. And what's crippled Obama's administration, as far as I'm concerned, is the financial crisis and it's prevented him from doing any new spending."[21]

Come again? What's that you say, Piggy Baldwin? Did you say Dear Leader hasn't done any new spending?! How's about racking up more debt than all the first forty-one presidents *combined*, fool![22]

But Baldwin the policy brainiac wasn't finished making a dunce of himself. He still had to do the obligatory Bush bashing.

"If the country was as flush as it was under Bill Clinton and he had money—these things cost money—he could have made more of a mark. . . . He inherited this crisis from Bush and Paulson [former U.S. Secretary of the Treasury]. He had to extend the TARP. I think it's been very difficult for him to spend his whole first term trying to, you know, correct our course financially. I think a second term of Obama, we'll see a lot more of what we want to see from him."[23]

Ominous words, to be sure.

Tax policy also gets Baldwin's ire up. That is, tax policy aimed at *his* wallet. According to the New York *Daily News,* "Alec Baldwin owns a residence in the city, but claims Hamptons is his home base. . . . That made him one of hundreds of people slapped with an audit in 2009." In response, the tax-and-spend progressive replied, "The moment you start working regularly [in the city], the city finance people come after you."[24]

For a man who advocates larger, more expansive and intrusive government every chance he gets, Baldwin should welcome the chance to make sure the government is squeezing every last penny it can from him. After all, isn't that precisely what he and his liberal pals are always complaining about—rich fat cats dodging taxes and not paying their "fair share"? Why the sour grapes?

In one of his *Huffington Post* screeds, Baldwin recounted a conversation he had with a "veteran Democratic member of Congress." According to Baldwin, the representative said, "It's the tax cuts that will kill us. These people [Republicans] want to make these cuts permanent. And that will mean the death of all entitlements in the budget. That will mean the death of a great deal of our social programming."[25]

In related news, the entire nation screamed out, "Hooray!"

Ever eager to position himself as a connected congressional "insider," Baldwin went on to say that *another* member of Congress told him, "Defend the seas and deliver the mail. That's all these guys [Republicans] want to pay for. Literally."[26]

Limited government. Hmmm . . . what a novel idea: follow the Founding Fathers' original intent. How radical!

Yet much of the Leftist lunacy Alec Baldwin has subjected America to could have been eliminated had the Hollywood hypocrite simply made good on his promise to move to Canada in the event that George W. Bush were elected president. Indeed, after Bush's presidential victory, the Republican Party of Florida was generous enough to purchase Baldwin a one-way bus ticket to Montreal, an invitation and kindness that Baldwin, unfortunately, refused. When reporters asked the Florida GOP why they chose Montreal, Republican communications director Daryl Duwe explained that the city was the cheapest and fastest route out of the country from New York City and that he is sorry to residents of Montreal for unloading Baldwin on an otherwise wonderful city. "We're sorry about that," said Duwe, "but he did promise to leave the country. The fastest way we could find a way out on a bus was to Montreal."[27]

It's depressing enough that the Florida GOP's attempt to jettison Alec Baldwin from America failed. But perhaps more unsettling is the fact that, as recently as 2010, far Left political groups have tried to recruit Baldwin to run for governor of New York. He's also hinted that he may run for mayor of NYC one day. Thankfully, Baldwin declined, sparing my home state further embarrassment and potential ruin. Baldwin's spokesman, Matthew Hiltzik, made sure to keep the door open, however. "It's flattering that people recognize Alec's strong sense of the issues, political perspectives, popularity and passion for New York," said that Baldwin butt boy. "But no, he has no current plans to run for office. But who knows what may happen in the future?"[28]

Fathers of the Year, unite!

Money-Grubbing Anti-Materialists

How Bono Hates Greed and Wealth by Loving Greed and Wealth

Preventing the poorest of the poor from selling their
products while we sing the virtues of the free market . . .
that's a justice issue.

—"Bono" (Paul David Hewson) at a prayer breakfast

attended by President George W. Bush, Jordan's King

Abdullah, and various members of Congress[1]

He is a living saint.

He is bigger than the pope.

Or Mother Teresa.

Or Gandhi.

A modern-day Robin Hood. A defender of the poor, the sick,

the impoverished. He is a perennial nominee for the Nobel Peace Prize, and one of the most important human beings (deities?) to ever walk the face of the earth.

Holiness, thy name is Paul David Hewson, more commonly known by the annoyingly self-important moniker "Bono," which, in Latin, means "good."

Gag.

If there's one thing Irishman Paul David Hewson wants you to know, it is that he is incredibly generous . . . with *your* money. As for the $900 million he's worth . . . well, not so much.

You see, despite having some decent pipes, Paul David Hewson (I'm sorry, I'm having a hard time calling a grown, fifty-one-year-old man "Bono"), U2's front man, is a grade-A hypocrite of the globalist variety. Known for his long-standing commitment to African "debt forgiveness" (otherwise known as "international welfare"), Hewson has spent over a decade galloping around the globe wagging his pious finger in the faces of those greedy, money-grubbing G-8 nations who have the audacity to want nations to whom they've loaned monies to—*gasp*—actually pay them back!

But we mere mortals should be grateful that the Savior of the Universe is willing to even grace us with such lectures. After all, Paul David Hewson has more important things to do. He has appeared on the cover of *Time* magazine with the headline "Can Bono Save the World?" and in 2005 was named, along with Bill and Melinda Gates, as a *Time* Person of the Year. He has performed in front of 130 million viewers during the Super Bowl. He regularly meets with the power players of the world, attends "prestigious" conferences like the World Economic Forum to hold forth on the continent of Africa's need to suck more money out of developed (if broke) countries, and meets with world leaders, presidents, and prime ministers.[2] He's even a recipient of an honorary British knighthood, for crying out loud! So we should all be grateful that the diminutive rocker would deign to issue antipoverty proclamations to trash like us.

"When you sing, you make people vulnerable to change in their lives," says the Irish sage. "You make yourself vulnerable to change in your life. But in the end, you've got to become the change you want to see in the world."[3] As Paul David Hewson put it in his *Time* Person of the Year spread, "This can be a generation in which we eradicate extreme poverty."[4]

(Cue the Obama "Yes, we can" track.)

"It's a scandal. The scale of the response does not match the scale of the problem," said Bono of the paltry billions America has shoveled into the hands of Third World countries. "You know, we're going to try, we're going to speak to Oprah Winfrey, we're going to try and get on her program, we're going to ask President Mandela to join us. We're going to get to the heartland in some way on this, because if Americans hear the facts on this, they'll respond to it like they have in Europe."[5]

See, folks, the solution among Hollywood hypocrites is always the same: be like Europe. Moreover, the underlying assumption dripping from Bono's message is that the African people are helpless and in need of a savior, which recalls the white man's burden and colonial unpleasantness. Hey, aren't liberals always trying to cast themselves as the enlightened ones on race relations? Right. And Lance Armstrong has two testicles.

Anyway, to make good on his "I am Jesus" proclamations, Bono cofounded something called the DATA organization, which stands for Debt, AIDS, Trade, Africa. DATA's aim was to end poverty and HIV in Third World countries. Bono's DATA group was then morphed into the ONE Campaign to Make Poverty History. Paul

David Hewson and his pal Bob Geldof were also the lead organizers of the Live 8 global concert events, the purpose of which was to get G-8 leaders to fork over even more cash for Africa. And indeed, based on the sheer might of celebrity star power and the lunacy that it induces, as *Time* reported, "Bono charmed and bullied and morally blackmailed the leaders of the world's richest countries into forgiving $40 billion in debt owed by the poorest."[6]

"But Jason," you say, "what could be wrong with such a blessed act of compassion on the part of Messiah Hewson? Are you so heartless that you can't see what a gift the benevolent Rock God hath bequeathed upon us common earth creatures?"

And to that I say, "Wake up, numbskull! International welfare stunts economic growth, fuels dependency, and, perhaps most horrible of all, strengthens thugocracies led by warlord dictators who take the lion's share of aid and use it to buy advanced weaponry to further oppress indigenous peoples before tossing a few crumbs to the starving in time for the photo op, only to then snatch the food back and give it to those in power or use it to feed their armies!"

Before we even get into what a fraud and scam artist Paul David Hewson is (and believe you me, you're going to puke when you see what a phony this guy truly is), let's address the painfully obvious fact that all serious scholars of foreign aid and economics have long recognized: foreign aid has been an unmitigated disaster and has made things far worse, not better. It's that pesky thing called the Law of Unintended Consequences that those evil conservatives are always talking about. But don't take my or the experts' word for it. Heck, ask the Africa aid organizations themselves.

"Aid has failed because campaigners, charities, and governments do not have the right plan and excluded African entrepreneurs and grassroots organizations from being part of the solution," says Jobs Selasie, head of African AIDS Action. "You can't impose change from without. It has to come from within and we won't end poverty with handouts. Africans need to fight corruption and work hard."[7]

Likewise, in an eye-opening 2010 open letter to Great Britain published in the *Telegraph*, six prominent Africans from Nigeria, Ghana, South Africa, and Uganda pleaded with foreigners to stop sending aid:

> As Africans, we urge the generous-spirited British to reconsider an aid programme they can ill afford, and which we do not want or need. A real offer from the British people to help our development would consist of the abolition of the Common Agricultural Policy, which keeps African agricultural exports out of the European marketplace. It is that egregious policy, combined with the weight of regulations, bad laws and stifling bureaucracy, subsidised by five decades of development aid, which prevents Africans from lifting themselves out of poverty . . . help Africa: please, ask your new government to stop your aid.[8]

Moreover, Kenyan economist James Shikwati has pleaded with the West to stop dumping truckloads of money on Africa's poor. Shikwati believes that the West's constant subsidizing of Africa's social services merely blunts Africans from having an opportunity to achieve constructive governmental engagement.[9] Worse, as former Malawi Peace Corps officer and noted author Paul Theroux points out, Bono and other rockers' naïve cries for debt relief and even more aid have only further entrenched existing problems.

"There are probably more annoying things than being hectored about African development by a wealthy Irish rock star in a cowboy hat, but I can't think of one at the moment. . . . When Malawi's minister of education was accused of stealing millions of dollars from the education budget in 2000, and the Zambian president was charged with stealing from the treasury, and Nigeria squandered its oil wealth, what happened?" asked Theroux. "The simplifiers of Africa's problems kept calling for debt relief and more aid. . . . Donors enable embezzlement by turning a blind eye to bad governance, rigged elections and the deeper reasons these countries are failing."[10]

Still, propelled by "good intentions," Hollywood hypocrites just can't keep themselves from their feel-good efforts that do exactly the *opposite* of what they claim to do. And, not surprisingly, the results are invariably bad. There's just something about progressive charities and celebrity-backed causes that makes every "charity" they create or touch turn into a money pit or a scandal.

Oprah's much-ballyhooed "school for girls" in Africa turned into a house of horrors, with several students testifying in a South African court that a female supervisor sexually abused them.[11]

Then there's Madonna's $15 million "Raising Malawi" Kabbalah boondoggle, which promised to build a school for impoverished girls, but never did get off the ground after independent audits revealed its executive director pissed away nearly $4 million on chauffeurs, golf memberships, lavish salaries, and office space.[12]

Or how about the massive oil-for-food scandal, which allowed Saddam Hussein to pocket more than $20 billion in kickbacks and illegal profits right under the United Nations' nose?

They all backfired. I guess when you hate capitalism that means you must, by default, hate "management," "executive leadership," and all that other icky business stuff.

But to see the Law of Unintended Consequences on ugly

display, all one has to do is look at the Ethiopian famine efforts in the 1980s and how our charity monies were spent. As a 2010 investigative report by that radical conservative news outlet the BBC revealed, "millions of dollars in Western aid for victims of the Ethiopian famine of 1984–85 was siphoned off by rebels to buy weapons." As former rebels told the BBC, an estimated $95 million from Western governments and charities was used by rebels to overthrow the government, and 95 percent of that "was allocated to buying weapons and building up a hard-line Marxist political party within the rebel movement."[13]

Peachy.

More recently, in 2011 the Bono-backed Global Fund to Fight AIDS, Tuberculosis, and Malaria found itself in big trouble. The right-wing zealots over at that GOP mouthpiece the Associated Press reported on the staggering corruption scandal that resulted in the pilfering of two-thirds of some of the Global Fund's grants. Championed as an "alternative to the bureaucracy of the United Nations," the Global Fund was created in 2002 and quickly became a darling of the Left celebrity Bono's charity brand, Product (RED), which donated a portion of its proceeds to the Global Fund. According to the Associated Press, the abuses and corruption uncovered by auditors have been "astonishing."[14] With Obama's America suffering under the weight of 15.2 percent underemployment, here's a small taste of all the good that our billions of dollars did for the Bono-backed "save the universe" syndicate:

- Tens of millions of dollars' worth of donated free malaria prescription drugs were stolen and sold on the black market.
- $5.3 million of the money given to Djibouti (which I'm sure all Americans could pick out on a map) was used

to purchase cars, motorcycles, and other things without receipts. A full $750,000 was transferred with nary an explanation.

- Mountains of forged documents and shady bookkeeping were discovered.

- 67 percent of the $4.1 million to combat AIDS in Mauritania was misspent, as well as $3.5 million of its tuberculosis funds, which were "eaten up by faked invoices and other requests for payment."

- $4 million of the $22.6 million that went to Mali was misappropriated and has sparked the arrest of fifteen people in that country alone.

- In total, an estimated two-thirds of some of the $21.7 billion in grants has been squandered due to massive corruption.[15]

On and on it goes. And the worst of it is that some of the most egregious corruption has yet to be uncovered because, ironically, the half of the Global Fund that was created to circumnavigate the United Nations' bureaucratic waste and red tape is run by—wait for it—the United Nations Development Program![16] So here now, a celebrity-studded fund that was billed and sold to all of us working-class chumps as a way to streamline aid and get it directly to the source without the corruption, scandal, and waste that is the United Nations juggernaut, was actually being run by the Lefty globalists at the United Nations. Ain't that rich.

Bono has funneled monies to the Global Fund, in part, through his ONE nonprofit, which sells itself as a nonpartisan "organization that fights extreme poverty and preventable disease, particularly in Africa, by raising public awareness and pressuring political leaders to support smart and effective policies and programs that are saving lives, helping to put kids in school and improving futures."[17] According to a report by the *New York Post*, Bono's nonprofit hauled in $14,993,873 in donations in 2008, which was the most recent year for which tax records were available. Out of the near $15 million Bono's outfit raked in, the nonprofit's IRS filings revealed that just $184,732 had been distributed to three charities. As for the rest, over $8 million had been spent on "executive and employee salaries."[18] You see, as Kimberly Hunter, spokeswoman for D.C.-based ONE, explained, ONE "does advocacy work, not charity work."[19]

Ah . . . we see. So ONE's 120 staff members yap all day on the phone in cushy offices and attend swank celebrity parties instead of actually getting their hands dirty with all those yucky poor people.[20] Well, at least we now know what "ONE" really stands for—one percent! Excellent. Got it. Where do we send the check?

But Bono's larger method of pumping money into the Global Fund's scandal-plagued corruption racket has been through the charity brand he cofounded, Product (RED), which partners with companies such as Starbucks, Gap, Motorola, and others and donates proceeds to the Global Fund. (RED) claims it "funds grants that currently go to HIV/AIDS programs in Ghana, Lesotho, Rwanda, South Africa, Swaziland, and Zambia" and brags that it "is the largest business sector contributor to the Global Fund." According to (RED)'s website, so far "(RED) partners and events have contributed more than $170 million. 100% goes to programs on the ground—no overhead is taken by either (RED) or the Global Fund."[21] No overhead, that is, but the graft and corruption. (RED) claims that, to its knowledge, none of its funds were implicated in the Global Fund scandal. But it's hard to know whom to believe when you read their incredibly laughable damage-control postings on the (RED) blog. There you will find wonderful spin-doctor postings with headlines like "Why the AP Story about the Global Fund Is Great" (corruption! yippee!) and "How the Global Fund Protects Its Grant Money" (it doesn't).[22] Ridiculous.

Some scholars, like Lisa Ann Richey and Stefano Ponte, believe that celebrity-supported charities actually create negative publicity for the causes they trumpet, because the ensuing scandals garner even greater attention than would have otherwise been the case. "The Global Fund is now known as 'celebrity backed,' and almost no news story of the recent corruption saga has been without reference to Irish rock star Bono and celebrity philanthropist Bill Gates. Celebrities draw attention and stir emotion," write Richey and Ponte. "But now, the opportunity to link development aid mismanagement or lavish spending with global celebrities has led to negative publicity. People all over the world are interested in what is happening to 'Bono's Fund' or 'Madonna's Malawi.'"[23]

In the case of Bono's Product (RED), the goal has been not only to garner greater awareness, but to shift the way people think about consumerism and development aid. In other words, the goal is to make people anti-materialistic by being . . . um . . . more materialistic. Makes perfect sense, right? Wrong, say Richey and Ponte in their case study of Product (RED), *Brand Aid: Shopping Well to Save the World:*

> In essence, aid celebrities are asking consumers to "do good" by buying iconic brands to help "distant others"— Africans affected by AIDS. This is very different from "helping Africa" by buying products actually made by Africans, in Africa, or by choosing products that claim to have been made under better social, labour and environmental conditions of production.
>
> In Product (RED), celebrities are moving attention

away from "conscious consumption" (based on product information) and towards "compassionate consumption" (based on emotional appeal). To us, this is even more problematic than the risk of negative media attention that celebrities bring to development aid.[24]

But the bigger concern, report those Republican Party hacks over at *Advertising Age* (because, as you know, the advertising industry is riddled with conservative plants), is how little money Bono's "cause marketing" approach has actually raised relative to how much it costs to roll out. *Ad Age* assessed the first year of the Product (RED) campaign and found that despite blowing $100 million in marketing expenses, it only brought in a paltry $18 million worldwide. And that was back in 2007.[25] By extrapolation, even if one accepts (RED)'s own 2011 figures, they have only raised $170 million—and in year one *alone* (five years ago) brands dropped $100 million. That may make for effective feel-good marketing for big brands like Motorola and Apple, but it's hardly the most efficient way to fund causes.

"Contributions don't seem to be living up to the hype," reported *Ad Age*'s Mya Frazier. Worse, some believe the call for people to buy products instead of giving directly to charities will undermine philanthropies or spawn a "we gave at the office" mentality. One group of San Francisco designers and artists got together and created a parody poking fun at Bono's (RED) and encouraging people to donate directly to the Global Fund. "Shopping is not a solution. Buy less. Give more." But others, like Trent Stamp of Charity Navigator, believe the (RED) campaign may be a mistake or, worse, will undermine long-term giving. "The Red campaign can be a good start or it can be a colossal waste of money, and it all depends on whether this edgy, innovative campaign inspires young people to be better citizens or just gives them an excuse to feel good about themselves while they buy an overpriced item they don't really need," said Stamp. Similarly, Ben Davis, creative director for Word Pictures Ideas, said, "The Red campaign proposes consumption as the cure to the world's evils. Can't we just focus on the real solution—giving money?"[26]

But that assumes one thing: that giving money actually helps, not *hurts,* African countries. As Dambisa Moyo, author of *Dead Aid: Why Aid Is Not Working and How There Is a Better Way for Africa,* explained in a *Wall Street Journal* editorial:

> Evidence overwhelmingly demonstrates that aid to Africa has made the poor poorer, and the growth slower. The insidious aid culture has left African countries more debt-laden, more inflation-prone, more vulnerable to the vagaries of the currency markets and more unattractive to higher-quality investment. It's increased the risk of civil conflict and unrest. . . . Aid is an unmitigated political, economic and humanitarian disaster.[27]

This is, of course, heartbreaking; no one wants to see people suffer in squalor or face intractable economic stagnation. But long-term solutions will require serious economic restructuring and allowing indigenous markets and producers to form from within, not stay hooked to the international welfare teat, where corruption and graft run rampant. The last sixty years have seen more than $1 trillion of development-related aid flow from rich nations to African nations. And the results have been a catastrophic failure. Real per capita income now is actually lower than in the 1970s, and more than half of Africans, roughly 350 million people, survive on less than a dollar a day—that's twice as many as did twenty years ago.[28]

In a *Los Angeles Times* op-ed titled "What Bono Doesn't Say about Africa," New York University economics professor William Easterly asks, "Could Africa be saving celebrity careers more than celebrities are saving Africa?" Easterly goes on to say that Africans will climb out of poverty using the same mix of entrepreneurship, democratic reform, and self-motivated effort that every other nation historically has used, not star-studded public relations campaigns. "The real Africa needs increased trade from the West more than it needs more aid handouts," concludes Easterly.[29]

Robert Calderisi, a thirty-year veteran in international development who held several senior positions at the World Bank and was its international spokesperson on Africa, agrees that trade and commerce is the pathway to African prosperity. "If not for their colorful national dress at international conferences, Africans would scarcely be noticed on the world stage," writes Calderisi. "Outside the oil and gas sector, most business people on the continent are monopolists, marathoners, or buccaneers. Serious investors have shunned the place for decades; stockbrokers do not think about Africa even in their sleep. In contrast, China attracts more private investment in a single year than Africa does in a decade."[30]

What all this means for Africa is more Bono-backed boondoggles. Sadly, as Charles Johnson has written, "Bono never considers the real barrier to Africans establishing their own business: government and the absence of the rule of law. . . . Bono will never challenge the actions of these governments because he doesn't want to incite their ire. Bono, ever the cultural relativist, is unwilling to upset those directly responsible for African poverty. . . . Implicitly, Bono's support for debt relief permits countries to experiment with systems of government—socialist, kleptocratic, or Islamic—historically known to fail."[31]

Sadly, though, it's even worse than that. The four decades of American foreign aid have bred not only a cycle of dependency and poverty, but *contempt*. The Reverend Gerald Zandstra, formerly with the Acton Institute, recounted during a keynote speech for the group's annual gathering a chilling true story from his visits to Kenya. Zandstra said that a few years before the Kenyan elections, he had a chance to listen to the then longtime president of Kenya, Daniel arap Moi, deliver a speech in the hotel Zandstra happened to be staying in. Moi told the crowd that the International Monetary Fund and the World Bank were demanding that Kenya repay the $3 billion it had borrowed from them. To that, President Moi said, "I look around Kenya and I don't see that we are three billion dollars better off. And until somebody from the IMF and the World Bank can come here and show me how we are three billion dollars better off, I say we don't pay one thin dime." The Kenyan crowd erupted in cheers and applause.

Using President Moi's rationale, the Reverend Zandstra vocalized this thought experiment: "I'm going to try this with a home improvement loan. . . . 'You gave me 25 grand, I was going to fix up the kitchen, but I went to Vegas, and I don't know where the money is. And I shouldn't have to repay it because my kitchen still looks the same.'" Zandstra noted that when Moi left office, his personal, direct, provable assets were worth $3.3 billion. "And yet Bono is traveling the world highlighting the problem but yet also highlighting the exact solution that has only exacerbated the problem."[32]

But none of this should worry the planet. The reason? A stubble-faced senior citizen rocker wearing eight-hundred-dollar Prada sunglasses stands ready to hector you and the rest of the developed world into handing over your hard-earned money so that he doesn't have to!

"People like Bono really annoy me," said Irish comedian Graham Norton. "He goes to hell and back to avoid paying tax. He has a special accountant. He works out Irish tax loopholes. And then he's asking me to buy a well for an African village."[33]

Yep. That's right. Paul Hewson, the savior of the galaxy, turns out to be a first-rate moneygrubber.

Debt and Development Coalition Ireland (DDCI), which is a coalition of seventy aid groups, including the likes of Oxfam and Concern Worldwide, has condemned the world's highest-grossing rock band for its blatant hypocrisy. Specifically, the DDCI has called out U2 for its tax-dodging ways and described the band as "robbing the world's poor" with its piratical business policies and raiding the very poverty and social justice causes they purport to champion.

"We wanted to raise our concern that while Bono has championed the cause of fighting poverty and injustice in the impoverished world, the fact is that his band has moved part of its business to a tax shelter," said DDCI's Nessa Ni Chasaide. "Tax avoidance and tax evasion costs the impoverished world at least $160 million every year. This is money urgently required to bring people out of poverty."[34]

The sordid tale of capitalist pig greed all began in 2006. That's when Ireland changed its tax laws. Today Ireland's corporate tax rate is one of the lowest in the world. Among European Union nations, the average corporate tax rate is 23 percent. That's a dream compared to America's tax rate for business! At a jaw-dropping 39.2 percent, the United States has the second-worst corporate tax rate in the world, second only to Japan, as in "lost-decade Japan." So at 12.5 percent, Ireland's corporate rates are the envy of much of the planet, and have produced strong gains for the nation in attracting businesses and entrepreneurs from around the world. But for the Irish-born U2 boys, their mother country's generous business tax rates were apparently not enough. Indeed, once Ireland's finance minister announced that its even more generous tax exemptions for artists would be replaced with a $319,000 ceiling for tax-free artist incomes, Paul Hewson and the boys hightailed it out of the Republic of Ireland and headed for the proverbial hills in Holland to set up corporate shop. Indeed, within just six months of the new law's enactment, U2 Ltd., the company the band created to handle all of its massive royalty payments, had relocated to take advantage of the Netherlands' wonderfully low tax rates, rates so low that U2 instantly cut its taxes on the band's songwriting royalties, which *Slate* estimates at $286 million, exactly in half![35]

Not surprisingly, Paul Hewson and David Evans (also known as "The Edge." Again, I refuse to call someone old enough to be my freaking father "The Edge." And besides, how the hell does one even appropriately address such a loon? Is it Mr. Edge? When calling him by his first name, are we to call him "The"? Hard to say. In any event, it's some of the most ridiculous, self-important, juvenile crap I've ever heard. But I digress . . .) don't see the hypocrisy of a band whose entire brand is built around its alleged concern for the world's poor, and which traipses around the globe lecturing and hectoring us working hacks to see to it that our governments cut a gargantuan check full of our money, and dodges taxes that would help the very same cause.

"Like any other business, U2 operates in a tax-efficient manner," says lead U2 flack, manager Paul McGuiness.[36]

Ohhhh . . . is that what it's called? A "tax-efficient manner." Ah, I see. So when the nations of the world refuse to wipe away billions and billions and billions of dollars of loans, that's not behaving in a "tax-efficient manner." No, that's straight-up evil, capitalistic greed and a lack of moral compassion. But when "Messiah Bono" and "Archangel Edge" turn their backs on their homeland and set up a massive corporate empire in the Netherlands to avoid paying taxes that would otherwise foot the bill for Third World debt forgiveness . . . well, you see . . . um . . . uh . . . that's just sound corporate policy carried out in—drum roll, please—a "tax-efficient manner."

It's so audaciously hypocritical it almost seems like a bad *Saturday Night Live* skit (and you know how *bad* they've been lately). But if all that isn't nauseating enough, perhaps even more outrageous has been Paul Hewson's feigned moral indignation and rhapsodic emotionalism at the suggestion that he might be a self-interested capitalist creature, just like the rest of the human race.

"We pay millions and millions of dollars in tax," whined the faux poverty crusader to the *Irish Times*. "The thing that stung us was the accusation of hypocrisy for my work as an activist."

Um, no, you washed-up leprechaun, no one finds your "work as an activist" (who talks like that, seriously?) hypocritical. What everyone but you and "The Edge" find hypocritical is the fact that you bully everyone else to pony up cash to pay off the debts of Third World nations (many of whom are led by corrupt warlord thugs) even as you command your army of tax accountants to invade and capture every tax loophole on the planet!

But St. Bono's absurd rant to the *Irish Times* continued. "I can understand how people outside the country wouldn't understand how Ireland got to its prosperity but everybody in Ireland knows that there are some very clever people in the Government and in the Revenue who created a financial architecture that prospered the entire nation. It was a way of attracting people to this country who wouldn't normally do business here and the financial services brought billions of dollars every year directly to the Exchequer." [37]

Okay, so where does one even begin to address this one? First of all, what Paul Hewson appears to be saying is that he's an even bigger supply-sider than the late great Jack Kemp, because he's right: Ireland's low corporate tax rate has done what any low tax rate does—it has created more, not less, revenue. And in fact, since Ireland's tax exemption scheme for artists made its appearance in 1969, the measure has helped attract numerous famous artists, including the Rolling Stones.[38] What's more, its low 12.5 percent corporate tax rate has helped Ireland snag investments from the likes of tech giants Intel and Dell.[39] Thus, if carried to its logical ends, Messiah Bono's comments suggest that if he *really* cared about helping poorer nations lift themselves out of poverty, what he should be doing is lobbying world governments to lower their corporate tax rates in order to attract businesses, create jobs, and thereby grow revenues that could be used to fund the kinds of international welfare programs he seems so fond of championing. Indeed, if Hewson's comments are correct, more, not less, capitalism is the solution. But Hollywood hypocrites aren't interested in logic, nor are they interested in supporting the most opportunity-creating economic system ever devised by human minds. And so, after a brief flashing moment of clarity, Bono returns to his regularly scheduled program of inane stupidity and senselessness.

"What's actually hypocritical is the idea that then you don't use a financial services centre in Holland. The real question people need to ask about Ireland's tax policy is: 'Was the nation a net gain benefactor?' and of course it was—hugely so. So there was no hypocrisy for me. We're just part of a system that has benefited the nation greatly and that's a system that will be closed down in time. Ireland will have to find other ways of being competitive and attractive."[40]

Again, understanding what the hell this merry leprechaun is attempting to say is about as easy as trying to cut one's own hair. But what the Deity appears to be saying is, "Hey, Irish government. If you want our money, keep your tax rates low and we'll park our corporate empire here on the mother soil. Otherwise, kiss our capitalist asses, you bunch of tax-hiking ingrates!" Put another way, comparatively, they are making Andrew Carnegie and John D. Rockefeller look like a bunch of wimps when it comes to hard-core capitalistic practices. But that doesn't stop the aging rocker from pretending to have his little feelers hurt.

"It hurts when the criticism comes internationally," says the Lucky Charms leprechaun reject. "But I can't speak up without betraying my relationship with the band. So you take the shit. People who don't know our music—it's very easy for them to take a position on us, they run with the stereotypes and caricature of us."

Gee, and what "stereotypes" and "caricatures" might those be, Sir "Bono"? Or shall we ask the equally puffed up "Mr. Edge"? What? That you are a bunch of capitalist charlatans who think your constant moral harangues and inflated egos make you impervious to charges of hypocrisy? If so, then you're absolutely right.

But actually, when confronted, "The Edge" was refreshingly candid about just what tax-dodging capitalist hypocrites the global poverty crusaders truly are. U2 Ltd., as Evans explained, is "our own private thing. We do business all over the world, we pay taxes all over the world and we are totally tax compliant." In another interview he said, "Our business is very complex. Of course we're trying to be tax-efficient. Who doesn't want to be tax-efficient?"[41]

Wow. Just . . . um . . . wow.

It's hard to decide which is more appalling: the sheer elitism ("Our business is very complex . . . you simple working class dolts can't wrap your minuscule minds around the complexity that is 'The Edge'") or the breathtaking "do as I say, not as I do" hypocrisy. When rich nations are trying to be wise about how taxpayers' hard-earned monies are doled out and therefore resist the pleas of over-the-hill rockers to ram money down the Third World hole, they are immoral moneygrubbers drunk on greed. But when rich rockers are trying to be wise about how much of their hard-earned money governments should get their hands on, they are simply being "tax-efficient." (There's that phrase again! Great phrase, that "tax-efficient.") After all, as "The Edge" points out, "Who doesn't want to be tax-efficient?"

Apparently, when "The Edge" issued these comments, as the *Observer*'s Nick Cohen described it, he "sounded as edgy as a plump accountant in the 19th hole" (whatever the heck that Eurocrap means).[42] Joan Burton, finance spokeswoman for the Labour Party, was more diplomatic in voicing her dismay. "It seems odd, in a situation where they enjoy an already favorable tax regime, they would move operations to the Netherlands to get an even more favorable rate."[43]

Actually, when you consider the fact that U2 Ltd. remaining in the Republic of Ireland would have meant that Paul Hewson, Dave Evans, and those other two dudes that no one knows or cares about would go from paying zero tax on earnings from their music publishing to 42 percent tax on the same earnings, it's really not terribly "odd" at all.[44] It's a neat thing the father of capitalism, Adam Smith, would have explained as the Invisible Hand of self-interest directing market decisions.

Still, among those in the "end global poverty" brigades, the idea of following one's self-interest to avoid the onerous hand of intrusive government is considered anathema to the sanctimonious goals of Hollywood hypocrites like Paul Hewson and Dave Evans. "There are trillions of dollars stashed in tax havens. If that money was taxed in the countries where it was earned," says Andy Storey of the "justice group" Afri, "governments would have their own resources to improve the lives of their people."[45] Indeed, according to the Leftist London-based Tax Justice Network, "Wealthy individuals have put about $11.5 trillion in tax havens around the world" and that means that "unpaid taxes on those assets could amount to $255 billion."[46]

Ignore for a moment the absurd notion these Lefty whack jobs espouse: namely, that *your* money belongs to the government (hard, I know, but just for the sake of argument). Just assume for a moment that one holds this view. By that standard, Bono, "The Edge," and those other two rich nameless dudes in the band are major-league scoundrels of the worst kind, betrayers of the cause, and, by proxy, foot soldiers for "The Man."

The *Observer*'s Nick Cohen agrees:

Here was a man who incited audiences to condemn Western politicians for not sending enough of their taxpayers' money to the wretched of the earth, avoiding tax himself. . . . If you say you care about Africa, why are you paying fees to international money movers who encourage Africa's "tax-efficient" kleptomaniacs to hide their loot in tax havens? You are also forcing fellow citizens, who didn't make U2's estimated $110 million in 2005, to pick up the bill, not only for foreign aid, but for education, health, law and order and defense. And all the time while others suffer on your behalf, you maintain that you are behaving reasonably.[47]

Other major-league rockers, like lead singer Brian Johnson of Australia's rock legends AC/DC, have found Bono's monetary moralizing equally obnoxious and wrongheaded. "I do it myself, I don't tell everybody I'm doing it," said Johnson. "I don't tell everybody they should give money—they can't afford it. When I was a working man I didn't want to go to a concert for some bastard to talk down to me that I should be thinking of some kid in Africa. I'm sorry mate, do it yourself, spend some of your own money and get it done. It just makes me angry."[48]

For conservatives, none of this is a surprise. Progressives love to confiscate money from others and then redirect it to their pet projects and social engineering programs. But for Bono to shake down the free world for cash, only to hoard all of his from the tax man is, well, uniquely hypocritical, even by Hollywood standards. "A familiar paradox about leftist celebrities in the entertainment industry," writes Timothy Noah for *Slate,* "is that their embrace of progressivism almost never includes a wholehearted embrace of progressive taxation, i.e., the principle that the richer you get, the larger the percentage of your income you ought to pay in taxes."[49]

To be sure, as even the Debt and Development Commission acknowledges, "There is nothing illegal about what they [U2] have done in taking advantage of more favorable tax laws but, given Bono has invested so much in promoting an end to poverty, we see a contradiction here."[50] In fact, the hypocrisy has been so glaring that activist group Art Uncut planned a large June 2011 concert protest against U2 at Glastonbury, England, complete with a huge inflatable "Bono Pay Up" sign and bundles of oversized money to be paraded in front of Bono while onstage.[51] "Bono claims to care about the developing world," said a spokesman for Art Uncut, "but U2 greedily indulges in the very kind of tax avoidance that is crippling poor nations. We will be showing the very real impact of U2's tax avoidance on hospitals and schools in Ireland. Anyone watching will be made very aware that Bono needs to pay up." Tax expert and anti-poverty campaigner Richard Murphy concurs: "If Bono thinks he is just like any other Irishman, he should pay his taxes like everyone else."[52]

In fact, the further into Bono's holdings and assets you delve, the more you realize just how different he is from any Irishman or human being. Paul Hewson's estimated worth exceeds $900 million. He owns a fleet of expensive automobiles, including a family-sized Maserati. He frequents New York's chicest restaurants and regularly drops thousands on a single bottle of his favorite wine. He, along with five former senior executives from major companies (including the former chief financial officer at Apple), set up Elevation Partners, which is named after one of U2's songs and has $1.9 billion of assets under management. The private equity group invests hundreds of millions in cash-churning ventures. His bandmates have also gotten in on the capitalist act, investing in *Vertigo 3*, an Airbus A230 that flies them all around the world they claim to be saving. Bono's equity firm even owns a 40 percent stake in *Forbes* magazine, the holy grail of capitalism, valued at between $250 million and $300 million! "Behind Bono's working-class, man-of-the people façade lies someone whose love of money is matched only by his obsession with making even more of it," writes *Daily Mail* reporter Paul Scott.[53]

Bono's commitment to fattening his own wallet while draining taxpayers' has even led him to applaud communist China's Internet censorship, in the name of reducing music sharing, which cuts into his profits. Writing in the *New York Times*, Bono said, "we know from America's noble effort to stop child pornography, not to mention China's ignoble effort to suppress online dissent, that it's perfectly possible to track content." A bone-crushing crackdown, China-style: now that's what America needs! I'll let Phil Elmore, writing in *WorldNetDaily*, address this mind-boggling hypocrisy: "A man whose band made its name writing whiny songs about human rights is now suggesting a totalitarian Communist regime just might have the right idea where policing the Internet is concerned. . . . Where pirating his band's music is concerned, Bono thinks China's despotic and often arbitrary censorship of the Internet is a fine idea. . . . 'Social justice' is only just when it concerns issues that don't benefit Bono. If totalitarian control of the Internet is what it takes to prevent piracy of his music, U2's front man is happy to stand the world's music consumers against the figurative wall of Communist China's firing squads."[54]

Bottom line: Paul Hewson isn't the Savior of the Universe. He's for stealing your money, hoarding his, and advocating the very feel-good foreign aid policies that have destroyed the continent of Africa, funded military muscle for warlord-led oppression, eradicated economic growth, and mired hundreds of millions of Africans in seemingly intractable and dire circumstances. And all while he clutches every last penny of U2's billion-dollar music empire.

Way to go, Bono. Way to go.

8

Be Healthy or Else!

How Hollywood Loons Follow Dear Leader's Lead in Lusting to Regulate What We Do, Buy, and Eat

One of the few things that John McCain's sorry 2008 presidential campaign did effectively was to create an awesome TV ad juxtaposing images of Barack Obama against those of Paris Hilton and Britney Spears to make the case that the community organizer candidate was, in actuality, "the biggest celebrity in the world." And so, given that fact, perhaps it should come as no surprise that Hollywood's celebrity sheep would follow in the hypocritical path of the biggest celebrity hypocrite of all—Obama himself.

Even as the man has his wife out waving her USDA organically approved finger into our faces and hectoring us to eat nuts, twigs, and berries, Obama has spent the past thirty years puffing like a smokestack. (Can you imagine how much earth-killing carbon his cigarette addiction has emitted?! Gasp!) His numerous attempts to quit smoking have been about as effective as his fiscal policies. In February 2011, however, his Food Nazi wife reported that he hadn't touched a cigarette in almost a year, and by "almost a year" she meant "four hours." Even if her estimate is accurate—and that's a big if—that would mean that Barack Obama, the Messiah who promised to heal the oceans (before overseeing the biggest oil spill in American history), was puffing away when Michelle began her "Let's Move" health campaign.[1]

Tofu for you, Marlboros for me!

But maybe we should be counting our lucky stars that the Celebrity in Chief's current addiction only involves cigarettes. After all, nicotine isn't the only drug the Anointed One has succumbed to. Writing about his high school and college days in his 1995 book, *Dreams from My Father*, Obama explained, "Pot had helped, and booze; maybe a little blow [cocaine] when you could afford it."

That's right, kids! Say no to cookies and yes to crack!

Then, in 2007, speaking about marijuana, Obama put his own twist on Bill Clinton's infamous "I didn't inhale" line. Obama told an interviewer, "When I was a kid I inhaled frequently. That was the point." Maybe this could help explain why Dear Leader, speaking in 2004, told Northwestern University students, "The War on Drugs has been an utter failure. We need to rethink and decriminalize our marijuana laws." And why, in 2006, he explained to a constituent: "I am aware of the argument that legalizing marijuana would make the drug more 'controlled' or safer, and that it may curb the violence associated with the sale of an illegal substance. I also appreciate that many physicians believe that medicinal marijuana can be helpful to some patients."[2]

Let's just hope this doesn't explain why he still shows all

those signs of having the munchies when he's out of Michelle's calorie-controlling sight.

Then again, in fairness to the Socialist in Chief, he's probably just mimicking the Food Witch's lead. Michelle Obama wasted no time in planting her famous vegetable garden, digging alongside public school kids. (They say she planted the garden in response to childhood obesity stats, but I can't help wondering if it's her emergency rations for when her hubby finally sends us into a full Depression-style food shortage.) And since she announced her "Let's Move!" initiative at the beginning of 2010,[3] healthy living and healthy eating have been a huge focus of the Obama White House.[4] There's just one problem: the woman wolfs down junk food like Obama spends taxpayers' money.

During a visit to South Africa, Michelle remained invested in children's health, speaking to Cape Town children with Archbishop Desmond Tutu about AIDS and the importance of staying healthy. She and the archbishop even took the time to do some push-ups with the kids.[5] But when a kid asked her about her favorite foods, Mrs. Obama resorted to stall tactics.

"My favorite? Oh, this is a tough one. It is tough, you know, because if I say something not healthy, people will be, like, you aren't really committed to health. If I say something healthy, you know—I do—honestly, I like all kinds of foods."

She then launched into the obligatory multicultural shout-outs, one to the Indian community via Indian food, and then another to the all-important Latino voting bloc via Mexican food. And then she dropped the bitter, artery-clogging truth.

"No, if I picked one favorite, favorite food, it's French fries. Okay? It's French fries. I can't stop eating them." Then, in characteristic Obama hypocrisy fashion, she added, "But eat your vegetables. And exercise." Elsewhere she confessed, "I love burgers and fries. And I love ice cream and cake. And so do most kids."

And all this from the calorie crusader whose "Let's Move!" initiative has as its goal solving childhood obesity within a generation.[6] That's a pretty ambitious goal if you ask me, especially given the fact that nearly one-third of children in America today (about 25 million) are overweight and obese and the average 8–18-year-old spends seven and a half hours a day consuming celebrity-flooded, sedentary-lifestyle-inducing entertainment media.[7]

But fear not. Mrs. Obama is fast on the job! And her chain-smoking, pot-loving, cocaine-using husband stands at the ready to get her back!

On the surface, Mrs. Community Organizer's plan to broadside childhood obesity sounds admirable. She touts a battery of strategies aimed at improving nutrition during children's early developmental stages, providing healthier foods in schools, making sure families have access to healthy and affordable foods near their homes, helping kids become more active, and ensuring that parents are better informed about the health-related choices they make for their kids. That all sounds swell—that is, until you find out how our nation's Dietary Dominatrix wants to accomplish all of this.

For one, she wants to see to it that *all* children are subjected to body mass index (BMI) measurements,[8] something that more and more schools have been incorporating into "weight grades" for students.[9] Think about how creepy this is. The government monitoring and tracking the weight of the nation's kids, as if they are boxers being weighed in before the big bout? Yeah, because fat kids don't already have enough crap to deal with!

Next, her plan will spend $25 million to renovate public school kitchens (private school kids be damned!) and ditch their deep fryers.[10] Vending machines in schools? Becoming a thing of the past, as long as they contain conventional snack foods (of course, she sees no reason why schools can't have vending machines stocked with water, healthy juice drinks, trail mix, granola bars, and whole-grain sandwiches).[11] This will, of course, do wonders for the thousands of jobs that depend on the vending machine industry. However, on a positive note, it will likely be a boon to enterprising kids who fill their backpacks with Snickers and sell them on the playground for a heavy markup. Gotta love the free market!

But worse, instead of simply having parents be responsible for teaching their kids how to make smart, healthy eating decisions, Mrs. Obama's approach does what Leftists always do: it squelches individual freedom all in the name of doing so "for the children." Newsflash: grocery stores and the gas station next to the school sell—gasp!—candy and soda! So rather than tossing the kiddos on some dirty public school scale to tell them the number of chins they're sporting, how about teaching them a little self-restraint and responsibility? Yet the message of self-control is only a minor part of Michelle's grand program.

Far more alarming are the Dietary Dominatrix's market-controlling ideas. They include a suggestion that the government regulate companies that produce junk food and soft drinks.[12] In addition to being a genuinely bad idea, it's breathtakingly hypo-critical. Why? Because Michelle Obama used to be on the board of directors of Treehouse Foods, a company that served as a leading supplier for McDonald's![13]

Still, as if regulating companies wouldn't drive up our food prices enough, Michelle has also proposed that the government subsidize the production of healthy foods and investigate the pos-sibility of *taxing* the unhealthy ones, like soft drinks, candy, snack foods, and fast foods.[14] (Tip for the eventual 2012 GOP hopeful: run on a pro-junk-food platform and you'll be in like Flynn, yo!)

But there is one spoonful of sugar to help all this food policing go down. In typical Obama fashion, Michelle enlisted the help of a celebrity to create a fun way for kids to exercise. Enter the gorgeous Beyoncé, who re-recorded her old hit "Get Me Bodied" and fashioned it into a dance-workout routine tune called "Move Your Body."[15] Beyoncé has now infiltrated schools across the nation with her "Move Your Body" music video, in which she coaches students in a school cafeteria through her dance routine while wearing knee socks, stiletto heels, and dress-code-violating short-shorts. The music video even ends with a patriotic dance step: "Wave the American Flag." Michelle liked the dance so much that when she made a surprise visit to the Alice Deal Middle School in Washington, she couldn't help herself and had to bust a move with the kids, going against her initial plan to not "embarrass" herself.[16]

Michelle has every reason to get into the groove of this campaign. See, for Mrs. Obama, childhood obesity is personal. During the interviews leading up to the launch of "Let's Move!," she traced her interest in the problem to when her own children were six and nine and experienced weight fluctuations that concerned their pediatrician. "I had a wake-up call," she said. And wake up she did. She reported that she responded to the threat that her daughters were getting—heaven forbid—"chubby" by putting them on a diet that wowed even the pediatrician.

First of all, let me go on record as saying that Sasha and Malia are not overweight. They're adorable, precious kids. So Mom needs to chill and stop with the kind of neurotic hectoring that sends girls into an eating disorder. Instead she should focus on teaching Barack how old their children are, since the genius can't seem to remember. Even *Psychology Today* questioned Michelle's wisdom in telling the whole civilized world that her daughters were "chubby." Nevertheless, even after bashing her daughters for being fatsos, she told America at the "Let's Move!" launch, "This isn't just about inches and pounds or how our kids look. It's about how our kids feel, and how they feel about themselves."[17] Yeah, because BMI report cards telling fat kids they're part of an epidemic targeted for eradication are going to do *wonders* for their self-esteem![18]

The problem is that we don't have a pediatrician or nutritionist pushing these policies. Instead we have a woman who actually made a point to include dried fruit among the trick-or-treat goodies she doled out at Halloween White House celebrations. But even the health nut Michelle isn't all she's cracked up to be.[19]

America's chief celebrity couple showed their commitment to clean eating at the Obamas' 2011 Super Bowl party. Their menu certainly didn't receive the same kind of scrutiny Michelle would advocate for us normal folk. No, it consisted of cheeseburgers, deep-dish pizza, buffalo wings, bratwurst, kielbasa, twice-baked potatoes, German potato salad, Snyder's potato chips, pretzels, chips and dips, ice cream, and—thank goodness—salad.[20] Salad excepted, how much of our tax dollars would the Obamas' buffet have cost with food taxes in place? No telling. And Michelle also has a penchant for an item not on this menu: ribs, that 141-fat-gram-per-serving of joy.[21] She also praised Charlotte, North Carolina, for its "great barbecue" in a letter she sent out about the 2012 Democratic National Convention, to be held there. The average total barbecue meal clocks in at around 2,500 calories. But as a rib-loving man myself, please, for the love of God, do not tell that to the Dietary Dominatrix, or else she might regulate it and tack on another fifty dollars per slab in fat-boy food taxes.[22] And in this disastrous Obama economy, who the hell can afford that?

Barack's no better. He has a penchant for junk food that no White House handler has been able to hide. Frequently photographed scarfing down tacos, burgers, giant roast beef sandwiches, and the like, the Skinny Socialist has developed such a reputation for eating trash that, during the 2008 elections, restaurants all over the country began crafting their own versions of a special menu item in his honor: the Obama burger. With the 2012 race just around the bend, Obama burgers are returning. And the first creation of this election cycle is the "Obama Pizza Burger" from Pops Restaurant in Boston. What could conjure up a clearer picture of nutritional piety than a "pizza burger?"[23]

Some of Barack's junk food binges have been timed worse than others. Like when he popped into Rudy's Hot Dog in Toledo with the city's mayor the day after Michelle unveiled "MyPlate," a replacement for the famous "My Pyramid." Doh! That day, the scrawny community organizer wolfed down two chili dogs, a side of chili, and an order of French fries, too.[24]

Eat that, Michelle!

Mrs. Obama plans to take her nutrition reforms to the world (maybe she'll draw the line at Ethiopia).[25] But in light of the Obamas' profligate eating, as well as the Snorting Socialist's substance abuse, the Obamas should shut their pie holes and stop lecturing us about healthy living and start practicing what they preach. These hypocrites merely make it easier for their Hollywood lackeys to mimic them.

If the Leftists have to regulate something, maybe they should start with the huge cash their Hollywood pals make by hawking harmful items through product placement in movies. Indeed, the impact of product placement in movies is significant. This was first proved in the eighties when the film *E.T.* caused 65 percent sales increase in Reese's Pieces for months following the film's release.

It has since been proved over and over by the fact that junk food companies continuously shell out large sums so that movies will feature their products.

A 2010 study published in the journal *Pediatrics* sheds some light on just how much junk food Hollywood actually feeds our eyes. The study analyzed the top twenty films in box office receipts for each year from 1996 to 2005. Sixty-nine percent of these two hundred total films contained at least one food, beverage, or food retailer brand placement. That covered one-third of all G-rated movies, 58 percent of PG movies, and 72 percent of PG-13 movies. And of course, the most featured types of food items were salty snacks, including chips, soft drinks, candy, and other sweets. Of these categories, salty snacks, candy, and sweets comprised 59 percent of food brands represented, and sugar-sweetened drinks accounted for three-fourths of beverages. A full 62 percent of restaurants featured were fast-food brands. So if America's biggest celebrity wants to help us change our eating habits, how about starting with spanking his big-money donors in Hollywood?[26]

We know the Hollywood Left knows nothing about foreign policy, domestic policy, environmental policy, world peace, or pretty much anything else they love to lecture us about. But when it comes to healthy living and making wise lifestyle and health decisions, the entertainment industry's "best and brightest" are far too often our lowest and most base. Nevertheless, these hypocrites still have the gall to tell us how to live our lives. They do antidrug PSAs and come to work too doped up to sit straight. They encourage us to party it up with them and tell us, "Oh, yeah, by the way, watch out for AIDS." They save the trees and trash the kids. But somehow they almost always get away with it. Every time I think of Leftists lecturing us about how to live, what to buy, and what the government should or shouldn't "allow" us to eat, my mind rewinds to that infamous moment in presidential history when NORML (National Organization for the Reform of Marijuana Laws) advisory board member and American tax cheat Willie Nelson sat on the roof of the White House during the Carter presidency and smoked a fat spliff.[27]

Classy. And tellingly emblematic.

If Obama really wants to promote an anti-tobacco agenda and wants to lower health-care costs associated with smoking he needs to point the finger at himself and his movie-making followers. After all, we all know smoking is bad for you. Cigarette smoke contains over four thousand different chemicals, and many of these cause cancer. Smoking is linked to around 85 percent of all lung cancer cases, and lung cancer is the leading cause of cancer death across all ethnic groups in the United States, responsible for one in three cancer deaths and over 123,000 deaths every year (about 440 a day). That's why the government stepped in during the 1970s and banned TV smoking ads.[28]

But a generation later, the proliferation of cigarettes remains one of Hollywood's biggest contributions to the world. The entertainment industry still gives Big Tobacco plenty of screen time. Of the 1,692 films produced by Hollywood from 1999 to 2008, 1,235 included smoking. That's almost 73 percent.[29] Over the past fifteen years, Marlboros have appeared in at least seventy-four of Hollywood's top-grossing films. What's more, movies give tobacco companies a nifty little loophole through which they can circumvent the TV commercial ban. If cigarettes make it into movie trailers (which they have a nasty habit of doing), and if that trailer gets aired on TV, then—voilà!—cigarettes get into television commercials. Isn't Hollywood great?

But the liberal entertainment industry's health-hurting wrecking ball doesn't stop swinging there. Exposure to smoking is linked to more positive attitudes toward smoking. In fact, nonsmoking teens are sixteen times more likely to have a positive attitude toward smoking in the future if their favorite stars smoke. Exposure to smoking in the movies triples the chances that a teen will try smoking and quadruples the chances of nonsmokers' kids taking up the vice. Smoking in movies has such a potent influence on youth that it accounts for 44 percent of adolescents who start smoking; this effect is even stronger than that of cigarette advertising. So it should come as no surprise that the U.S. Centers for Disease Control and Prevention named tobacco in movies as a major factor in teen smoking in 2002, 2004, 2005, 2006, 2008, and 2010.[30]

Now, does that mean we need even more government intervention in the cigarette market? Or bureaucrats to regulate the number of Lay's potato chips some actor stuffs in his face while on the big screen, for that matter? Heck no. That's the type of Nanny Statism that would make liberals happy in their pants. With all the information we know about cigarettes today, it's silly for anyone to puff on those bad boys. But addictions are hard to break. I get that. Still, it's nothing short of hypocritical for this White House to be giving us lectures on healthy living habits when their biggest backers encourage adolescents to light up stogies in a misguided attempt to be down with the coolness.

What is the response from Obama's beloved movie stars, who flood his campaign coffers with fat celebrity cash? Not much. Many of Obama's Hollywood pals smoke far more offstage than they do onstage. I'm thinking of actors like Colin Farrell, who used to blaze eighty cigs a day. They're constantly being photographed puffing away on their cancer sticks. Worst of all, approximately half of young stars smoke.[31] The reason this matters, say antismoking experts, is that images of offscreen smoking are just as bad as onscreen, particularly in our tabloid Internet culture, which prizes celebrity video and images.[32] Just a few of the innumerable smokers include Brad and Angelina, Cameron Diaz, Drew Barrymore, Ben Affleck, Leonardo DiCaprio, Paris Hilton, Mary Kate Olsen, and even waning teen sensation Miley Cyrus.[33]

YOU'D THINK THAT no self-respecting star would dare do anything that looked remotely like preaching in favor of smoking. Especially not an Oscar winner like the aforementioned racist bigot Whoopi Goldberg. But when it comes to health double standards, Whoopi is a prime example of the kind of "save the world, kill the children" hypocrisy one might expect from an Obama supporter.

Now let's be clear: Whoopi is no slouch when it comes to charitable work. She's received the Gay and Lesbian Alliance Against Defamation Vanguard Award for her LGBT community advocacy, she's been named a UNICEF Goodwill Ambassador, she serves on the board of Garden of Dreams, and she's been hosting the Comic Relief TV specials to benefit charities for the homeless since 1986.[34] She's also done plenty of health-related work. There's her work for AIDS-related charities, such as chairing the largest fundraiser event for Project Angel Food, an organization that gives food to housebound Los Angeles AIDS victims and gave Goldberg an award for her generous service.[35] She's also active in the fight against breast cancer.[36] Not just through advocacy, either; when agent and close friend Cara Stein was diagnosed, Whoopi lent her friendship and strength to Stein's recovery, so she knows the disease personally.[37] Additionally, she's taken a stand against substance abuse,[38] as when she recently put out a PSA against crystal meth.[39]

Whoopi personally knows the pain of addiction. Big-time.

While Charlie Sheen was sharing his plans of skipping rehab and resuming his acting career (what's the point of rehab when your Adonis DNA let's you blink and be cured?), Whoopi candidly let us in on her own battle with drugs, during an episode of *The View*. Explaining the kind of lifestyle she chose to lead while working and doing drugs, she recalled how her addiction drove her to work, to push through till that next paycheck. "I ended up sitting on a bed for three or four days scared there was something under the bed. I wet the bed, I pooped the bed . . . I was so scared. I hit bottom. I did that a long time ago." Wow . . . That story makes Charlie Sheen look like a droopy-eyed, armless child, as he would put it. But thankfully, she's "straight as an arrow," she says.[40]

In 2011, a nineteen-year-old video emerged on YouTube in which Whoopi spilled the beans about the night she received her Oscar for her role in *Ghost*. Unbeknownst to the rest of America (except her observant mother), Whoopi was high as a kite on pot when she took the statuette from Denzel Washington. Wanting "to relax," she'd "smoked this wonderful joint that was the last of my homegrown." But she said she learned a valuable lesson: "Never smoke pot before there's the possibility of having to talk to a hundred million people." And, just in case there would be any kids watching, she concluded the footage with "Well, just 'cause I do it doesn't mean you should, too. Do as I say, not as I do. I'm the adult, goddamnit."[41]

Anyone can see why Whoopi would want to make an example out of herself, why she would want to be a voice of health and sobriety to the younger generation of malleable American minds who could save so much hassle by learning from the poop stains of her fetid past. And at least her story ended well, and she's "straight as an arrow."[42]

"Straight as an arrow" she may be by her own estimation,

but Whoopi still smokes, albeit these smokes are legal. So rather than promoting public health and fighting the vices of substance abuse as she would in other cases, she released a furious attack on authorities who enforce public antismoking laws. And it's not like Goldberg opposed the regulation due to limited-government convictions. I'd join her on that. But nah, she just can't live without the nicotine. Instead she demanded that legislators take up the Big Brother environmental cause of cracking down on greenhouse gases that are emitted from vehicles. To drive home her save-the-trees-and-kill-the-children message, she vowed to violate the smoking ban and pay the fifty-dollar fine for puffing in public.[43]

And while conservatives can sympathize with Goldberg's frustration that police officers are being put on cigarette duty in parks (cops have more pressing matters), what do you call someone with a passion for fighting breast cancer who sees no problem promoting a practice that will inevitably lead to lung cancer? And what do you call an ex-druggy who knows the pain of addictions and speaks out against drug abuse, but would prefer that others remain vulnerable to the addiction of nicotine so she can brag about her fifty-buck smoke in the park? Um, I'm thinking "hypocrite" should work just fine.

With Whoopi's mega-platform, it's too bad she doesn't share these "inconvenient" facts with her audience: Lung cancer kills more people than breast cancer. Actually, more than breast, prostate, colon, liver, kidney, and melanoma cancers combined.[44]

Pot may be a thing of the past for Whoopi, but the same can hardly be said for the rest of Tinseltown. Drugs run rampant among the stars, of course, but weed seems to evoke a certain public passion not seen for other substances.

"Some people are just better high," says Justin Timberlake,[45] a strong Obama supporter.[46] Justin served up this little nugget of wisdom after he'd had the misfortune of being punk'd by Ashton Kutcher and caught—unsuspecting—totally stoned on TV.[47] Better in what way, Justin? You mean the concentration-killing effects that rob weed freaks of the ability to retain information?[48]

Then there's *Transformers* movie star Shia LaBeouf. His hippie parents had him trying weed before he had his first drink. And he's proudly sported an "Everybody must get stoned" shirt. One of Shia's contributions to cannabis crosstalk: "My parents always thought weed was healthier than alcohol. If you look at the science of it, it's the truth," says the toxicological expert. "Nobody has ever died smoking weed."[49]

Genius logic there, *Transformer* boy. As if contracting lung cancer, experiencing memory loss, and, for teenagers with developing brains, suffering panic attacks, depression, increased anxiety, and other mental health problems does wonders for extending longevity. It also can impair motor skills and other faculties. That's why one in five car-crash victims under eighteen test positive for marijuana.[50] But why look at facts when you can get your information from a dude raised by hippies who plays with pretend robots for a living?

Johnny Depp, whose friend River Phoenix died from a heroin overdose in front of the Viper Room, a nightclub Depp previously owned, made the same kind of full-o'-crap argument: "I'm not a great pothead or anything like that . . . but weed is much, much less dangerous than alcohol." Yes, Johnny, shooting yourself in the chest is much, much less dangerous than shooting yourself in the head, so, by all means, blast away at your rib cage!

Idiots.

And then there are those sages like *Spider-Man* starlet Kirsten Dunst who sidestep logic and facts altogether and openly advocate the utopian effects that a world on weed would bring. She says she wishes "everyone smoked weed. I do like weed," she said.[51] Imagine the wonders that mass smoke inhalation would do for our skyrocketing health-care costs! Oh yeah . . . but that's right, ObamaCare solved all that. Whew. Good thing we have Dear Leader to save us.

Cameron Diaz is another pothead who should keep her drug-loving, eco-preaching yap shut. She was listed among the "Top 100 Women of Weed" by Canada's leading marijuana magazine, *Skunk* magazine (quite an accomplishment, really, when you factor in the magazine's strong bias toward Canadians).[52] Cameron looks like she could be a credible Hollywood health advocate with her trim, yoga-toned frame.[53] This comes in handy for sure, because as a prominent Hollywood environmentalist, she has a passion for making sure we average Americans know how to protect our bodies from pollutants in our environment.

That's why back in 2009 Diaz put together a five-and-a-half-minute, untitled documentary wherein she goes around pestering unsuspecting Americans with questions like "Do you have a say in whether or not your water, air, and food are clean?" One lady living next to a billowing factory smokestack tells Cameron that maybe the plumes of smoke are what made her kid sick, and Cameron reacts like a scared child trying to reconcile herself to a hard truth when she tells the camera, "I don't think that the people who are working at those jobs are bad people. I don't think people wanna believe that they're hurting other people." The message is clear: evil corporations, such as the kind who back her movies and buy product placements in them, are out to get you.[54]

But of course we should take any of Cameron's admonitions about protecting our bodies with a grain of salt. This, after all, is the woman who in 2004 appeared on a panel on the *Oprah* show with P. Diddy, Christina Aguilera, and Drew Barrymore to motivate America's youth to get out and vote (for—cough, cough—John Kerry). Cameron sobbed about how scared she was of another four years of Bush. The political genius then framed the choice between Bush and Kerry as a matter of . . . preventing rape? She told Americans that depending on how we voted, citizens "could lose the right to their bodies." Then, with wisdom well beyond her years, the arbiter of all things personal health offered up this maxim of age-old wisdom: "If you think rape should be legal, then don't vote!"[55]

Crickets chirping.

All the same, no one can contest that Diaz is a bona fide naturalist when it comes to health. She's also a tree-hugger. No, I mean literally: the chick loves to physically cuddle with trees. She summed it up pretty well to the *Huffington Post:* "And I like hugging trees too! I do! I'm just going to say it! I like to hug trees! It's awesome! They're alive! They're brilliant so I'm not going to be afraid to say it! I hug trees." And if these trees could talk back to Diaz, they'd promptly say: "Stop humping us, you crazy beast!"

Diaz also believes in keeping her surroundings healthy for humans. She recycles, drives a Prius, buys carbon offsets for her extensive travels, and worships Al Gore. (She's called him "amazing," "charismatic," "wonderful," and "a great teacher," and she did a press conference with him to announce Live Earth.) She also took a year off to dedicate herself to "the movement" and made a hajj to one of Al Gore's slide show presentations. (No word yet on if Gore asked her to tickle his lower chakra). That's how she started her current mission to inform and empower people about what she calls "the only issue in the history of mankind that affects every single one of us."[56] Never mind mankind's immortal yearnings for freedom, justice, or truth, or any of that other "universal" crap. No, the important thing, explains Cameron, is that she become Mother Earth's . . . publicist?

"The planet needs a publicist," says the Obama backer. "I had this cartoon in my head a couple of years ago. . . . There's a woman at a desk talking to planet Earth, and she's like, 'I'm going to make you a star!' And it says, 'But I'm a planet.' And she's like 'No, I can tell, you're going to be bigger than Paris and Britney.'"[57]

Cute, Cameron. Now scamper along and leave running the world to the adults so we can keep your liberal butt safe from the Islamic terrorists who seek to murder you, sweetie.

As the self-appointed publicist of planet earth, Cameron has made tremendous strides in averting worldwide apocalypse by telling us average people how to improve our health by issuing toilet rules. Like when she went on *The Tonight Show* and enlightened Americans on how to save water with this saying-for-life: "If it's yellow, leave it mellow. If it's brown, flush it down. I believe in that 100 percent."[58] Some of Cameron's other efforts have included helping develop a book of practical green lifestyle choices, shooting environmental PSAs with other celebrities, and doing an MTV show called *Trippin'* in which she traipses around the world to educate its diverse peoples about the environment. I'm still waiting to hear what her carbon footprint was by the end of the show.[59]

So, surely a woman who wants us all to ask ourselves about what we eat, drink, and breathe and to improve our health through activism and conscientious living would object to contaminating our bodies with, say, marijuana smoke, just as much as she would object to that smokestack that made the lady's kid sick in her documentary. Right?

Wrong.

Recently Diaz appeared on *Late Night with Jimmy Fallon* to

promote her movie *Bad Teacher.* After some insincere (one hopes) banter about how her character comes in drunk to her junior high class ("If you were a teacher and you had 30 kids in front of you all day long, wouldn't you drink? . . . They have to learn about life at some point, Jimmy!") Fallon shifted the dialogue to a scene where Cameron's character smokes marijuana with another teacher. "I made the other teacher smoke. I'm like, 'Hold it in, hold it in!'" "Weed is awesome!" she exclaimed to a cheering studio audience. At least seven seconds later she rebutted her pro-pot infomercial by adding, "That was what my character says, that's not what I say." Phew! Clean-living image preserved! Or, as Fallon put it, "Nice save there." That is until she opened her mouth again and this little bit of eloquence spilled out: "I think this weed . . . this movie . . . Freudian slip!"[60]

Bad Teacher. Starring Cameron Diaz as her liberal idiot self. Rated R.

It turns out that *Bad Teacher* was hardly Cameron's first experience with weed in the classroom. She'd learned plenty "about life" on the other side of the teacher's desk at Long Beach Polytechnic High School. She reminisced on *Lopez Tonight* about how she and professional stoner/rapper/porn filmmaker Snoop Dogg attended the same high school, which explains a lot—about Diaz, Snoop, and the American public education system more generally. "He was a year older than me. . . . I remember him, he was very tall and skinny. He wore lots of ponytails." Only the starlet was more intentional with George Lopez about how she addressed the pot issue: "I'm pretty sure I bought weed from him. . . . I was green even in high school!" No Freudian slip necessary this time.[61]

Photographers confirmed as much when Diaz, along with her BFF Drew Barrymore, vacationed in Hawaii. Photographers snapped shots of Cameron lounging in a sunhat beside her bestie, propping herself up on her elbows to fully enjoy a good whiff.[62] Another snapshot shows Drew passing a joint to her friend. And Cameron's no stranger to smoking on the beach, either. She remembers her days growing up in San Diego. "It took two hours to get [to the beach] on the bus. You stayed all day, ate corn dogs. It wasn't the 'California Dreamin' thing. We had only $2 for a joint." You'd think that over all these years she might've learned to look out for the paparazzi while puffing the magic dragon down by the sea.[63]

So there you have it. In one breath Cameron tells us to take ownership of our health by taking ownership of our environment, and in another she tells us that "weed is awesome" and exhales a smoke ring or five. But that's not all. She also recently told *Maxim* magazine that marriage is "a dying institution." The guru of life, mind, and spirit balance added: "I think we have to make our own rules. I don't think we should live our lives in relationships based off of old traditions that don't suit our world any longer."[64]

Special, this one.

As a writer for *Big Hollywood* put it, "Who better to expound on the institution of marriage than a promiscuous, never-been-married Hollywood liberal out promoting a movie about an oversexed teacher 'saving up cash for a boob job?'"[65] I would only add that it's highly unfortunate that my junior high teachers looked nothing like Diaz. Mom and Dad wouldn't have had to drag me out of bed each morning if they did. But I digress. The reality is that Hollywood liberals may frown upon marriage as an outmoded way of living, but that doesn't undermine the fact that it's still the best environment in which to raise children and prevent poverty.[66]

The upward acceptance of cohabitating and "open" relationships these days has led not only to a decline in marriage rates,[67] but also an explosion of sexually transmitted diseases. Because nothing says clean, responsible living like getting pile-driven by a different dude each week, all in the name of feminist progressivism. Isn't that right, Ms. Diaz?[68]

America has some of the highest STD (I know, an icky subject, but bear with me) and teen pregnancy rates in the Western world. STDs other than AIDS cost us $8 billion a year to diagnose and treat. One in five Americans has an STD, but the numbers are far worse for the younger generation that makes up the legions of Obama Zombies. In fact, two-thirds of infected Americans are twenty-five or younger. The CDC says a quarter of teenage girls in the United States have an STD, and one-quarter of new STD infections are occurring in teens. The total number of infections is growing by 19 million new cases a year among 15–24-year-olds. One in five American teens will be infected with an STD, which is especially bleak when juxtaposed with the 1-out-of-47 chance their parents have. In fact, it's hard to find sexually transmitted diseases that are in decline; most are climbing. That's especially true among adolescents. Even syphilis is making a national comeback.[69] You see, playing hide-the-salami wantonly can be cool and all . . . until you start peeing blood. Then it sucks. Just like Charlie Sheen's goddesses.

But there are some compassionate souls in Hollywood who would like to make a difference. Even a few Obama-loving partiers/ sex icons seem to think they can roll back the STD stats and teach real sexual health values to kids.

Take Sean "P. Diddy" Combs. He's a fashionable guy. Not just because he's always pimped out with huge furs, blinding bling, giant cigars, and a posse, but also because he's dedicated plenty of his music to Bush bashing, and as we know, you can't be cool and like Bush, especially not if you're a rapper.[70] He also stayed with the in-crowd through Dear Leader's grand ascension, helping Cameron Diaz and a host of other stars commemorate the end of "Rape King" Bush by shooting a PSA wherein each star pledges to support their new Messiah and personally change America. The propaganda piece ends with a slow zoom shot that gradually pans out from a single celebrity to more and more of them until they all fade into pixels in a glorious blue and red print of the visage of the Savior of Socialism, the Messiah of the Universe, Barack Obama.[71]

But P. Diddy wears a lot more hats than just rapper and Obama boot licker. He's also a fashion designer, producer, label boss, and hip-hop mogul, just to name a few. And that's where the hypocrisy comes in. On the one hand, he's a promoter of AIDS awareness. "Once you know about it," he said, "it's almost like being an accessory to genocide if you turn your back on it." Then, in the next breath, he turns around and dashes into the studio to lay down mad beats and phat lyrics about sexing up all his "bitches" and "hos." Holla, dawg!

And I wonder if personal health is what's in the forefront of his mind when he parties. And boy oh boy does Diddy love to party, homey. Wherever he goes, he brings a cordless mic so nobody can forget that he's there (as if he didn't dress loud enough already). If he's not asserting his presence by projecting the word *yo* over the mix, he's probably using his mic to call on the bitches and hos to "get butt naked." And for whatever reason, they listen. Hardly a study in sexual health.[72]

And what about self-professed celibate Lady Gaga? Surely she represents a paragon of public health virtue, right? I mean, she said she's practiced abstinence herself, so surely the Obama-loving liberal promotes abstinence to the public at large. Nope. Gaga, who zealously celebrated Obama's repeal of "Don't Ask, Don't Tell,"[73] and even co-headlined an event for Human Rights Campaign (the country's largest gay rights group) with Dear Leader,[74] regularly talks about safe sex with her fans. "I want to get people started at home at a younger age with their children, talking about HIV, talking about AIDS, talking about safe sex." And of course, who could possibly forget her attempt to promote AIDS awareness on *Good Morning America*? The eccentric starlet appeared wearing a flesh-tone "latex condom–inspired" dress, topped off with visor-like sunglasses and a ridiculous white hat vaguely reminiscent of the Flying Nun.[75]

But let's get real. No one should be taking health advice (or fashion advice, for that matter) from Lady Gaga. Homegirl is just straight-up weird. And not just because she went to the 2010 MTV Video Music Awards wearing a dress and matching purse made of raw, artery-clogging red meat (almost enough to last the Obama family through a whole Super Bowl party).[76] Remember the 2009 American Music Awards? She performed in a nude bodysuit, accompanied by six pansexual dancers, all gyrating onstage as though they were getting booty-slammed under the sheets. At a certain juncture in the act, she grabbed her mic stand, approached a glass-encased piano, and smashed her way through the barrier. Surrounded by broken glass, she began to play, even after her piano burst into flames. At the end she struck a pose and held it, covered in glass and roasting in the flames of her piano.[77]

Like I said, Gaga is weird. But then again, she's Gaga. Weird is her thing. She's good for an entertaining performance, but I'm going to take a wild stab at this one and say she's not exactly the type of person who should be lecturing her teen fans on when and how they should lose their virginity. Perhaps I'm wrong. But if your daughter turns out to be a human vacuum cleaner by the time she graduates from high school, you'll look back and say, "Damn, that Jason was right. I shouldn't have let Gaga teach little Kimmy about getting knocked to the next century."

Then of course there is one of Gaga's inspirations, Madonna. She's been promoting safe sex and AIDS awareness for more than two decades now. "Avoid casual sex and you'll avoid AIDS," she told schoolkids in a 1988 ad. "And stay away from people who shoot drugs."[78] Good advice. Then, for the next two decades, she's cranked out slutty album after slutty album and has fanned the flames of sexual revolution with pornographic books and videos.

With health-loving "friends" like these, who needs enemies? The very entertainment industry that lines up lockstep behind the cigarette-puffing, junk-food-eating, pot-smoking, cocaine-using Barack Obama is the same bunch that joins him in preaching to us dumb, unwashed, God-fearing, Wal-Mart–shopping, gun-owning dolts about what the government should *allow* us to eat, buy, and do. Worse, they double down on foolishness by having the Food Witch, Michelle Obama, launch a campaign to regulate everything in sight, down to what little kids can munch on—even as she herself admits that she devours yummy, unhealthy crap like the rest of us. Parents, not government agents, should be the ones in charge of ensuring that their kids grow up to make smart, healthy decisions. It's a neat thing called "freedom" and "personal responsibility."

It's more than a little nauseating to hear Hollywood—the industry that makes billions off promoting unhealthy lifestyles, actions, and choices—lecturing us dumb yokels about how we can be "healthy" like Obama's worshippers. Spare us the lectures on organic foods, the cleaning power of colonics, the ironclad safety of "safe" sex, and the diatribes about when we're allowed to flush our doo-doo and instead focus on cleaning up your own crap—both personally and on the screen.

Do that first, and then we'll listen to you nag us all day long about eating fruits and berries and twigs and the wonderful health effects of drugs and orgies.

Be Peaceful or I'll Shoot Yo Ass!

Why Leftists Do Not Good Nonviolence Spokespersons Make

They bring a knife to the fight, we bring a gun.

—President Barack Obama

FACT: Liberals love peace and conservatives are uneducated, ignorant, pistol-packing, hatemongering, homophobic, xenophobic fundamentalists who export global terrorism, only care about saving a life until it passes through the birth canal, and get a kick out of waterboarding anyone in a turban.

FACT: Dear Leader ascended to his throne to bring the world's citizens justice, unity, and strawberry-scented peace treaties.

FACT: Conservatives are bloodthirsty warmongers who live to blow things and people (especially those non-Christians) up, start wars, and saw off the horns of unicorns.

Hollywood progressives hold these truths to be self-evident (though certainly not endowed by a Creator). In fact, the prophets of the entertainment industry are so tolerant, so compassionate, and so desirous of peace . . . that they will *beat your ass* if you dare disagree with them! And God help the conservatives if and when any act of violence does erupt, because when it does, progressives will make sure Sarah Palin, Glenn Beck, or Rush Limbaugh gets stuck with the blame.

Case in point: the horrific national outrage that was the gunning down of Congresswoman Gabrielle Giffords and her many Arizona constituents. On the morning of January 8, 2011, twenty-two-year-old Jared Loughner went on a shooting rampage at a political event for Giffords outside a supermarket in Tucson.[1] The murderer fired up to twenty shots at Giffords, eventually dealing her a point-blank shot to the head. Miraculously, she survived.[2] Eleven others, however, were wounded by the gunman and six, including a judge and a nine-year-old little girl, were killed.

Within hours, crime investigator and forensics expert Jane Fonda had already identified the responsible parties and tweeted their names: Glenn Beck, Sarah Palin, and the Tea Party movement. Fonda fired off her tweets with no knowledge of what had motivated the still unidentified shooter—and very little knowledge of how to spell Beck's name.[3]

So how exactly did Hanoi Jane, the woman who stood in solidarity with the North Vietnamese as American warriors came home in body bags, come up with her hit list of conservative culprits?

No telling. What soon became clear, though, was that America's far Left loons almost *immediately* concluded that the gut-churning slaughter of innocent human lives was a symptom of a volatile political climate that had boiled over from . . . the health-care debate?[4]

No sooner had the dead been counted than did the media castigate conservatives for their ubiquitous use of violent images and martial metaphors—clear proof that those Jesus-worshipping, Constitution-loving conservatives were unmistakably responsible for the Tucson death and carnage. Exhibit number one, said the liberal media, was the Alaskan assassin, Sarah Palin. Why? Because almost a year earlier Palin had released a map on her Facebook page with crosshairs over key congressional districts where incumbent Democrats were vulnerable to a Republican challenger. Moreover, Palin had employed a gun metaphor—"Common-sense conservatives and lovers of America: Don't retreat . . . instead, reload"—after Obama's health-care bill was passed by Congress.

The Left was sure they had identified the mystery shooter on the grassy knoll, and her name was former governor Sarah Palin.[5] Of course, the use of combatant analogies is nothing new in politics, and certainly doesn't spark killing sprees. Just ask the Democratic Congressional Campaign Committee. Two years prior to the Giffords shooting, the DCCC, which calls itself "the official campaign arm of Democrats in the House," unveiled a list of Republicans whom they considered to be at risk. Those districts had bull's-eyes on them. And when you clicked on the district, the "Targeted Republican" popped up with a picture and dossier.[6]

No matter. Liberals had a heyday spouting their usual hypocrisy about how conservatives are hatemongers. ABC's Jane Cowan prefaced a segment about Palin's website with the opener: "Political candidates, especially those aligned with the grassroots Tea

Party movement, have increasingly invoked violent imagery." Daily Kos founder Markos Moulitsas tastelessly tweeted: "Mission accomplished, Sarah Palin."[7] On ABC's talk show *The View*, Joy "Daddy Never Hugged Me" Behar said Palin's opponents map "looks like an al Qaeda Christmas card."[8] (Heads up, Joy: Radical Muslim jihadists do not celebrate the birth of Jesus Christ . . . but I digress.)

Still, it doesn't take a journalism degree to see how thin the mainstream liberal media's slander was, or how little homework they had done before embarking on their massive, national smear campaign. After Loughner was identified as the gunman, it didn't take too much sleuthing to discover that the nutjob in question was *far* from the Tea Party activist the Left had hoped for. After a few Google searches, phone calls, and a visit to the murderer's MySpace page, it quickly became clear that, if anything, the idiot was a Leftist. In fact, Loughner was, in one of his classmates' words, a "left-wing pot head" who was "quite liberal."[9] It was also revealed that he hates religion,[10] has a soft spot in his heart for both *The Communist Manifesto* and Hitler's *Mein Kampf*, considers a film clip showing an American flag burning one of his favorites, and claims that the United States government is full of "treasonous laws."

Hmmm . . . let's see . . . a God-hating, pot-smoking, flag-burning communist . . . yep, sounds like your garden-variety Republican, all right!

Not surprisingly, in May 2011 the murderer was found mentally incompetent to stand trial for his crimes.[11] Thankfully, Giffords has made a miraculous recovery.[12] The Left, however, shows no signs of recovering from its pathological obsessive hatred of conservatives, nor anyone who would dare to cross their enlightened, peace-loving, compassionate ways.

The reason: Progressives are allowed to use violent rhetoric against conservatives, but not the other way around. For instance, liberal comedienne Sandra Bernhard warned Sarah Palin not to enter Manhattan lest she be "gang-raped by my big black brothers."[13] What a hoot, that Bernhard!

And when Leftist talk radio hosts blast conservatives with graphic, violent salvos, they're just doing it in good fun. For instance, Obama worshipper Ed Schultz said, "I really think there are conservative broadcasters in this country who would love to see Obama taken out."

Or when Mike Malloy taught us unwashed masses that, in point of fact, conservative radio hosts are actually members of al-Qaeda: "Do you not understand that the people you hold up as heroes bombed your goddamn country? Do you not understand that Glenn Beck and Sean Hannity and Rush Limbaugh and Bill O'Reilly are as complicit of the September 11, 2001, terror attack as any one of the dumbass 15 who came from Saudi Arabia?"

Or the always illuminating Montel Williams, who explained that Republicans—the people who fight to save the lives of the 1.2 million babies who are murdered in the womb each year—are actually eager to kill you. "If, in fact, the GOP doesn't like any form of healthcare reform, what do we do with those 40 to 60 million uninsured? . . . When they show up in the emergency room, just shoot 'em! Kill them! . . . Do we have enough body bags? I don't know." Montel was apparently feeling a bit more peaceful that day, because on another show he advocated the killing of Congresswoman Michele Bachmann. "So, Michele, slit your wrist! Go ahead! I mean, you know, why not? I mean, if you want to—or, you know, do us all a better thing. Move that knife up about two feet. I mean, start right at the collarbone." Indeed, it seems Bachmann inspires a special ire from peace-loving, compassionate Leftists, such as when Mike Malloy deemed the foster mom of twenty-three a "hatemonger" and said, "she's the type of person that would have gladly rounded up the Jews in Germany and shipped them off to death camps. . . . This is an evil bitch from hell."[14]

Ah yes . . . can't you just feel the warm Obama goodness and Leftist love?

But few of Obama's celebrity constituencies can quite match the Left's "I will shoot yo ass if you don't love peace" schizophrenic mentality with quite the panache of that Democrat juggernaut of vote-getting surety: rappers.

Take Obama backer Kanye "Bush Hates Black People" West. West turned out a profanity-packed, racial-slur-infested music video for a song on his *My Beautiful Dark Twisted Fantasy* album. This peace-inspiring doozy depicts images of female corpses hanging from the ceiling, Kanye holding a woman's blood-soaked severed head, women held captive, women in nooses, and severed appendages oozing blood.[15] The album's sexually explicit cover art alone got Kanye's album axed from Wal-Mart, but the ban barely registered a shrug from the always self-assured West.[16] He calls his music "medicine," "a cure for cancer musically," and an attempt to "touch people" and "give them what they need."[17]

Others, like Yana Walton of the Women's Media Center, see it differently. "His imagery and lyrics go beyond legitimizing violence to women," said Walton. "They fetishize it. Since gender based violence is a daily reality in our country, I urge Kanye to examine the harmful effects of using his fame in this manner."[18] Dan Gainor of the Media Research Center agreed. "This is a new low for Kanye and that's the essence of the pop culture right now— everything has to out-shock the thing that came before. In this case, Kanye did his best to out-vile the competition. What next? Live human sacrifice?"[19]

Shut up, Dan! Don't give Kanye any more ideas!

Where the rapper's woman-hating, racialist tendencies come from is up for debate. But perhaps the fact that his father, Ray West, is a former Black Panther may have been a contributing factor. Other thug rappers, like the deceased Tupac, were raised by Black Panther parents, too.[20] So who knows.

What is clear, however, is that in addition to Kanye's insane lyrics and serial-killer-style videos, West also has a penchant for unruly behavior. And I'm not just talking about the 2009 Video Music Awards, where, in the middle of giving Taylor Swift her award for Best Female Video, he grabbed her microphone, told everyone that she didn't deserve the award because Beyoncé's video was better, and reportedly flipped off the disapproving audience once he was no longer being filmed.[21] Kanye has also faced criminal charges. In 2008 he was charged with grand theft, misdemeanor battery, and vandalism after his manager smashed a photographer's camera at Los Angeles International Airport.[22]

And by the way, when Obama called West a "jackass" for how he treated Taylor (a PR tactic designed to appeal to mainstream U.S.A., no doubt), Kanye said he didn't mind. After all, Obama had "way more important things to worry about," like the health-care bill, said Kanye.[23]

Now that's one loyal Obama Zombie!

It doesn't matter that Kanye's a loose-cannon criminal or that his music is moral arsenic. No. He still thinks he can oppose war[24] *and* promote social justice. But not always with much success. For example, in another famous Kanye-style showjack, he derailed a fundraising telethon for Hurricane Katrina victims to tell America that "George Bush doesn't care about black people." Way to go, Kanye! I'm sure that brought in tons of donations for those poor black people Bush hates! No chance that it encouraged millions of viewers who like or respect Bush to flip the channel, thereby forgoing any chance of donating to the cause. But hey, at least you made Bush feel the burn, right?

Fool.

President Bush later called West's disgraceful racist rant the worst—and "one of the most disgusting"—moments of his presidency.[25] (Kanye apologized to W. five years later.)

More proactive than most rappers, West uses his Kanye West Foundation to "combat the severe dropout problem plaguing America's communities."[26] An interesting choice for the guy who rocketed to stardom with a debut album called *The College Dropout*.[27] Just as he fails to see the disconnect between violent lyrics and war opposition, or the connection between impulse and any semblance of proper time and place, West fails to realize the hypocrisy of promoting education while also partnering with Nike, a company whose infamous child labor practices make education an empty dream for kids all over the world. Kanye even has his own line of Nike sneakers, the overpriced "Nike Air Yeezys."[28] He played the villain opposite controversial basketball star Kobe Bryant in Nike's "Black Mamba" commercial, among other contributions to the oppressive corporate giant.[29] Kanye, here's a tip: stick to what you're good at—glamorizing violence and interrupting people.

But, in fairness, bigot rappers like West aren't terribly unique for the musical genre; the ubiquitous use of the N-word, odes to violence, rape, drug use, bitches and hos, murder, gunfights, and every other social pathology known to mankind are common fare for those in the rap hustle. But hey, at least those musical beats get the booties grinding in the clubs. So there is that.

Not surprisingly, Dear Leader has given the obligatory tongue lashings to the hip-hop industry's overall baseness. According to White House spokesman Jay Carney, Obama has "spoken very forcefully out against violent and misogynist lyrics."[30] Prez set those rappa thugz straight when he said on the campaign trail that rappers who use derogatory language are "degrading their sisters."[31] Obama has also complained of being "troubled sometimes by the misogyny and materialism" in rap music. "It would be nice," Obama said, "if I could have my daughters [whose ages I know not] listen to their music without me worrying they were getting bad images of themselves."[32]

Ever the one to find a "Sister Souljah" opportunity, as Bill Clinton did when he pandered to family values voters in 1992 by castigating rapper Sister Souljah, who talked about killing whitey, Obama has rapped the rap industry on other occasions as well. Doing his best to mimic Tipper Gore and Joe Lieberman, Obama said, "I do think we've seen a coarsening of the culture. I think that we have not talked enough about the harmful images and messages that are sent," and "I think that all of us have become a little complicit in this kind of relaxed attitude toward some pretty offensive things. And I hope this prompts some self-reflection on the part of all of us."[33]

Awww . . . how tender.

Now the reality: Obama has taken boatloads of rapper donations and has more rap music on his iPod than Pamela Anderson has silicone in her body.

During the 2008 primaries, Obama enjoyed strong public support from hip-hop artists like will.i.am, Talib Kweli, Common, Mos Def, 50 Cent, the Game, and Jay-Z. They thought Barack was mad sick, yo. As 50 Cent said after hearing Obama speak, "He hit me with that he-just-got-done-watching-'Malcolm X' [thing], and I swear to God, I'm like, 'Yo, Obama!' I'm Obama to the end now, baby!"

Alas, the grandiloquence that is 50 Cent. Only in America could people who crucify the English language become multimillionaires. Ain't freedom great, cuz?!

Or Sean "P. Diddy" Combs. When Obama won the Democrat nomination, Diddy said it was "one of the greatest and proudest moments of my life. Not just as a black man, but as an American."[34] (I'm guessing his acquittal for gun charges and bribery was one of the other "greatest and proudest moments" in his life.) But Mr. Diddy went on to throw his weight behind the Obama campaign and was moved to tears at his inauguration.[35]

In 2008, Jay-Z, a drug dealer turned rapper turned mega-capitalist businessman whom *Forbes* calls "one of the most successful musicians ever" and whose net worth it estimates to be $450 million, said the following when he pledged support to Obama at the Uptown Theatre in Philadelphia: "Rosa Parks sat so Martin Luther King could walk. Martin Luther King walked so Obama could run. Obama's running so we all can fly."[36]

Now that sounds pretty inspirational and nice, right? That is, until you hear what else Jay-Z and rapper Young Jeezy had to say at an inauguration-eve gathering. Because copyright laws don't allow me to reprint Jay-Z's lyrics verbatim, I cannot express the fullness of his "commitment" to racial harmony. But, suffice it to say that Rosa Parks and Dr. Martin Luther King are both rolling over in their graves. Obama worshipper Young Jeezy, however, was kind enough to speak, not rap, the following words of Hope and Change, reprinted here for your unity-inspiring edification:

> I know ya'll thankin a lot of people right now. . . . I want to thank two people. I want to thank the motherfucker overseas that threw two shoes at George Bush, and I want to thank the motherfuckers who helped them move they

shit up out the White House. Get it moving, bitch! Because my president is motherfucking black, nigga![37]

Isn't that special? How postracial. Don't you just feel the "Yes, we can!" unity, peace, and love?

Young Jeezy's song "My President Is Black" is just one of many sweet musical offerings paying homage to Dear Leader. Rapper Nas started the trend with his 2008 song "Black President" (which appeared on a mixtape bearing two covers, one with a photo of police brutality)[38] and recorded "Election Night," an ode to Obama featuring Dear Leader's voice, in November of that year.[39] Other pro-Obama rap songs include Joell Ortiz's "Letter to Obama," Jin's "Open Letter to Obama," Ti$a's "Obamaway," 6th Sense's "Ignite the People (Like Obama)," Jay-Z and Mary J. Blige's "You're All Welcome," and Common's "The People," just to name a few.[40]

We should, of course, take these celebrity endorsements with a grain of salt; not all pro-Obama artists are known to be the best judges of character. After all, a number of them have done private shows for none other than—you ready for this one?—Libyan strongman dictator the late Muammar Gadaffi and/or his family. As international geopolitical expert turned rapper Nas tried to explain, Muammar Gadaffi was actually a really swell guy, it's just that he was "misunderstood."[41] And Obama backers like Usher, Jay-Z's wife, Beyoncé, Nellie Furtado, Mariah Carey, and others performed private shows for up to $1 million for the Gadaffi clan.[42] Later, under the pressure of negative publicity, these human rights celebrity heroes allegedly donated the proceeds from said venues. However, I wonder how many of them would draw the line at doing a gig at the Bush ranch? Just sayin'.

Rapper Nas (born Nasir bin Olu Dara Jones) says he saw his share of violence growing up in New York City's Queensbridge housing project.[43] The rapper's been praised for doing such a good job capturing the worst of it in his music. Nas explains that his raps were influenced by kidnappings, stickups, drug dealings, killings, and the like.[44] Besides his knack for coming up with creative ways to retell his life experience (like blasting us with the word *kill* in three-round bursts in his song "Shoot 'Em Up"),[45] he has a passion for, you guessed it, peace. Like rapper Jay-Z and pop rock singer airhead Sheryl Crow, Nas is a member of Musicians United to Win Without War and was seen in one of its ads that read "War On Iraq Is Wrong And We Know It" and "Don't let Bush, Cheney, and Rumsfeld drown out the voices of reason."[46] Nas is such a peace advocate, in fact, that he even opposed the Libyan people's hateful rebellion against dictator Gaddafi. The rapper believed the United States should have intervened to end protests against Gaddafi because he "just doesn't like" seeing the people and their leader against each other. So we should have helped bring peace by using *our* military forces to help Gaddafi suppress his people even more?

Genius!

What makes Nas's asinine position even more pathetic is the fact that he voiced it at a time when other artists who had performed for Gaddafi's clan were giving the huge sums he had paid them to charity.[47]

In addition to solving the world's conflicts, Nas is in the business of bringing relief to the war-torn and traumatized. He helped bring healing to injured Liberian child soldiers by working with the Liberian national amputee soccer team and worked with Damian Marley on a collaborative record intended to draw attention to the plight of Africa.[48] But in one of his attempts to alleviate the suffering of those traumatized by violence, the violence of his lyrics came back to bite him pretty hard. To put the graphic nature of music in perspective, consider what happened when he decided to join the Dave Matthews Band, John Mayer, and Phil Vassar in the lineup for a free concert at Virginia Tech. The concert was a good-will show intended to help lift the spirits of VT students less than half a year after the April 16, 2007, mass murder. But so brutish are Nas's lyrics that the thought of bringing his violent message to the traumatized campus provoked outrage from victims' families. A spokesman for some of the victims' parents said the rapper's lyrics are "indicative of the moral decay in our society that contributes to acts of violence" and called his appearance "unconscionable beyond belief." Even students thought he was a bad choice, like a twenty-six-year-old sister of one of the victims. She said she understands that there is a time and place for aggressive music, but that featuring Nas's rhymes is "the most inappropriate thing I could imagine hearing at such an event."[49]

But it's not just Nas's lyrics that are so over the line, it's his actions as well. Nas has a gun conviction. When Bill O'Reilly called Nas a bad choice for the Virginia Tech benefit concert and pointed to the rapper's record and song lyrics, the peace-loving Nas went ballistic.[50] First he called Bill O'Reilly—I'll give you three guesses—a racist. This from the guy who drops the N-word as frequently as most people say "the."[51] Heck, it's so egregious, the dude even named one of his albums *Nigger!*[52] Oh the artistry and creativity of it all!

The peace and harmony rapper also challenged O'Reilly to a debate before machine-gunning him with a string of threats: "I will tell him [O'Reilly] I'm an American psycho, I'm his worst nightmare. . . . When he wants to come holla at me, be ready for Hannibal Lecter. He don't deserve an intelligent explanation. I'll bite his nose off! He wants to talk to me like a animal? I will be—but only to him. With everybody else I'll be a gentleman, including his wife. That's right—I'm crazy. That's how we should be to him."[53]

Not satisfied that he'd made his point, Nas picketed Fox's building later that year and presented a 600,000-person petition to prove that Fox is racist. He also explained that Fox only loves black men when they're dead or in jail.[54]

But for many members of the Obama hip-hop brigade, exalting and glorifying violence is a common practice. After all, how could they be offended by criminality when many of the Obama campaign rap regiment have criminal records themselves?

Take Diddy. He was arrested for assaulting Nas's manager after Nas turned out a video for his song "Hate Me Now" that involved footage of Diddy being crucified. Diddy was also arrested and indicted for bribery and weapons charges after he and then girlfriend Jennifer Lopez fled the scene of a shooting in a Bronx club. Police pulled them over and found a 9mm pistol in their front seat. Diddy had some 'splainin' to do before a grand jury after that—not just because of the gun, but also about why he allegedly offered their driver fifty g's and a diamond ring to pretend the gun was his. Diddy was smart, though: he hired O. J. Simpson's attorney, the late Johnnie Cochran, who got him acquitted for his bribery and weapons charges in 2001. But the events influenced Puffy so much that he changed his stage name from "Puffy" to "P. Diddy" not long afterward.[55]

And then there's rapper Maino, whose hit "All the Above" talks about how envisioning Obama helps him face impossible things.[56] This Brooklyn rapper spent over ten years in the slammer for kidnapping. And he's still got a violent streak. In the debut episode of the MTV documentary-style series *World of Jenks*, host Andrew Jenks spent some time living with Maino (don't ask), following him around, and, as it turned out, apparently getting a little too personal with Mr. Maino. Jenks made the mistake of asking the former inmate questions about a few of his life choices. The result: the Obama-loving rapper attacked him.

"People don't realize Maino is a big guy," Jenks recounted. "It hurt. If you look, after he choked me a little bit, you see my neck is really red because he is a forceful man." About three months later, Maino was taken in briefly for driving on a suspended license after refusing to follow police directions about where to drive in a congested area.[57] I wonder if he was envisioning Dear Leader when the po-po asked for his license and registration.

Then there is the sordid tale of Obama's favorite rapper, Ludacris. Or at least that's what Ludacris boasts in one of his songs.[58] In any event, Ludacris wasn't exactly the single greatest ally early on to the Obama campaign. Not for lack of effort, though. His 2007 song "Politics," another great American hymn to Obama, crossed the line when it called Hillary "irrelevant" and a "bitch," declared Bush mentally impaired and Dick Cheney unworthy of sitting in any chair but a wheelchair, and even threw in a Jesse Jackson put-down for good measure (hey, why not?). Neither Hillary nor Obama was amused. Obama's spokesman said Ludacris should be "ashamed of those lyrics."[59] But seriously, should Obama expect better from his favorite rapper, Luda? After all, this is a guy whose hits include a song about a drunk guy beating up his girlfriend.

So freaking nuts are Luda's lyrics that Bill O'Reilly called for the rapper's ouster from his Pepsi sponsorship perch. Bill called on "all responsible Americans to fight back and punish Pepsi for using a man who degrades women, who encourages substance abuse and does all the things that hurt particularly the poor in our society." Pepsi fired Ludacris the next morning. Ludacris retaliated by charging Pepsi with—wait for it—racism. And when the Hip-Hop

Summit Action Network encouraged African Americans to boycott Pepsi products, the soda maker had little choice but to agree to pay for their carbonated crime by giving $1 million a year for three years to Ludacris's charity, the Ludacris Foundation.[60] Now *that's* ludicrous!

Now, with all this thuggery, violence, hatred of women, and glorification of drugs, you might think the Obamas would try to keep their rapper fan base at arm's length. Instead they give unrepentant former drug dealers like Jay-Z (a man with a net worth of almost half a billion dollars can be a fundraising game changer) one of the highest honors any American could receive—a personal invitation to the White House. In fact, Jay-Z has been photographed in Obama's chair in the Situation Room.[61]

There's more. In an attempt to bring some "relevant" culture to a May 2011 White House poetry event, the Obamas invited rapper Common to read some rhymes. Common is no Boy Scout. In one of his antiwar jams, Common suggests we should "Burn a Bush," since all Bush wants is oil. Common also celebrates the peaceful legacy of convicted cop killers. There's the Left's longtime favorite cop killer (and really, that's saying something, because there are so many lovely cop killers to choose from), Mumia Abu-Jamal, whom Common praised in a Def Poetry Jam session by rhyming about how "Free Mumia" flyers adorn his freezer.

Then there's Common's adoration of that other progressive heroine of peace, Assata Shakur (previously named Joanne Chesimard), an FBI-branded domestic terrorist who executed New Jersey trooper Werner Foerster with his own gun. Afterward, she literally kicked Foerster's brains out before going on to be sentenced to life in prison for armed robbery, illegal possession of a weapon, assault with a dangerous weapon, assault and battery of a police officer, assault with intent to kill, and first-degree murder. Rapper Common calls Shakur innocent and beautiful and rhymes about their kinship in his song "A Song for Assata." Today Assata is at large, having escaped from prison to Cuba. Needless to say, when First Lady Michelle Obama invited Common to come kick it with her in the White House, members of the New Jersey State Trooper Fraternal Association objected. Obama officials claimed they'd never heard of Assata, a horrifying fact given that she is listed on the FBI's Wanted list on its website, along with a $1 million reward.[62]

These thugs haven't just infiltrated America's White House, but also our president's iPod playlists. Like millions of Americans, Obama has an iPod. A quick glance at his playlist reveals just what a hypocrite he is. He's not ashamed of it, either. "My rap palate has greatly improved," Obama boasted in über-cool fashion to *Rolling Stone.* "Jay-Z used to be sort of what predominated, but now I've got a little Nas and a little Lil Wayne and some other stuff, but I would not claim to be an expert."[63]

We've already covered the lovely lyrics and antics of Nas and Jay-Z. As for Lil Wayne, at the time of the president's comments, the rapper was serving a one-year sentence for possession of drugs and guns at Rikers Island. His lyrics explore things like round-the-clock drug hustling, getting high on weed, shooting porno flicks, and the sheer fun you enjoy when capping someone.[64] Black author Thomas Chatterton Williams, writing in the *Wall Street Journal,* was hardly amused. "Lil Wayne is emblematic of a hip-hop culture that is ignorant, misogynistic, casually criminal and often violent. A self-described gangster, he is a modern-day minstrel who embodies the most virulent racist stereotypes that generations of blacks have fought to overcome. His music is a vigorous endorsement of the pathologies that still haunt and cripple far too many in the black underclass."[65]

Using violent rappers for political advantage is one thing.

Inviting them over for a poetry reading or letting them sit in your chair is another. But what about savoring their rants on hate, sex, guns, and killing when you've denounced all of these things? There's a name for that: hyp-hop-crisy. Oh, snap! Sign me to a record label, son!

Furthermore, Obama's endorsement of his rap star campaign supporters has an effect on precisely the people Obama claims he longs to save and help—the black underclass. As Juan Williams points out in his book *Enough,* while young middle-class white kids (mostly males) are the largest buyers of rap music, the middle-class values of self-empowerment and educational achievement they are largely raised with buffer the majority of them from the corrosive effects caused by a musical genre that preaches victimology, "keepin' it real" (i.e., not "acting white" and valuing educational excellence), misogyny, drugs, gang life, etc. Put simply, for white kids gangsta rap is an act of rebellion and mischievous fantasy. For black kids it's an identity, a prism through which to view the world, and a proxy for the absence of male role models, given that 72 percent of black babies in America are born out of wedlock (versus just 28 percent for whites and 51 percent for Latinos).[66]

Given that Obama himself grew up without a dad, you would think he would be more sensitive and cautious to the caustic influence of gangsta rap on America's black, fatherless culture. But why bash black rappers when they've got millions to donate to your campaign? And why challenge black voters who consider rappers their heroes when you can instead pander to them and poach more votes?

The entertainment industry's love of violence appears to have also spilled over into the way Obama speaks. After all, he can really dish it like a hata' when he gets going. At a 2008 fundraising event in Philadelphia he quoted Sean Connery's "Chicago Way" monologue: "If they bring a knife to the fight, we bring a gun," adding, "Because from what I understand folks in Philly like a good brawl." (Dag, homes! Obama goin' bus' a cap!) In February 2009, Obama sent this message to special interest groups who disagreed with his health-care reform plan: "I know they [the special interests and lobbyists] are gearing up for a fight as we speak. My message to them is this: so am I."[67] Speaking about the national debt in January 2011 he said, "The debt ceiling should not be something that is used as a gun against the heads of the American people to extract tax breaks. . . ."[68]

Of course, comments like these are merely playing to his far Left base. For all progressives' yapping about being lovers of peace, they sure are ready to rumble when things don't break their way. When Obama urged his thug union supporters to "gear up for a fight" and "hit back twice as hard" against health-care opposition, members of Service Employees International Union (SEIU) flocked to a town hall meeting in purple shirts, singled out Kenneth Gladney, a black man who was selling flags and other patriotic merchandise outside the meeting, and beat him to within an inch of his life. Without even talking to him (except to yell at him and call him the N-word), their mass attack left Gladney confined to recover in a wheelchair. Did Obama intend for this to happen? No. But one thing's certain: Obama, who comes out of the Chicago machine, used to work for ACORN, training their "rent-a-mobs."[69] So he knows how to "take it to the street," Lil Wayne–style.

Indeed, in the aftermath of the Gabby Giffords shooting, progressives administered endless lectures about how conservatives must turn from their militaristic rhetoric and restore civility and peacefulness to our political discourse. But the person they should have been lecturing is Obama, not conservatives. Obama has amassed quite the list of violent quotes, some of which are very polarizing. He told Latino voters in 2010 to vote Democrat in the midterm elections to "punish our enemies." In 2010 he told minority voters that Republican victory in the midterm elections would mean two years of "hand-to-hand combat," and later that year he told his party he was "itching for a fight" with Republicans.[70] In 2008 he urged supporters, "Argue with [people], get in their faces." And after sitting idly by as the biggest natural disaster in American history took place on his watch, our calm, cool, and collected president told NBC's Matt Lauer that he's looking for "whose ass to kick."[71]

Sound like a Nobel Peace Prize winner to you?

The progressive pose of loving peace is as obnoxious as it is hypocritical. But few things are as nauseating as having to listen to Hollywood peaceniks wax eloquent about what unity-loving, harmony-valuing doves they are . . . before heading over to the studio to film a gore-riddled bloodbath of a movie. Violence rules in movies. And if a picture is worth a thousand words, the stars would best shut up when it comes to violence because all the hot air of the West Coast can't measure up to the gruesome imagery Hollywood churns out year after year.

Seriously, what could be more annoying than getting gun control lectures from multimillionaire action heroes who blast bad guys and blow things up? Something is definitely wrong in the world when Rambo trashes the Second Amendment. While in London, Sylvester Stallone told *Access Hollywood* that American criminality would persist "until America, door to door, takes every handgun." Sly continued: "It's pathetic. It really is pathetic. It's sad. We're living in the Dark Ages over there."[72] Then, in an *Access Hollywood* segment, Stallone said, "I know we use guns in films" but insisted the time has come "to be a little more accountable and realize that this is an escalating problem that's eventually going to lead to, I think, urban warfare." [73]

Then there's Daniel Craig, the current James Bond. For Craig, playing 007 was especially problematic because it meant confronting a personal fear of handguns. "I hate handguns," he told Britain's *OK!* magazine. "They are used to shoot people and as long as they are around, people will shoot each other. I've seen a bullet wound and it was a mess." Hey, Bond, don't be such an octopussy. (I'm of course referring to the 1983 James Bond movie, *Octopussy*.) Craig, by the way, also confessed that he doesn't like martinis shaken, but rather stirred.

And then there's Sarah Palin basher and Noam Chomsky worshipper Matt Damon. Damon is emblematic of the kind of hyperelitist smugness often found in liberal academia. And no wonder. The *Independent* newspaper describes Damon's mother, Nancy Carlsson-Paige, as "an author 'hippie' college professor who lectures on child psychology" and encouraged him to be "totally carried away" growing up. When young Matt was reprimanded by a schoolteacher for staring out a window, Carlsson-Paige "told the teacher off" and "proceeded to complete her son's schoolwork herself while he played outside, under the belief that he was daydreaming in class because he already knew how to do it all." [74]

Gee, I wonder where Damon got his "know-it-all" self-righteousness?

One of the other parenting gems Carlsson-Paige imparted was to neuter Damon's boys-will-be-boys recreational activities by discouraging him from playing with toy guns and to instead play peacefully (no wonder the dude has so much pent-up rage and anger). In fact, his professor mom specializes in teaching "nonviolent conflict resolution." [75] When Damon struck it big in the film industry, his mom bashed his success as merely a triumph of capitalism over humanity. "He's not a human being anymore," said Damon's mom. "He's a cog in the capitalist system."

A real nurturer, that Carlsson-Paige.

Not surprisingly, growing up granola has taken its toll on Damon. Damon says he remains committed to the code of nonviolence and peace-loving progressivism his mother indoctrinated him with. "Now I always look at the violence [in a script]. I don't want it to be gratuitous. Because I do believe that that has an effect on people's behavior. I really do believe that. And I have turned down movies because of that."[76] But apparently Damon's disdain for violence ends where his lust for dirty lucre begins. He has appeared in numerous action-packed, violence-drenched box office hits. Chief among them are *The Departed, True Grit, Saving Private Ryan, The Bourne Supremacy, The Bourne Identity,* and *The Bourne Ultimatum.* The last three of these, often called the Bourne Trilogy, are orgies of violence. According to *Forbes,* Damon hauled in $26 million for *The Bourne Supremacy* alone.[77] Go take a look at the Blu-Ray or DVD cover art for any of the three movies—every single one features a picture of the hard-core Obama backer with a gun in his hand.

To prepare for his violent roles, the antiviolence Lefty says he learned martial arts and "got all this expensive firearms training."[78]

Hypocrisy? What hypocrisy? I don't see any hypocrisy here!

In fairness, the dude really had no chance but to become a major-league hypocrite; he was influenced by progressivism *and* Hollywood, the two biggest reservoirs of hypocrisy this side of Anthony Weiner's Twitter account! But laughably, he has proudly declared to have taken an antiviolence stand by refusing to lend his voice to the Bourne video games based on the films. How courageous. The dude won't appear in the pissant video games that

Matt Damon promoting peace and protesting gun violence by aiming a rifle at your face (and banking $26 million in the process).

would make him peanuts compared to the megabucks he makes on the big screen, but he's happy to appear in movies that gross $290 million with vast audience reach, provided he makes fat coin. How noble.

The actor's mommy, the hippy professor, says she and momma's boy Damon are in agreement on the negative effects of video game violence. "I am very wary of violent video games," she said. "Research shows they desensitize kids to violence, even more because they engage kids in committing violence." Carlsson-Paige continued: "Matt and I don't share the same views about violence in adult films, but we do see eye-to-eye on the importance of protecting children. We both support regulations to stop the marketing of violence in films to children through violent toys, products, and video games."[79] Well, at least the mom is consistent in her views. The same cannot be said for her progressive star son, who talks peace and love and hippy goodness one minute, and then makes millions killing people in movies the next.

Oscar winner Sean Penn is another celebrity whose love for peace leads him to violence. Penn hates Bush, the Iraq War, and basically anything that makes America stronger. While receiving the first annual Christopher Reeve First Amendment Award in 2006, Penn seized the opportunity to call for the impeachment of Bush and Cheney.[80] He went a lot further in a 2007 op-ed, addressed to President Bush, wherein he called Bush "our country's and our constitution's most devastating enemy." Still not satisfied, Penn went on to say, "But now, we are encouraged to self-censor any words that might be perceived as inflammatory—if our belief is that this war should stop today. We cower as you point fingers telling us to 'support our troops.' Well, you and the smarmy pundits in your pocket, those who bathe in the moisture of your soiled and bloodstained underwear, can take that noise and shove it."[81]

Penn's superior wisdom comes in part from his work as a part-time journalist. In 2004 Penn put off his film career to work as a journalist in Iraq and went to Iran the following year. He's interviewed dictator Hugo Chavez (a friend of his), Raul Castro, and traveled to Cuba in an effort to interview Fidel Castro.[82] He displayed remarkable courage (and deplorable judgment) when he said that anyone who calls Chavez a dictator should be sent "to prison for these kinds of lies." No wonder he and Chavez get along so well.[83]

One more thing about Penn: he doesn't like guns. Except for his own. He was packin' a .38-caliber Smith & Wesson and a loaded 9mm Glock handgun in his trunk when his car was stolen outside a Berkeley, California, restaurant. Scared that an ex-employee had been stalking him, he got a concealed weapons permit, which is plenty hard to do if you're like Penn and have a history of marijuana abuse, plus a couple of arrests for reckless driving and assault. He got around these obstacles by getting FBI and State Department clearance and undergoing firearms training. Clearly, a lot of trouble, and a lot of reason to believe that Penn highly values his personal right to bear arms. As for the rest of us . . . well, we're not nearly as important as he is, so we can just get murdered by stalkers, I guess.[84]

And how can anyone talk about gun hypocrisy without mentioning that actress and menace of the talk-show and talk-radio airwaves, Rosie O'Donnell? Rosie may have taken on the nickname "queen of nice," but this soubriquet ignores that she is an extreme antiwar hater with a track record of displaying equally extreme mean-spiritedness (her antics have included screaming at guests and bullying former cohost Elisabeth Hasselbeck). Throughout the course of her talk career, Rosie has displayed quite a talent for trashing our leaders (provided they're Republicans), defending our enemies, and otherwise spewing her Leftist propaganda and milder forms of idiocy.

First there's the run-of-the-mill, garden-variety liberal venting, like how she loves to call Bush a "war criminal" and said he should be impeached and tried at The Hague. And there's been lots of hyperbole, such as when she likened post-9/11 America to the McCarthy era (apparently people were "blacklisted" for disagreeing with Bush) and also compared the Patriot Act to South African apartheid. (Don't we all miss our pre-9/11 freedoms?) But you really start to worry for her when she contends that America is the real terrorist threat, that Khalid Sheikh Mohammed was innocent and was only tortured into confessing to be the brains behind 9/11, and that "radical Christianity is just as threatening as radical Islam in a country like America."[85]

It should come as no surprise, therefore, that she also complained that Osama bin Laden was assassinated without due process of law. In this she joined the 11 percent of Americans who think it was wrong to kill him on the spot versus the 80 percent of Americans who say his assassination was handled well.[86] Nor should it be too surprising that when Helen Thomas attacked our ally Israel by telling Jews to "get the hell out of Palestine" and return to Poland and Germany, Rosie defended Helen the Jew-hater because, as she sees it, telling Jews to go back to Germany in 2010 wasn't like telling them to "go back to the ovens" of World War II.[87]

And just in case there's anyone left on planet earth who still doesn't think Rosie is totally off her rocker, she believes—and has frequently tried to make *us* believe—that 9/11 was staged and that al-Qaeda was not responsible. Her argument: it's "physically impossible" for steel to melt in fire, but the World Trade towers' steel did—so the building's steel had to have been tampered with by someone on the inside (cough—cough—Bush!). She went so far as to claim that Rudy Giuliani had shipped all the twin towers' steel to China so it couldn't be tested.[88]

Rosie's status as one of America's foremost terrorism experts has also come in handy when assessing the oil spill catastrophe that happened on her beloved Oilbama's watch. In reaction to the oil spill, she called BP "environmental terrorists" guilty of "criminal behavior" and said they should be taken over by the government so their money could be spent on repairing damages. Good luck seeing that resolution succeed, Rosie, especially with Obama having been the biggest recipient of BP's campaign donations![89]

Rosie has also channeled her boundless rage into fighting for gun control, a cause that she has aggressively advocated for years. In 2000 she emceed the "Million Mom March," a gun control protest that set records as America's largest-ever gun control rally and America's largest gathering of women and girls.[90] So passionate on this issue is the whalelike comedienne that she has savagely attacked her own guests over it,[91] as when she subjected National Rifle Association supporter Tom Selleck to a verbal lashing of nearly ten minutes when he appeared on the now-defunct *Rosie O'Donnell Show* to promote his latest romantic comedy. She had promised Selleck beforehand to keep calm "to show everyone how people who have opposing views can compromise." Selleck decided to leave before the next segment,[92] but not until Rosie got the chance to add this extremist statement: "I think the Second Amendment is in the Constitution so that we can have muskets when the British people come over in 1800. I don't think it's in the Constitution so we can have assault weapons in the year 2000!"[93] She made her rigid approach to gun control even more lucid on another occasion when she said, "I don't care if you want to hunt,

I don't care if you think it's your right. I say 'Sorry.'" In her ideal scenario, "you are not allowed to own a gun, and if you do own a gun I think you should go to prison."[94]

But in the midst of all Rosie's antigun rhetoric she failed to mention something very important: one of her own bodyguards had applied for a gun permit! Initially she suggested that her bodyguard had been prompted by the company he represented to apply for the license. Later she admitted that she did feel that she and her family needed to be protected from—who else—Second Amendment advocates.[95] Paranoid much? This coming from a woman who, on Halloween, actually had a security guard separate trick-or-treaters from their parents at the gate of her Nyack, New York, house.[96]

In one of many attempts to explain her use of a bodyguard, she said, "I chose to have a 'bodyguard' for my children."[97] But that doesn't make her any less of a hypocrite. Less than two weeks before the gun permit request was discovered, Rosie had railed against the NRA in an interview where she admitted that maybe the NRA cares about "their own kids, but not kids in general. The only life that is important to them is white, Republican life."[98] So how would that make the NRA any different from a talk-show host who wants only her kids to be protected by an armed bodyguard while she works to make the Second Amendment as antiquated as a rusty musket for everyone else?

Eventually Rosie had to concede some rhetorical ground over this issue. She felt compelled to make the cop-out claim that having an occasionally armed guard didn't violate her gun-hating, NRA-bashing, talk-show-guest-pummeling stance. "I don't personally own a gun," she said, "but if you are qualified, licensed and registered, I have no problem." Not exactly the kind of open-mindedness she showed to poor Tom Selleck.[99]

Another musket-ball-sized hole in Rosie's rhetoric: her affiliation with Kmart. When ABC's *This Week* asked Rosie how she felt about concealed-handgun laws, she replied, "Of course, I'm against them. I also think you should not buy a gun anywhere." (Hollywood and Handguns . . .) Yet one item on O'Donnell's résumé of hypocrisies is that she worked as pitchwoman for Kmart, which happens to have an extensive retail gun sales division. Her relationship with Kmart ended because of these criticisms. She claimed that this was her idea, saying, "It's only fair to Kmart that I stop doing commercials." But the New York *Daily News* presented a different story: Kmart fired the talk-show host because her gun talk was bringing the company too much negative publicity.[100]

What all this Hollywood hypocrisy proves is this: instead of Obama and his celebrity drones lecturing us to "give peace a chance," perhaps they need to give *silence* a chance. Before Professor Obama delivers his mind-numbing lectures about the proliferation of violence and misogyny, he would do well to pull all his rapper pals aside and give them a talking-to. After that, MC Prez might well do some deleting from his iPod.

Furthermore, before progressives blast conservatives for using words like *blast* (violent imagery alert!), maybe they should muzzle their violent celebrity minions, like Montel Williams, who advocate things like slitting the throat of Michele Bachmann.

And before Obama's big-money Tinseltown campaign backers try to steal away our Second Amendment right to bear arms, maybe they should look in the mirror and address the gun culture they themselves promote and glorify to the tune of billions of dollars at the box office. Moreover, they need to ask their bodyguards to disarm themselves, hand over their own concealed weapons, and refuse to ever appear in any film or television show that features a gun or any form of violence.

To do all that would, of course, be ridiculous and stupid. It would also make movies suck. Conservatives believe in freedom. Celebrities should have a right to do as they please and own weapons to protect their families. So why the hell won't they support the same rights for everyone else?

Hmmm . . . could it be . . . hypocrisy?

Conclusion

Tinseltown and Its Emperor Have No Clothes

Here's the rub: the only group powerful enough publicly to resuscitate and resurrect Obama's 2008 mass popularity is the mob of Hollywood Leftists who got him elected the first time. Last presidential cycle, the McCain campaign ignored the power of "cool" and lost. For conservatives who think we can't lose in 2012 because of Obama's disastrous record, here's my reply: "Yes, we can!"

Anyone who thinks Barack Obama's abysmal first term in office will be enough to demoralize the Hollywood Left from flexing their media-savvy political muscle is a fool. Sure, from time to time, stars pop off some emotionally charged quip about being disenchanted and disappointed that Obama hasn't brought about America's destruction with quite the rapidity that most progressives desire. But in the end, when the presidential election kicks into high gear, Hollywood will put its money, star power, and media dominance on the line to "make history again" by reelecting the most radical socialist ever to occupy the White House.

As we've seen, Hollywood matters—big-time. And no, not just because Ronald Reagan was a Hollywood actor turned president. The Hollywood Left dictates who and what is "cool." As 2008 revealed, they also hold major sway on younger voters and those who take their political cues more from pop culture than the six o'clock news. The temptation will be to dismiss Hollywood's power and importance as less relevant this time because of the consequences and realities of Obama's disastrous policies. But here again, conservatives play themselves for the fool; the mainstream media's love affair with Obama, while presently strained, will roar back with a vengeance when their guy is against the wall and the heat is on. And since Team Obama knows it can only win by replicating its strong showing among young voters and independents, you can be sure that Obama's Hollywood hit squad will continue to be called upon to raise boatloads of cash and mobilize key constituencies and get them to the polls.

So what to do?

Answer: Go and stay on offense by humiliating Hollywood progressives into silence. When celebrities don't pay a public price for opening their ignorant yaps, they keep talking. But when they perceive that the public considers their endorsement a liability rather than an asset, they clam up and fade from sight. That means the eventual Republican presidential nominee's campaign should publicly challenge and shame Hollywood endorsements of Barack Obama by using the celebrity's outrageous statements and hypocritical positions, such as the scores of them chronicled in this book, to make the celeb a liability for Obama.

For example, when Bon Jovi or The Boss announces that he will be hosting the obligatory Obama fundraiser or host a concert in honor of Dear Leader, GOP surrogates should immediately be dispatched to demand that the Obama campaign return the donations of a tax dodger like "bee farmer" Bon Jovi and a union buster like Bruce Springsteen. Introducing wedge issues that pit Democrat voters against their Hollywood hypocrite heroes on the one hand, and the progressive values they claim to champion on the other, explodes Leftist lies and flips the celebrity's star power on its head; what was once a positive quickly becomes a negative.

I'd also love to see some college kids donning bee costumes to ask Jon "Bee Farmer" Bon Jovi to sign their jars of honey. Just sayin'.

As we've seen throughout this book, Hollywood hypocrites are the perfect embodiment of all that is wrong with the Left's ideas and policies. Not only do progressive positions fail, but they are so bankrupt that even their loudest adherents live lives that stand in direct opposition to their ideology.

Michael Moore blasts capitalism and the profit motive . . . then sidesteps hiring union members to cut costs, demands full payment from studios, and maximizes every inch of existing tax laws to squeeze every last dime of profit he can out of his movies.

Sting and Trudie Styler lecture us common folk on our need to repent from our carbon-spewing ways . . . then hop on their private jet, with their massive concert trailer trucks in tow, and hopscotch around the globe lugging their 750-person entourage and leave a Sasquatch-sized carbon footprint in their wake.

Arianna Huffington writes bestselling books denouncing the "pigs at the trough" whose appetite for greed and profit destroys the rights and livelihoods of workers . . . then turns around and pulls off one of the shrewdest media mergers in recent memory by converting the free labor of nine thousand bloggers into a $100 million payday for herself.

Bono travels the globe shaking down nations who are in debt to hand over even more of taxpayers' hard-earned money in the name of African "debt relief" . . . then plays a shell game with his band's corporate structure to avoid paying higher taxes—the very same taxes that would otherwise be used for, well, African debt relief.

Matt Damon holds forth on the corrosive effects of violence in media . . . then makes movies wherein he brandishes weapons and kills people with his bare hands if necessary to make fat bank at the box office.

On and on it goes . . .

The point isn't that Michael Moore shouldn't maximize profits, Sting and Trudie Styler shouldn't travel, Arianna Huffington shouldn't be hard-nosed in business, Bono shouldn't be as tax-efficient as possible, or that Matt Damon shouldn't be free to make movies depicting violence. Quite the contrary! The point is that these and the scores of celebrities I've exposed throughout this book advocate that the heavy and crushing hand of government denies us the very liberties that they use to catapult themselves to prosperity and stardom.

And that's the point: since progressives see government as the solution to every social ill, the Left's hypocrisies bring with them a unique danger, because they carry with them the oppressive weight of governmental laws that control human behaviors and limit freedoms. As author Peter Schweizer has noted, "conservatives who abandon their principles and engage in hypocrisy usually end up harming themselves and their families . . . liberals who do the same usually benefit."[1]

That's certainly the case for many of Obama's biggest Hollywood supporters, and it's precisely why their hypocrisies must be exposed, their ideas challenged, and their idiocy called out at every turn.

Last go around, Republicans sat back like wimps and let Barack Obama's celebrity-fueled cool machine steamroll them into electoral smithereens.

This time around, we must be the ones doing the steamrolling.

Notes

Introduction

1. http://www.cnsnews.com/news/article/obama-has-now-increased
-debt-more-all-presidents-george-washington-through-george-hw.
2. http://www.weeklystandard.com/blogs/obama-vs-bush-debt
_537207.html.
3. http://www.salon.com/life/broadsheet/feature/2009/11/03/pelosi
_smile; http://www.politico.com/news/stories/0211/49273.html.
4. http://www.newsweek.com/blogs/the-gaggle/2010/05/26/the
-problem-with-james-carville-s-criticism-of-obama.html.
5. http://www.whitehousedossier.com/2011/03/15/president-obamas-
trivial-pursuits-2/; http://www.dailymail.co.uk/news/worldnews/
article-1300852/Spanish-police-close-public-beach-Michelle
-Obamas-250k-Spanish-holiday.html.
6. http://www.washingtonpost.com/wp-dyn/content/article/2010/
12/12/AR2010121203181.html?hpid=moreheadlines.

7. http://latimesblogs.latimes.com/the_big_picture/2008/11/geffen-on-obama.html.

8. John Heilemann and Mark Halperin, *Game Change: Obama and the Clintons, McCain and Palin, and the Race of a Lifetime* (New York: Harper, 2010), 86.

9. Ibid, 86–87.

10. Ibid.

11. http://latimesblogs.latimes.com/the_big_picture/2008/11/geffen-on-obama.html.

12. Heilemann and Halperin, *Game Change*, 87.

13. http://latimesblogs.latimes.com/the_big_picture/2008/11/geffen-on-obama.html.

14. Heilemann and Halperin, *Game Change*, 87.

15. http://latimesblogs.latimes.com/the_big_picture/2008/11/geffen-on-obama.html.

16. Heilemann and Halperin, *Game Change,* 86.

17. Maureen Dowd, "Obama's Big Screen Test," *New York Times*, February 21, 2007.

18. Heilemann and Halperin, *Game Change*, 89.

19. http://gawker.com/#!5412344/meet-the-hot-boyfriend-david-geffen-took-to-obamas-state-dinner/gallery/2.

20. http://blogs.wsj.com/washwire/2011/09/27/obama-turns-to-hollywood-for-fund-raising/.

21. http://news.yahoo.com/obama-mingles-stars-raises-cash-03164 8460.html; http://www.hollywoodreporter.com/news/president-obama-hollywood-meeting-253151.

22. Sara Lipka and Reeves Wiedeman, "Young Voters Overwhelmingly Favored Obama, Swinging Some Battleground States," *Chronicle of Higher Education*, November 14, 2008.

Chapter 1: Hollywood Welfare

1. http://www.backstage.com/bso/esearch/article_display.jsp?vnu_content_id=1002116907.

2. Robert Tannenwald, "State Film Subsidies: Not Much Bang for Too Many Bucks," Center on Budget and Policy Priorities, December 9, 2010.

3. Ibid.

4. Ibid.

5. Sharon Silke Carty, "Michigan Tax Credit Courts Film Industry to Lure Money, Jobs," *USA Today*, August 17, 2009, http://www.usatoday .com/money/media/2009-08-16-michigan-movies_N.htm.

6. Tannenwald, "State Film Subsidies."

7. "Tax Me If You Can," *Wall Street Journal*, March 14, 2009.

8. Pete Winn, "After Attacking Tax Credit for Movie Makers, Michael Moore Asks Struggling Michigan to Give Him the Tax Credit to Help Cover Cost of Anti-Capitalist Movie," *CNSNews.com,* January 31, 2010, http://www.cnsnews.com/node/60743.

9. http://boxofficemojo.com/movies/?id=michaelmoore09.htm.

10. Winn, "After Attacking Tax Credit."

11. Ibid.

12. Ibid.

13. Josh Barro, "Voodoo Economics of the Silver Screen," *RealClearMar kets.com,* September 21, 2010, http://www.realclearmarkets.com/ articles/2010/09/21/voodoo_economics_of_the_silver_screen_98678 .html.

14. James M. Hohman, "Michigan Film Subsidies: Two Years, $117 Mil- lion and No Film Job Growth," Mackinac Center for Public Policy, April 20, 2010, http://www.mackinac.org/12495.

15. http://www.boston.com/news/globe/magazine/articles/2005/ 10/02/to_be_frank/.

16. Navjeet K. Bal, "A Report on the Massachusetts Film Industry Tax Incen- tives," Massachusetts Department of Revenue, July 12, 2009, http:// www.mass.gov/Ador/docs/dor/News/2009FilmIncentiveReport.pdf.

17. Ibid.

18. Peter Enrich, "Lights. Camera. Stop the Film Subsidies Action," *Boston Globe,* February 19, 2011, http://www.boston.com/boston globe/editorial_opinion/oped/articles/2011/02/19/lights_camera _stop_the_film_subsidies_action/.

19. Shelley Geballe, "Fiddling While Rome Burns: Connecticut's Multi- Million Dollar, Money-Losing Subsidy to the Entertainment Indus- try," Connecticut Voices for Children, June 2009, http://www.ctkids link.org/publications/bud09filmtax.pdf.

20. Ibid.

21. Ibid.

22. Ibid.

23. Katherine Gregg, "Hollywood Is Here, But Is Price Too High for State?" *Providence Journal*, March 2, 2008, http://www.projo.com/news/content/film_credits_02_03-02-08_LM957VT_v77.365ac0a.html.

24. Ibid.

25. Joe Kristan, "Iowa Film Tax Credit Scandal: A Warning to Other States," 9, in "Special Report: Movie Production Incentives: Blockbuster Support for Lackluster Policy," Tax Foundation No. 173, January 2010, http://www.taxfoundation.org/files/sr173.pdf.

26. http://wvcommerce.org/business/industries/wvfilm/incentives/default.aspx.

27. Ibid. Also see William Luther, "Special Report: Movie Production Incentives: Blockbuster Support for Lackluster Policy," Tax Foundation No. 173, January 2010, http://www.taxfoundation.org/files/sr173.pdf.

28. "Tax Me If You Can," *Wall Street Journal*, March 14, 2009.

29. "The Money Shot: Why Government Handouts to Hollywood Are Growing," *Economist*, August 13, 2009, http://www.economist.com/node/1421482.

30. http://michellemalkin.com/2009/01/21/ailing-chrysler-wants-another-3-billion-of-your-money-while-underwriting-a-movie/; http://www.politico.com/news/stories/0711/59582.html.

31. "Tax Me If You Can," *Wall Street Journal*, March 14, 2009.

32. Robert Tannenwald, "State Film Subsidies: Not Much Bang for Too Many Bucks," Center on Budget and Policy Priorities, December 9, 2010.

33. Ibid.

Chapter 2: Private Jets Against Global Warming

1. J. Freedom du Lac and Joshua Zumbrun, "All Together Now; The Rockers of Live Earth Lift Their Voices in Support of a Greener Globe," *Washington Post*, July 8, 2007, D01.

2. http://abcnews.go.com/WN/bp-oil-spill-crude-mother-nature
-breaks-slick/story?id=11254252; http://www.time.com/time/health/
article/0,8599,2066031,00.html; http://www.humanevents.com/article
.php?id=38734.

3. http://www.whitehouse.gov/the-press-office/remarks-president-a
-discussion-jobs-and-economy-charlotte-north-carolina.

4. http://articles.nydailynews.com/2010-06-10/news/29437606_1
_oil-spill-gulf-relief-efforts.

5. http://www.aolnews.com/2010/05/25/why-is-hollywood-sitting
-out-gulf-oil-spill-relief.

6. http://www.time.com/time/health/article/0,8599,2066031,00.html
#ixzz1KJR2BtBP.

7. http://abcnews.go.com/WN/bp-oil-spill-crude-mother-nature
-breaks-slick/story?id=11254252.

8. http://oils.gpa.unep.org/facts/natural-sources.htm.

9. http://www.psychologytoday.com/blog/how-risky-is-it-really/
201005/it-s-not-just-about-oil-in-the-ocean-it-s-how-it-got-there.

10. http://www.independent.co.uk/environment/climate-change/
whos-cool-in-the-great-celebrity-green-rush-444719.html.

11. http://www.telegraph.co.uk/earth/copenhagen-climate-change
-confe/6599568/Copenhagen-climate-conference-celebrity-support
ers.html.

12. http://www.dailymail.co.uk/tvshowbiz/article-506906/Hypocrite
-Eco-warrior-Sting-Police-list-bands-worst-carbon-footprint.html.

13. http://www.ecorazzi.com/2009/12/03/sting-rejects-eco-hyprocrisy
-label/.

14. http://www.dailymail.co.uk/tvshowbiz/article-562149/Its-true
--hypocrites-huge-carbon-footprint-confesses-Stings-wife.html.

15. Ibid.; http://women.timesonline.co.uk/tol/life_and_style/women/
celebrity/article6931572.ece.

16. http://www.imdb.com/news/ni0781053/.

17. http://newsbusters.org/blogs/noel-sheppard/2010/04/26/sting
-calls-earth-day-climate-rally-green-tea-party-wants-big-government.

18. http://www.telegraph.co.uk/earth/energy/6491195/Al-Gore-could
-become-worlds-first-carbon-billionaire.html.

19. http://www.nytimes.com/2009/11/03/business/energy-environ
    ment/03gore.html.

20. Ibid.

21. Ibid.

22. http://www.huffingtonpost.com/2011/04/21/apple-green-ranking
    -greenpeace_n_851939.html.

23. http://www.nytimes.com/2009/11/03/business/energy-environ
    ment/03gore.html.

24. http://www.foxnews.com/story/0,2933,592263,00.html.

25. Catherine Elsworth, "Al Gore's Own Inconvenient Truth: 20-Room
    Mansion Uses 20 Times the Yearly U.S. Average of Electricity," *Daily
    Telegraph*, March 7, 2007, D16.

26. Ed Pilkington, "An Inconvenient Truth: Eco-Warrior Al Gore's
    Bloated Gas and Electricity Bills," *Guardian*, February 28, 2007.

27. http://www.canadafreepress.com/2007/global-warming080607.htm.

28. http://www.aei.org/article/26610.

29. http://www.guardian.co.uk/world/2007/feb/28/film.usa2.

30. http://www.aei.org/article/26610.

31. http://www.mvgazette.com/article.php?21124.

32. Ibid.

33. http://gawker.com/#!281714/is.

34. http://www.foxnews.com/story/0,2933,361721,00.html.

35. Stephen Adam, "Harrison Ford has chest waxed for rainforests,"
    Telegraph, May 22, 2008, http://www.telegraph.co.uk/news/celeb
    ritynews/2007500/Harrison-Ford-has-chest-waxed-for-rain-forests
    .html; http://www.huffingtonpost.com/harrison-ford/team-earth-are
    -you-in_b_293316.html.

36. http://stossel.blogs.foxbusiness.com/2010/03/01/wax-your
    -chest-for-the-environment; http://blog.seattlepi.com/people/2010/
    02/24/harrison-ford-slammed-for-unnecessary-flights/.

37. http://www.cnsnews.com/node/64907. Given Harrison Ford's
    thousand-dollar donation to then–GOP primary candidate Senator
    John McCain, one might be inclined to think this eco-crite was a
    Republican. That is until you learn that Ford, a lifelong Democrat,
    was also joined by progressive donors Michael Douglas and Obama's
    Hollywood kingmaker, David Geffen. Translation: get McLame nomi-

nated over George W. Bush so Democrats could enjoy a cakewalk in the general election.

38. http://www.dailymail.co.uk/sciencetech/article-1018182/0h-hippy -crites-Just-green-ARE-legions-holier-thou-stars.html.

39. "Saving the Planet," *Miami Herald*, December 7, 2005, A, 4.

40. http://www.foxnews.com/story/0,2933,361721,00.html.

41. http://www.breitbart.com/article.php?id=070519184436.x9vgvtk2 &show_article=1.

42. "Saving the Planet," *Miami Herald*, December 7, 2005, A, 4.

43. Nick Harding, " 'Our Kids Will Suffer if We Don't Act NOW,' " *News of the World* (England), July 8, 2007.

44. http://abclocal.go.com/kabc/story?section=news/local&id=4759345.

45. Dudley J. Hughes, "Carbon Dioxide Levels Are a Blessing, Not a Problem," Heartland Institute, May 1, 2007, http://news.heartland.org/ newspaper-article/2007/05/01/carbon-dioxide-levels-are-blessing -not-problem.

46. Audrey Hudson, "Global Warming Link to Drowned Polar Bears Melts Under Searing Fed Probe," *Human Events,* August 11, 2011, http:// www.humanevents.com/article.php?id=45447.

47. Nicholas Dawidoff, "The Civil Heretic," *New York Times Magazine,* May 25, 2009.

48. Bruce Kirkland, "Filmmaking's a Beach: Leonardo DiCaprio Unhappy with Movie Rumours," *Toronto Sun,* January 18, 2000, 41.

49. "DiCaprio Pledges to Preserve Beach," *Calgary Herald,* January 19, 1999, B12.

50. "Thais Sue DiCaprio Producers for Ruining Beach," *Ottawa Citizen,* January 5, 1999, A7.

51. Kirkland, "Filmmaking's a Beach."

52. Ibid.

53. Ibid.

54. http://www.time.com/time/specials/2007/article/0,28804, 1663317_1663319_1669890,00.html; http://www.independent.co.uk/ arts-entertainment/films/news/robert-redford-is-an-ecohypocrite -film-claims-2198447.html.

55. http://green.blogs.nytimes.com/2009/04/29/is-a-green-housing -development-too-close-to-home-for-robert-redford/.

56. http://www.independent.co.uk/arts-entertainment/films/news/robert-redford-is-an-ecohypocrite-film-claims-2198447.html.

57. http://www.sfgate.com/cgi-bin/blogs/ontheblock/detail?entry_id=39541.

58. http://www.independent.co.uk/arts-entertainment/films/news/robert-redford-is-an-ecohypocrite-film-claims-2198447.html.

59. http://www.dailymail.co.uk/sciencetech/article-1018182/Oh-hippy-crites-Just-green-ARE-legions-holier-thou-stars.html#ixzz1JjVE4SPK.

60. Ibid.

61. Andrew Fenton, "How Can We Believe Celebrities Flying Around in Private Jets?" *Advertiser* (Australia), October 13, 2007, W18.

62. http://www.foxnews.com/story/0,2933,361721,00.html.

63. Ibid.

64. Ibid.

65. http://www.tmz.com/2006/10/18/celebs-who-claim-theyre-green-but-guzzle-gas/.

66. http://realestate.aol.com/blog/2010/04/28/giseles-earth-unfriendly-home-shame-on-this-un-ambassador; http://news.bostonherald.com/news/regional/view/20100425home_field_advantage_bradys_pigskin_palace_slammed/srvc=home&position=0.

67. http://www.tmz.com/2006/10/18/celebs-who-claim-theyre-green-but-guzzle-gas/.

68. http://www.radaronline.com/exclusives/2007/07/jann-wenner-green-in-word-brown-in-deed.php; http://www.radaronline.com/exclusives/2007/07/rolling-stone-owner-is-a-global-warmer.php; and http://newsbusters.org/node/13949.

69. http://www.tmz.com/2006/10/18/celebs-who-claim-theyre-green-but-guzzle-gas/.

70. http://www.telegraph.co.uk/finance/newsbysector/energy/oilandgas/7719941/Gulf-of-Mexico-oil-spill-James-Cameron-offers-private-submarines-to-help-BP-clean-up.html. See also Ann McElhinney and Phelim McAleer's great short film on James Cameron's environmental hypocrisy: http://www.youtube.com/watch?v=TKZ4RolQxec.

71. http://articles.nydailynews.com/2010-06-10/news/29437606_1_oil-spill-gulf-relief-efforts.

72. http://nymag.com/daily/entertainment/2009/10/the_truth_about _james_cameron.html.

73. http://www.usnews.com/news/blogs/washington-whispers/2011/ 04/22/earth-day-ends-obamas-53300-gallon-trip.

74. http://www.dailymail.co.uk/tvshowbiz/article-445490/With-private -jets-Travolta-lectures-global-warming.html.

75. http://www.people.com/people/article/0,,625104,00.html.

76. http://www.dailymail.co.uk/tvshowbiz/article-445490/With-private -jets-Travolta-lectures-global-warming.html.

77. http://www.dailymail.co.uk/sciencetech/article-1018182/Oh-hippy -crites-Just-green-ARE-legions-holier-thou-stars.html.

78. http://www.dailymail.co.uk/sciencetech/article-1018182/Oh-hippy -crites-Just-green-ARE-legions-holier-thou-stars.html#ixzz1JjVE 4SPK.

79. http://www.dailymail.co.uk/sciencetech/article-1018182/Oh-hippy -crites-Just-green-ARE-legions-holier-thou-stars.html#ixzz1Jjh 7b2je.

80. http://www.telegraph.co.uk/earth/copenhagen-climate-change -confe/6599568/Copenhagen-climate-conference-celebrity-supporters .html.

81. http://www.dailymail.co.uk/tvshowbiz/article-447677/Climate -change-concert-star-Madonna-accused-hypocrisy.html.

82. http://www.huffingtonpost.com/2006/05/01/madonna-go-to -texas-and-s_n_20158.html; http://www.youtube.com/watch?v=Mq S6hBsFDnU.

83. http://www.dailymail.co.uk/tvshowbiz/article-447677/Climate -change-concert-star-Madonna-accused-hypocrisy.html.

84. Felicity Barringer, "Scientists Want Publisher to Refreeze Green-land," *New York Times,* September 24, 2011.

Chapter 3: Working-Class ~~Heroes~~ Zeroes

1. http://www.foxnews.com/story/0,2933,128219,00.html.

2. http://www.nytimes.com/2009/02/01/arts/music/01pare.html.

3. Ibid.

4. http://www.nytimes.com/2004/08/05/opinion/05bruce.html.

5. http://archive.newsmax.com/archives/ic/2004/8/6/134636.shtml.

6. http://articles.nydailynews.com/2000-06-10/news/18133660_1
   _american-skin-shooting-of-amadou-diallo-police-bullets.

7. http://www.nytimes.com/2004/08/05/opinion/05bruce.html.

8. http://www.myfoxny.com/dpp/news/investigative/farm-tax-breaks
   -for-nj-celebrities-20110209.

9. Ibid.

10. http://www.trentonian.com/articles/2010/12/11/news/doc4d0456
    c2882d6484823134.txt?viewmode=fullstory.

11. http://www.myfoxny.com/dpp/news/investigative/farm-tax-breaks
    -for-nj-celebrities-20110209.

12. http://online.wsj.com/article/SB120787592935506791.html?mod
    =todays_us_nonsub_weekendjournal.

13. http://en.wikipedia.org/wiki/Bruce_Springsteen_discography.

14. http://www.nytimes.com/2009/02/01/arts/music/01pare.html.

15. Ibid.; Walker Simon, "Boss Takes a Walk on Sunny Side," *Toronto Sun*, January 30, 2009.

16. Ibid.

17. Nick Rufford, "I'm Just a Regular Multi-Millionaire," *Sunday Times* (London), November 21, 2010.

18. http://www.forbes.com/lists/2010/53/celeb-100-10_Bruce-Spring
    steen_Y6W8.html.

19. Rufford, "I'm Just a Regular Multi-Millionaire."

20. http://blogs.forbes.com/zackomalleygreenburg/2011/01/03/inside
    -bon-jovi-200-million-payday-music-business/.

21. http://www.myfoxny.com/dpp/news/investigative/farm-tax-breaks
    -for-nj-celebrities-20110209.

22. Ibid.

23. http://music.msn.com/music/article.aspx?news=635420&affid
    =100055.

24. http://nymag.com/daily/entertainment/2011/03/jon_bon_jov
    i_steve_jobs.html.

Chapter 4: The Priestess of Pigs *(Capitalist, That Is)*

1. Arianna Huffington, *Pigs at the Trough: How Corporate Greed and Political Corruption Are Undermining America* (New York: Broadway, 2004), 27.

2. http://www.syracuse.com/news/index.ssf/2011/02/how_the_huff ington_post_became.html.

3. http://abcnews.go.com/2020/Stossel/story?id=4716938&page=1; http://www.syracuse.com/news/index.ssf/2011/02/how_the_huff ington_post_became.html.

4. http://www.amny.com/urbanite-1.812039/arianna-huffington-the -making-of-a-mogul-1.2683922.

5. http://www.syracuse.com/news/index.ssf/2011/02/how_the_huff ington_post_became.html.

6. http://www.rawstory.com/rs/2011/02/09/bloggers-readers-band -quit-huffington-post/.

7. http://www.guardian.co.uk/media/2011/feb/27/arianna-huffington -post-aol-deal.

8. Ibid.

9. http://articles.latimes.com/2011/feb/09/opinion/la-oe-rutten -column-huffington-aol-20110209.

10. http://www.amny.com/urbanite-1.812039/arianna-huffington-the -making-of-a-mogul-1.2683922.

11. Huffington, *Pigs at the Trough,* 15.

12. Maureen Orth, "Arianna's Virtual Candidate," *Vanity Fair,* November 1994, http://www.vanityfair.com/culture/features/1994/11/huffing ton-199411.

13. Ibid.

14. Ibid.

15. Ibid.

16. Ibid.

17. Ibid.

18. Ibid.

19. Ibid.

20. http://articles.chicagotribune.com/1994-10-12/news/9410120075 _1_roger-hinkins-arianna-huffington-rep-michael-huffington.

21. http://www.vanityfair.com/culture/features/1994/11/huffington
-199411.

22. Ibid.

23. http://www.usatoday.com/life/columnist/mediamix/2006-05-07
-media-mix_x.htm.

24. http://abcnews.go.com/2020/Stossel/story?id=4716938&page=1.

25. Gay Alcorn, "Daaarling, I've Come to Save Democracy: United
States," *Sydney Morning Herald* (Australia), July 22, 2000, 23.

26. Ibid.

27. http://www.syracuse.com/news/index.ssf/2011/02/how_the_huff
ington_post_became.html.

28. Ibid.

29. http://articles.latimes.com/2011/feb/09/opinion/la-oe-rutten
-column-huffington-aol-20110209.

30. http://www.washingtonpost.com/wp-dyn/content/article/2011/
02/08/AR2011020805179.html.

31. http://www.creators.com/conservative/debra-saunders/aol-huffpo
-meet-corporate-greed.html.

32. http://www.rawstory.com/rs/2011/02/09/bloggers-readers-band
-quit-huffington-post/.

33. Ibid.

34. http://www.guardian.co.uk/media/2011/feb/27/arianna-huffing
ton-post-aol-deal.

35. http://blogs.forbes.com/jeffbercovici/2011/04/12/aol-arianna
-huffington-hit-with-class-action-suit/.

36. http://blogs.forbes.com/jeffbercovici/2011/04/12/aol-huffpo-suit
-seeks-105m-this-is-about-justice/.

37. http://www.newyorker.com/reporting/2008/10/13/081013fa_fact
_collins?currentPage=all.

38. http://www.creators.com/conservative/debra-saunders/aol-huffpo
-meet-corporate-greed.html.

39. http://abcnews.go.com/2020/Stossel/story?id=4716938&page=1.

40. http://www.washingtonpost.com/wp-dyn/content/article/2011/
02/08/AR2011020805179.html.

41. http://www.thedailybeast.com/blogs-and-stories/2011-02-07/aol
-buys-huffington-post-arianna-huffington-calls-it-her-last-act/.

Chapter 5: Hollywood Hatemongers

1. Ruth Picardie, "Feuds Corner: Spike Lee V The World," *Guardian* (London), October 27, 1992, 7.

2. Angela McGlowan, *Bamboozled: How Americans Are Being Exploited by the Lies of the Liberal Agenda* (Nashville: Thomas Nelson, 2007), 134.

3. Ibid., 136–37.

4. Allen W. Trelease, *White Terror: The Ku Klux Klan Conspiracy and Southern Reconstruction* (Baton Rouge: Louisiana State University Press, 1995), xlvii.

5. Eric Foner, *A Short History of Reconstruction* (New York: Harper & Row, 1990), 146.

6. Ibid. For an excellent look at the jaw-dropping hypocrisy of the Democrat Party's disgraceful, racist history, check out Angela McGlowan's excellent book *Bamboozled*, cited above.

7. http://www.huffingtonpost.com/2008/04/07/spike-lee-hillary-and -mas_n_95450.html.

8. Ibid.

9. Ruth Picardie, "Feuds Corner: Spike Lee V The World," *Guardian* (London), October 27, 1992, 7.

10. Shane Danielsen, "Spike Lee's Older Ego," *Sydney Morning Herald*, August 24, 1996, Arts, 15.

11. Steve Persall, "Spike on Race," *St. Petersburg Times*, February 4, 1994, 1B.

12. Hugh Murray, "What About the Nation of Islam's Historical Ties to Fascism," *New York Times*, February 23, 1994, A18.

13. Frank Walker, "Kicking Up a Storm," *Sun Herald*, January 3, 1993, 7.

14. Picardie, "Feuds Corner."

15. Christopher Hitchens, "Inside the Minds of the Fanatics in Bow Ties," *Evening Standard* (London), July 1, 1998, 8.

16. Danielsen, "Spike Lee's Older Ego."

17. Ibid.

18. Ibid.; Shlomo Schwartzberg, "Mo' Better Jew-Baiting," *Jerusalem Report*, December 18, 2000, 54.

19. Danielsen, "Spike Lee's Older Ego."

20. Ibid.

21. Paul Lewis, "Spike Lee Gets in Clint Eastwood's Line of Fire," *Guardian* (London), June 6, 2008, 17.

22. Ibid.

23. http://newsone.com/entertainment/cganemccalla/spike-lee-compares -tyler-perry-to-amos-and-andy/.

24. http://www.huffingtonpost.com/2011/04/20/tyler-perry-spike-lee -go-to-hell_n_851344.html.

25. Doug Camilli, "Spike Lee Stirs the Pot with Ads: Image Is Cooking Up Lucrative Trouble," *Gazette* (Montreal, Quebec), September 12, 2000, F6.

26. Reuters, "Promoting Racial Harmony; Nike Plans Commercial That Features Spike Lee," *New York Times*, May 23, 1992, 37.

27. Michael Goldfarb, "Basketball: One Man's Shoe Is Another Man's Murder," *Guardian* (London), June 4, 1990.

28. Reuters, "Promoting Racial Harmony."

29. Jake Pearson, "Teens Trash Spike Over Vodka Promo," *Daily News* (New York), November 2, 2010, 2.

30. Hilary De Vries, "Spike's Driven," *St. Petersburg Times*, June 3, 1991, 1D.

31. James Barron with Joe Brescia, "Public Lives: Defending Humor Among Uniforms," *New York Times*, May 28, 1999, B2.

32. Ibid.

33. http://abcnews.go.com/print?+101153.

34. http://voices.washingtonpost.com/channel-08/2008/03/your _obama_ad_oliver_stone_app.html.

35. http://newsbusters.org/blogs/alana-goodman/2010/07/25/oliver -stone-jewish-dominated-media-prevents-hitler-being-portrayed-c.

36. Ibid.

37. http://www.jpost.com/ArtsAndCulture/Entertainment/Article .aspx?id=182744.

38. http://www.adl.org/PresRele/ASUS_12/5816_12.htm.

39. Ibid.

40. http://newsbusters.org/blogs/brad-wilmouth/2010/09/22/oliver -stone-invokes-kkk-know-nothings-cheney-was-very-dangerous -man-.

41. McGlowan, *Bamboozled*, 161.

42. http://newsbusters.org/blogs/brad-wilmouth/2010/09/22/oliver -stone-invokes-kkk-know-nothings-cheney-was-very-dangerous -man-.

43. http://www.reuters.com/article/2010/03/14/us-venezuela-chavez -idUSTRE62D05I20100314.

44. http://www.cnsnews.com/node/68358.

45. Ibid.

46. http://latino.foxnews.com/latino/news/2011/01/06/chvez-ambas sador-suggestions-says-thanks/.

47. http://www.commentarymagazine.com/2010/07/28/why-no-out rage-over-oliver-stone/.

48. http://abcnews.go.com/Entertainment/story?id=101846&page=1.

49. http://www.commentarymagazine.com/2010/07/28/why-no-out rage-over-oliver-stone/.

50. http://www.jpost.com/ArtsAndCulture/Entertainment/Article.aspx ?id=182744.

51. http://www.washingtontimes.com/news/2010/jul/27/stone-cold -anti-semitism/; http://online.wsj.com/article/SB100014240527487 03578104575397550901748306.html.

52. http://pajamasmedia.com/ronradosh/2010/01/12/i-thought-howard -zinn-was-bad-enough now we have-to-learn-our-history-from -oliver-stone/; http://www.telegraph.co.uk/news/celebritynews/69 62475/oliver-stone-suggests-hitler-is-easy-scapegoat.html.

53. http://www.debbieschlussel.com/columns/120204p.htm.

54. http://pajamasmedia.com/eddriscoll/2011/04/27/whoopi-goldberg -im-playing-the-damn-race-card-now/.

55. "Whoopi Goldberg Defends Ted Danson's Blackface Act at Friars Club Roast," *Jet*, October 25, 1993, http://findarticles.com/p/articles/mi _m1355/is_n26_v84/ai_14488564/.

56. Ibid.

57. Ibid.

58. "Blacks Fail to See Humor in Ted Danson's Blackface Tribute to Whoopi Goldberg," *Jet*, November 1, 1993, http://findarticles.com/p/articles/ mi_m1355/is_n1_v85/ai_14515746/.

59. http://articles.latimes.com/1993-10-12/local/me-44785_1_whoopi -goldberg.

60. "Blacks Fail to See Humor in Ted Danson's Blackface Tribute to Whoopi Goldberg," *Jet*, November 1, 1993, http://findarticles.com/p/articles/mi_m1355/is_n1_v85/ai_14515746/.

61. http://articles.sun-sentinel.com/1993-10-19/lifestyle/9310150951 _1_ted-danson-friars-club-black-women/3.

62. "Blacks Fail to See Humor in Ted Danson's Blackface Tribute to Whoopi Goldberg," *Jet*, November 1, 1993, http://findarticles.com/p/articles/mi_m1355/is_n1_v85/ai_14515746/.

63. "Whoopi Goldberg Defends Ted Danson's Blackface Act at Friars Club Roast," *Jet*, October 25, 1993, http://findarticles.com/p/articles/mi _m1355/is_n26_v84/ai_14488564/.

64. http://www.cbsnews.com/8301-31749_162-20029718-10391698 .html.

65. http://hollywooddiversity.org/2011/01/2011-oscars-may-be-more -reverse-than-diverse/.

66. http://www.variety.com/article/VR1118010361?refCatId=1055.

67. http://www.hollywoodreporter.com/news/whitest-oscars-10-years -28551.

68. http://articles.cnn.com/2011-01-26/entertainment/diversity .academy.awards_1_roger-ross-williams-oscar-nominations-geoffrey -fletcher?_s=PM:SHOWBIZ.

69. http://jezebel.com/5570545/comedy-of-errors-behind-the-scenes -of-the--daily-shows-lady-problem.

70. http://www.huffingtonpost.com/2010/07/06/the-women-of-the -daily-sh_n_636743.html.

71. http://www.variety.com/article/VR1118011500?refCatId=14.

72. Ibid.

73. http://articles.cnn.com/2011-01-26/entertainment/diversity .academy.awards_1_roger-ross-williams-oscar-nominations-geoffrey -fletcher?_s=PM:SHOWBIZ.

74. Ibid.

75. http://www.psychologytoday.com/blog/are-we-born-racist/ 201102/whitewash-is-hollywood-really-racist.

Chapter 6: Hollywood Leftist Loon Lifetime Achievement Award

1. http://www.babble.com/CS/blogs/strollerderby/archive/2007/04/
   19/alec-baldwin-s-raging-abuse-filled-message-to-daughter-may
   -cost-him-his-parental-rights.aspx.

2. Erik Hedegaard, "How Hollywood's Bad Boy Grew Up," *Times* (London), Magazine Features, 28–32.

3. Ibid.

4. Ibid.

5. http://newsbusters.org/blogs/kyle-drennen/2008/05/12/cbs-alec
   -baldwin-easy-target-conservative-junkyard-dog-sean-hannity.

6. Ibid.

7. http://www.wnd.com/index.php?fa=PAGE.printable&pageId=1271.

8. Christopher Stern, "Baldwin's Comments Drawing Ire from D.C.,"
   Variety, December 18, 1998, 6.

9. http://www.wnd.com/news/article.asp?ARTICLE_ID=14641.

10. "Senator Baldwin—Not!" *Washington Times*, January 23, 1999, A13.

11. Ibid.; http://www.variety.com/article/VR117489560.

12. John McCaslin, "Inside the Beltway," *Washington Times*, October 30,
    2000, A8.

13. http://www.opensecrets.org/news/2011/01/his-future-unknown
    -alec-baldwin-a-m.html.

14. http://www.huffingtonpost.com/alec-baldwin/to-hell-with-wall
    -street_b_130850.html.

15. http://extratv.warnerbros.com/2011/04/capital_idea_alec_baldwin
    _supports_the_arts.php.

16. http://online.wsj.com/article/SB100014240527487043969045762 2
    7023423795528.html.

17. http://www.huffingtonpost.com/don-mcnay/the-person-we
    -should-be-m_b_841520.html.

18. http://www.huffingtonpost.com/alec-baldwin/what-occupy-wall
    -street-h_b_1096920.html?ref=tw.

19. http://www.nytimes.com/2011/03/25/business/economy/25tax
    .html?pagewanted=all; http://www.mogulite.com/richest-celebrities
    -ows/?pid=794#image.

20. http://spectator.org/archives/2011/10/11/alec-baldwin-fund-tied
    -to-wall/.

21. http://www.cnsnews.com/news/article/alec-baldwin-financial-crisis
    -has-crippl.

22. http://www.cnsnews.com/news/article/obama-has-now-increased
    -debt-more-all-presidents-george-washington-through-george-hw.

23. http://www.cnsnews.com/news/article/alec-baldwin-financial-crisis
    -has-crippl.

24. http://articles.nydailynews.com/2011-01-23/local/27096359_1
    _residency-rules-audits-tax-bill.

25. http://www.huffingtonpost.com/alec-baldwin/tax-cuts-and-the
    -republic_b_17379.html.

26. Ibid.

27. Jason Chow, "Anti-Bush Boast Earns Baldwin One-Way Trip to Montreal," *National Post*, April 15, 2002, A5.

28. Elizabeth Benjamin, "Would Alec 'Rock' WFP Ballot Line?" *Daily News* (New York), May 24, 2010, 8.

Chapter 7: Money-Grubbing Anti-Materialists

1. http://www.slate.com/id/2152580/.

2. http://www.time.com/time/covers/1101020304/story.html.

3. Ibid.

4. http://articles.cnn.com/2005-12-18/us/time.poy_1_bill-and-melinda
   -gates-global-health-time-names?_s=PM:US.

5. http://abcnews.go.com/Entertainment/story?id=105757&page=1.

6. http://articles.cnn.com/2005-12-18/us/time.poy_1_bill-and-melinda
   -gates-global-health-time-names?_s=PM:US.

7. http://www.nme.com/news/bono/32704.

8. http://www.telegraph.co.uk/comment/letters/7958485/What-is
   -the-best-way-to-help-the-worlds-deserving-poor.html.

9. http://media.www.claremontindependent.com/media/storage/
   paper1031/news/2007/10/14/News/Bono-Friend.Of.Poverty.Not
   .The.Poor-3065764.shtml.

10. Ibid.; http://www.nytimes.com/2005/12/15/opinion/15theroux.html.

11. http://www.time.com/time/world/article/0,8599,1680715,00.html.

12. http://www.nytimes.com/2011/03/25/us/25madonna.html.

13. http://news.bbc.co.uk/2/hi/africa/8535189.stm.

14. http://www.msnbc.msn.com/id/41221202/ns/health-health_care/ t/fraud-plagues-global-health-fund-backed-bono-others/.

15. Ibid.

16. Ibid.

17. http://www.one.org/us/about/.

18. http://www.nypost.com/p/news/national/poor_idea_bono_bsUzJM fT2mBJbqyXgp6YoO.

19. Ibid.

20. http://www.dailymail.co.uk/news/article-1314543/Bonos-ONE -foundation-giving-tiny-percentage-funds-charity.html.

21. http://www.joinred.com/red/.

22. http://blog.joinred.com/search?updated-max=2011-04-28T08%A55 %3A00-07%3A00; http://blog.joinred.com/2011/01/why-ap-story -about-global-fund-is-great.html; http://blog.joinred.com/2011/01/ how-global-fund-protects-its-grant.html.com.

23. http://aidwatchers.com/2011/04/are-celebrities-good-for-develop ment-aid/.

24. Ibid. See also Lisa Ann Richey and Stefano Ponte, *Brand Aid: Shopping Well to Save the World* (Minneapolis: University of Minnesota Press, 2011).

25. http://adage.com/article/news/costly-red-campaign-reaps-meager -18-million/115287/.

26. Ibid.

27. http://online.wsj.com/article/SB123758895999200083.html.

28. Ibid.

29. http://www.latimes.com/news/opinion/commentary/la-oe-easterly 6jul06,0,5290414.story.

30. Robert Calderisi, *The Trouble with Africa: Why Foreign Aid Isn't Working* (New York: Palgrave, 2006), 5.

31. http://media.www.claremontindependent.com/media/storage/ paper1031/news/2007/10/14/News/Bono-Friend.Of.Poverty.Not .The.Poor-3065764.shtml.

32. http://blog.acton.org/archives/196-bono-aid-or-trade.html.

33. http://www.contactmusic.com/news.nsf/story/norton-hits-out-at
-bonos-tax-dodge_1008508.

34. http://www.guardian.co.uk/music/2009/feb/27/u2-irish-aid-group
-coalition.

35. http://www.slate.com/id/2152580/.

36. http://www.guardian.co.uk/music/2009/feb/27/u2-irish-aid-group
-coalition.

37. http://entertainment.timesonline.co.uk/tol/arts_and_entertain
ment/music/article5814498.ece.

38. Ibid.

39. http://www.bloomberg.com/apps/news?pid=newsarchive&sid=aef6s
R60oDgM.

40. http://entertainment.timesonline.co.uk/tol/arts_and_entertain
ment/music/article5814498.ece.

41. http://www.slate.com/id/2152580/; http://entertainment.timeson
line.co.uk/tol/arts_and_entertainment/music/article5814
498.ece.

42. http://www.slate.com/id/2152580/.

43. http://www.bloomberg.com/apps/news?pid=newsarchive&sid=aef6s
R60oDgM.

44. Ibid.

45. http://www.belfasttelegraph.co.uk/entertainment/music/news/u2
-frontman-bonos-tax-avoidance-depriving-poor-14203187.html.

46. http://www.bloomberg.com/apps/news?pid=newsarchive&sid=aef6s
R60oDgM.

47. http://www.guardian.co.uk/commentisfree/2006/oct/22/comment
.theobserver.

48. http://entertainment.timesonline.co.uk/tol/arts_and_entertain
ment/music/article7013075.ece.

49. http://www.slate.com/id/2152580/.

50. http://entertainment.timesonline.co.uk/tol/arts_and_entertain
ment/music/article5814498.ece.

51. http://www.dailymail.co.uk/news/article-1394422/Saint-Bono
-facing-huge-Glastonbury-protest--avoiding-tax.html.

52. Ibid.

53. http://www.dailymail.co.uk/femail/article-400188/St-Bono-hypo crite.html; http://en.wikipedia.org/wiki/Elevation_Partners.

54. http://www.wnd.com/index.php?fa=PAGE.view&pageId=121143.

Chapter 8: Be Healthy or Else!

1. Alex Spillius, "Obama quits his 30-year smoking habit," *Daily Telegraph*, February 10, 2011, 20.

2. http://www.celebstoner.com/20080304602/celebstoners/top-celeb stoners/barack-obama.html.

3. Silvia Ayuso, "The First Lady's Controversial Rib," *Nation*, February 27, 2011.

4. http://www.dailymail.co.uk/news/article-1394099/Obama-eats-2 -chili-dogs-fries-day-wife-Michelle-unveils-new-dietary-guide.html.

5. http://www.whitehouse.gov/blog/2011/06/24/push-ups-arch bishop-and-more-cape-town-first-lady; http://www.washingtonexam iner.com/blogs/beltway-confidential/2011/06/michelle-obama-i -cant-stop-eating-french-fries-eat-your-vegetable.

6. http://www.letsmove.gov/.

7. http://latimesblogs.latimes.com/washington/2010/02/first-lady -michelle-obamas-rollout.html.

8. http://www.whitehouse.gov/the-press-office/childhood-obesity -task-force-unveils-action-plan-solving-problem-childhood-obesity-.

9. http://www.huffingtonpost.com/2011/04/19/bmi-schools_n _850776.html.

10. http://www.usatoday.com/news/health/weightloss/2010-02-09-1 Afirstlady09_CV_N.htm.

11. http://atlantapost.com/2011/06/15/the-not-so-celebrated-side-of -the-lets-move-campaign/.

12. http://washingtonexaminer.com/politics/blogs/beltway-confiden tial/michelle-obama039s-obesity-report-tax-pop-and-candy-subsi dize-fru.

13. http://www.foxnews.com/story/0,2933,592802,00.html.

14. http://washingtonexaminer.com/politics/blogs/beltway-confiden tial/michelle-obama039s-obesity-report-tax-pop-and-candy-subsi dize-fru.

15. Chris Richards, "Beyonce is poppin', but can she lock down votes?" *Washington Post*, April 28, 2011, C01.

16. "Michelle's moves; Let's dance," *Daily Telegraph*, May 4, 2011.

17. http://www.usatoday.com/news/health/weightloss/2010-02-09-1 Afirstlady09_CV_N.htm.

18. http://latimesblogs.latimes.com/washington/2010/02/first-lady -michelle-obamas-rollout.html.

19. Amy Argetsinger and Roxanne Roberts, "Any witches here? It's scary time at the White House," *Washington Post*, November 1, 2010, C01; http://www.huffingtonpost.com/2009/10/31/white-house-trick ortreate_n_341235.html.

20. http://www.huffingtonpost.com/2011/02/06/white-house-super -bowl-menu_n_819312.html.

21. Silvia Ayuso, "The First Lady's Controversial Rib," *Nation*, February 27, 2011.

22. http://nation.foxnews.com/michelle-obama/2011/02/01/not -known-be-diet-food-michelle-obama-hails-great-barbecue-nc.

23. http://thestir.cafemom.com/food_party/120515/does_new_obama _pizza_burger.

24. http://www.dailymail.co.uk/news/article-1394099/Obama-eats -2-chili-dogs-fries-day-wife-Michelle-unveils-new-dietary-guide .html; http://www.whitehouse.gov/blog?page=6.

25. Alex Spillius, "Obama Quits his 30-Year Smoking Habit," *Daily Telegraph*, February 10, 2011, 20.

26. http://www.reuters.com/article/2010/02/09/us-junk-food-idUS TRE6184HZ20100209.

27. http://www.foxnews.com/slideshow/entertainment/2009/10/29/ celebrities-stars-who-smoke-pot-marijuana#slide=13.

28. http://theview.abc.go.com/forum/whoopi-goldberg-and-smoking.

29. http://www.stateoftheusa.org/content/smoking-on-the-silver -screen.php.

30. http://www.smokefreemovies.ucsf.edu/problem/moviessell.html.

31. Paul Martin, "Farrell Is Biggest Influence on Kids When It Comes to Smoking," *Mirror*, March 21, 2007, 8.

32. http://www.nytimes.com/2005/09/20/arts/20iht-smoking.html.

33. http://stopsmokinghownotto.com/celebrity-smokers/.

34. http://www.looktothestars.org/celebrity/312-whoopi-goldberg.

35. http://www.usatoday.com/news/health/spotlight/2001-08-23 -goldberg-aids.htm08/23/2001.

36. http://breastcancernews.breastcancerawareness.ws/2011/01/24/ watch-stop-breast-cancer-for-life-psa-ronde-barber/.

37. http://community.comcast.net/t5/Breast-Cancer-Hope/Lifetime -Interview-A-New-View-of-Whoopi-Goldberg/td-p/684002.

38. http://www.looktothestars.org/celebrity/312-whoopi-goldberg.

39. http://howcocaine.com/47114/crystal-meth-psa-whoopi-goldberg/.

40 http://watching-tv.ew.com/2011/02/02/whoopi-goldberg-drugs -charlie-sheen-the-view/.

41. http://articles.nydailynews.com/2011-03-24/gossip/29358635_1 _smoke-camera-tape.

42. http://watching-tv.ew.com/2011/02/02/whoopi-goldberg-drugs -charlie-sheen-the-view/.

43. "New Law Lights Up Whoopi," *Northern Territory News*, February 5, 2011, 34.

44. http://theview.abc.go.com/forum/whoopi-goldberg-and-smoking.

45. http://www.foxnews.com/slideshow/entertainment/2009/10/29/ celebrities-stars-who-smoke-pot-marijuana#slide=13.

46. http://www.mtv.com/news/articles/1596923/justin-timberlake -jessica-biel-speak-at-obama-rally.jhtml.

47. http://act.mtv.com/posts/justin-timberlake-confesses-to-smokin -the-pot/.

48. http://checkyourself.com/fivemyths.aspx.

49. http://www.foxnews.com/slideshow/entertainment/2009/10/29/ celebrities-stars-who-smoke-pot-marijuana#slide=13.

50. http://checkyourself.com/fivemyths.aspx.

51. http://www.foxnews.com/slideshow/entertainment/2009/10/29/ celebrities-stars-who-smoke-pot-marijuana#slide=13.

52. http://www.celebstoner.com/201008314774/news/celebstoner -news/top-100-women-of-weed.html.

53. Elisa Roche, "Yoga Queen Diaz Dazzles at Full Stretch," *Express*, Scottish edition, February 3, 2010, 126, 130.

54. http://hlifemedia.com/2009/10/168/.

55. Anthony Harwood, "Diaz Tears; Star Cries on TV at Voter Apathy," *Mirror*, October 1, 2004, 30; Rex Murphy, "Hark! I Hear a Celebrity Oracle," *Globe and Mail* (Toronto), November 1, 2008, A23.

56. http://www.huffingtonpost.com/marianne-schnall/talking-green -with-camero_b_95784.html.

57. http://hlifemedia.com/2009/10/168/.

58. Leora Broydo Vestel, "A Mellow Approach to Green; In the Blogs: Green Inc.," *International Herald Tribune,* May 27, 2009, 17.

59. http://www.huffingtonpost.com/marianne-schnall/talking-green -with-camero_b_95784.html.

60. http://www.postchronicle.com/news/original/article_212371769 .shtml.

61. http://today.msnbc.msn.com/id/41178614/ns/today-entertain ment/t/cameron-diaz-bought-weed-snoop-dogg/.

62. http://theblemish.com/2007/02/drew-and-cameron-smoke-the -weed/.

63. http://www.celebstoner.com/20080521720/celebstoner/celeb stoner/top-celebstoner.html.

64. http://newsbusters.org/blogs/lachlan-markay/2011/05/25/ actress-cameron-diaz-marriage-dying-institution-doesnt-suit-our -worl.

65. http://bighollywood.breitbart.com/jdeangelis/2011/05/10/ thoughts-on-marriage-from-cameron-diaz/.

66. http://www.heritage.org/research/reports/2010/09/marriage -america-s-greatest-weapon-against-child-poverty; http://downloads .frc.org/EF/EF11E70.pdf.

67. http://pewresearch.org/pubs/1802/decline-marriage-rise-new-fam ilies.

68. http://justjared.buzznet.com/2010/06/15/cameron-diaz-alex -rodriguez/.

69. http://www.everydayhealth.com/sexual-health-pictures/celebrity -advocates-for-safe-sex-and-abstinence.aspx; http://host.madison .com/ct/news/local/health_med_fit/article_96d0ee57-e3dc-59d7 -a5ec-e5cbc5b71ffc.html; http://www.livestrong.com/article/13924 -std-information/.

70. Andrew Dembina, "P. Diddy," *South China Morning Post*, November 12, 2006, 2.

71. http://latimesblogs.latimes.com/entertainmentnewsbuzz/2009/01/video-cameron-d.html.

72. Dembina, "P. Diddy," 2; Neil McCormick, "The Thoughts of Statesman Diddy: Feminists are unlikely to warm to his invitation to females at his soirees to 'get butt naked,'" *Daily Telegraph*, November 28, 2002, 24.

73. Cian Traynor, "Give me a crash course in . . . ," *Irish Times*, December 24, 2010, 5.

74. http://blogs.cbn.com/thebrodyfile/archive/2009/10/05/gay-dinner -special-lady-gaga-and-president-obama.aspx.

75. "Gaga's condom couture," *Northern Territory News*, February 19, 2011, 35.

76. "Gaga explains beefy outfit (sort of)," *Toronto Star*, September 14, 2010, E7.

77. http://www.mtv.com/news/articles/1626837/lady-gaga-shatters -glass-braves-flames-at-american-music-awards.jhtml.

78. "Madonna joins AIDS fight," *Advertiser*, September 27, 1988.

Chapter 9: Be Peaceful or I'll Shoot Yo Ass!

1. "My Daughter's Enemies? The Whole Tea Party; Shot Politician's Dad Blames Palin Jibes," *Mirror*, January 10, 2011, 6.

2. "Giffords Is Able to Stand," *Daily Telegraph*, June 29, 2011, 18.

3. http://newsbusters.org/blogs/noel-sheppard/2011/01/08/jane -fonda-blames-giffords-shooting-sarah-palin-glenn-beck-and-tea -pa#ixzz1Rb3RwlRL.

4. "Quick to Pull the Trigger over a Massacre Motive," *Daily Telegraph* (Australia), January 10, 2011, 20.

5. "My Daughter's Enemies?" *Mirror*, January 10, 2011, 6.

6. http://www.verumserum.com/?p=13647.

7. "Deranged Left Quick to Point the Gun at Palin," *Daily Telegraph* (Australia), January 11, 2011, 22.

8. http://www.youtube.com/watch?v=5mlYHiJCqBI.

9. http://blogs.phoenixnewtimes.com/valleyfever/2011/01/jared _loughner_alleged_shooter.php.

10. "My Daughter's Enemies?" *Mirror*, January 10, 2011, 6.

11. "Giffords Is Able to Stand," *Daily Telegraph*, June 29, 2011, 18.

12. Ibid.

13. "Deranged Left Quick to Point the Gun at Palin," *Daily Telegraph* (Australia), January 11, 2011, 22.

14. http://www.mrc.org/specialreports/2010/RealRadioHatemongers/ExecSumm.aspx.

15. http://www.youtube.com/watch?v=qLnS-2h_nog.

16. http://newsbusters.org/blogs/erin-brown/2010/10/20/daily-beast-wal-mart%E2%80%99s-morals-victimize-kanye.

17. http://www.bmi.com/news/entry/533098.

18. http://www.foxnews.com/entertainment/2011/06/07/kanye-wests-new-dead-model-music-video-called-misogynistic-vile/.

19. Ibid.

20. http://popcrush.com/kanye-west-things/.

21. http://www.mtv.com/news/articles/1621389/kanye-west-crashes-vma-stage-during-taylor-swifts-award-speech.jhtml.

22. http://www.tampabay.com/blogs/juice/content/kanye-west-charged-battery-theft-vandalism.

23. http://www.hiphopdx.com/index/news/id.12337/title.kanye-west-reacts-to-president-obamas-remark-ep-with-jay-z-may-be-with-def-jam.

24. http://www.eliminatewarforever.org/stop-war/well-known-against-war.html.

25. http://articles.nydailynews.com/2010-11-03/news/27080134_1_world-trade-center-bush-s-nbc-care-about-black-people.

26. http://www.reuters.com/article/2009/05/18/idUS175847+18-May-2009+PRN20090518.

27. http://www.contactmusic.com/info/kanye_west.

28. "West Begs Nike to Give Him Design Deal," WENN Entertainment News Wire Service, April 7, 2009.

29. "Kobe Courts the Big Dogs for Big-Budget Sneaker Ad," *San Antonio Express-News*, February 17, 2011, 12CX.

30. http://www.mrc.org/bozellcolumns/columns/2011/2011051601 4725.aspx.

31. "Dems Facing a Rap. Hil & Obama Got Help from Foul Musicians," *New York Daily News*, April 15, 2007.

32. http://www.mrc.org/bozellcolumns/columns/2011/2011051601 4725.aspx.

33. "Dems Facing a Rap."

34. http://www.mtv.com/news/articles/1588694/check-out-nas-new -obamainspired-song-black-president.jhtml.

35. http://www.huffingtonpost.com/2011/01/31/diddy-on-obama -calls-out-president-asks-to-do-better-for-black-people_n_816473 .html.

36. http://www.guardian.co.uk/music/2008/nov/05/jayz-falloutboy; http://www.forbes.com/2010/09/21/forbes-400-ones-to-watch -seinfeld-tiger-jay-z-rich-list-10-watch_slide_13.html; http://blogs .forbes.com/davidewalt/2010/09/22/jay-z-vs-warren-buffett-in -the-forbes-400/.

37. http://bighollywood.breitbart.com/abreitbart/2009/01/21/feelin -the-healin-young-jeezy-jay-z-perform-%E2%80%9Cmy-president -is-black%E2%80%9D-remix-on-inauguration-eve.

38. http://www.mtv.com/news/articles/1588694/check-out-nas-new -obamainspired-song-black-president.jhtml.

39. http://www.mtv.com/news/articles/1598568/check-out-nas-new -song-election-night-right-here.jhtml.

40. http://rap.about.com/od/songs/tp/ObamaRapSongs.htm.

41. http://www.xxlmag.com/news/2011/03/nas-says-moammar-gad hafi-is-%E2%80%9Cmisunderstood%E2%80%9D.

42. http://www.vh1.com/news/articles/1659301/20110305/index.jhtml.

43. http://articles.cnn.com/2010-05-04/entertainment/nas.espn.liberia _1_nas-cnn-new-perspective?_s=PM:SHOWBIZ.

44. "Concert Lineup Angers Some Va. Tech Families; Rapper's Violent Lyrics Draw Protests," *Washington Post,* August 3, 2007, B01.

45. "Factor Flashback: Rapper Not Appropriate for Virginia Tech Concert?" Fox News Network, August 30, 2007.

46. http://www.billboard.com/news/musicians-band-together-against -war-threat-1826821.story#/news/musicians-band-together-against -war-threat-1826821.story.

47. Ibid.; http://www.yoraps.com/news1.php?subaction=showful&id=1
    300287998&archive=&start_from=&ucat=1&.

48. http://articles.cnn.com/2010-05-04/entertainment/nas.espn.liberia
    _1_nas-cnn-new-perspective?_s=PM:SHOWBIZ.

49. "Concert Lineup Angers Some Va. Tech Families"; "Factor Flashback:
    Rapper Not Appropriate for Virginia Tech Concert?," Fox News Net-
    work, August 30, 2007.

50. Ibid.

51. http://www.mtv.com/bands/m/mixtape_monday/091707/.

52. http://www.mtv.com/news/articles/1572287/nas-explains-contro
    versial-album-title.jhtml.

53. http://www.mtv.com/bands/m/mixtape_monday/091707/.

54. "The Guide: Music 2008: 6 rock star feuds," *Guardian*, December 13,
    2008, 10.

55. http://www.mtv.com/news/articles/1441789/puffy-combs-acquit
    ted-shyne-guilty-assault-gun-possession.jhtml; http://crime.about
    .com/od/famousdiduno/ig/mugshots_rap_hip_rb/rap_puffymug
    shot.htm.

56. http://blogs.reuters.com/frontrow/2010/09/23/from-will-i-am-to
    -b-o-b-obama-looks-to-get-his-groove-back/.

57. http://www.xxlmag.com/news/2010/12/maino-busted-for-driving
    -with-suspended-license/.

58. "Ludacris Provides Obama with More Unwelcome Help," *Washington
    Post*, July 31, 2008, C07.

59. "Song's Ludacris-ly 'offensive,' Sez Bam Flack," *Daily News* (New
    York), July 31, 2008, 5.

60. "Word of Mouf Turns Against Pepsi," *Times* (London), February 22,
    2003, 24.

61. http://online.wsj.com/article/SB10001424052748703859204575 52
    6401852413266.html.

62. http://www.fbi.gov/wanted/dt/joanne-deborah-chesimard.

63. http://gawker.com/5650176/president-obama-is-a-nas-and-lil
    -wayne-fan-these-days.

64. http://online.wsj.com/article/SB10001424052748703859204575 52
    6401852413266.html.

65. Ibid.

66. http://articles.cnn.com/2009-04-08/living/out.of.wedlock.births_1_out-of-wedlock-unwed-mothers-wedding-dress/2?_s=PM:LIVING.

67. http://www.therightperspective.org/2010/06/12/a-history-of-obamas-violent-rhetoric/.

68. http://www.realclearpolitics.com/video/2011/07/06/obama_debt_ceiling_fight_should_not_be_a_gun_used_at_the_heads_of_the_american_people_to_extract_tax_breaks_for_corporate_jet_owners.html.

69. http://thespeechatimeforchoosing.wordpress.com/2011/01/10/did-barack-obamas-violent-rhetoric-inspire-mass-murder-in-arizona/.

70. http://www.therightperspective.org/2011/01/10/a-history-of-obamas-violent-rhetoric-pt-2/.

71. http://www.therightperspective.org/2010/06/12/a-history-of-obamas-violent-rhetoric/.

72. http://www.mediaresearch.org/cyberalerts/1998/cyb19980612.asp#3.

73. Ibid.

74. http://www.independent.co.uk/news/people/profiles/matt-damon-i-have-turned-down-scripts-if-the-violence-is-gratuitous-i-do-believe-it-has-an-effect-on-peoples-behaviour-1803189.html.

75. Ibid.

76. Ibid.

77. http://www.forbes.com/2007/08/03/celebrities-hollywood-movies-biz-cz_dp_0806starpayback.html.

78. http://www.femail.com.au/mattdamon.htm.

79. http://multiplayerblog.mtv.com/2008/04/28/developer-bourne-game-too-violent-for-matt-damons-liking/.

80. http://www.foxnews.com/story/0,2933,237357,00.html#ixzzlRaCYSiYO.

81. http://www.huffingtonpost.com/sean-penn/an-open-letter-to-the-pre_2_b_44172.html.

82. http://www.guardian.co.uk/film/2009/oct/27/sean-penn-fidel-castro-vanity-fair.

83. "Crusader of Controversy," *Courier Mail* (Australia), November 25, 2010, 45.

84. http://articles.sfgate.com/2003-04-30/bay-area/17487611_1_con cealed-permit-guns.

85. http://www.mrc.org/Profiles/odonnell/welcome.asp.

86. http://hotair.com/archives/2011/05/09/rosie-odonnell-we-didnt -give-bin-laden-due-process/.

87. http://newsbusters.org/blogs/tim-graham/2010/06/13/rosie-odonnell -helen-thomas-wasnt-saying-go-back-ovens-so-sit-and-spin-h.

88. http://www.mrc.org/Profiles/odonnell/welcome.asp; http://www .politico.com/news/stories/0510/36783.html.

89. http://newsbusters.org/blogs/tim-graham/2010/06/13/rosie-odonnell -helen-thomas-wasnt-saying-go-back-ovens-so-sit-and-spin-h.

90. "Mothers March for Gun Control: Historic Rally Fills U.S. Capital," *Toronto Star*, May 15, 2000.

91. http://newsbusters.org/node/12120.

92. "Gun Battle Pits Rosie vs. Selleck," *Daily News* (New York), May 20, 1999, 8.

93. http://www.mrc.org/Profiles/odonnell/welcome.asp.

94. http://old.nationalreview.com/comment/comment052500c.html.

95. http://newsbusters.org/node/12120.

96. http://old.nationalreview.com/comment/comment052500c.html.

97. http://www.nrawinningteam.com/0006/rosie.html.

98. http://www.mrc.org/Profiles/odonnell/welcome.asp.

99. http://newsbusters.org/node/12120.

100. http://www.wnd.com/news/article.asp?ARTICLE_ID=15370.

Conclusion

1. Peter Schweizer, *Do as I Say (Not as I Do): Profiles in Liberal Hypocrisy* (New York: Doubleday, 2005), 215.

Printed in the United States
By Bookmasters